Media in Europe Today

Edited on behalf of the Euromedia Research Group by Josef Trappel,
Werner A. Meier, Leen d'Haenens, Jeanette Steemers and Barbara Thomass

With an introduction by Denis McQuail

intellect Bristol, UK / Chicago, USA

First published in the UK in 2011 by
Intellect, The Mill, Parnall Road, Fishponds, Bristol, BS16 3JG, UK

First published in the USA in 2011 by
Intellect, The University of Chicago Press, 1427 E. 60th Street,
Chicago, IL 60637, USA

A catalogue record for this book is available from the
British Library.

Library of Congress Cataloging-in-Publication Data

Media in Europe today / edited for the Euromedia Research Group by Josef
Trappel ... [et al.] ; with an introduction by Denis McQuail.
    p. cm.
  ISBN 978-1-84150-403-2 (alk. paper)
1. Mass media--Europe. I. Trappel, Josef, 1963- II. McQuail, Denis. III.
Euromedia Research Group.
  P92.E9M395 2011
  02.23094--dc22
                    2010035361

Cover designer: Jenny Scott
Copy-editor: Elena Fysentzou
Typesetting: Mac Style, Beverley, E. Yorkshire

ISBN 978-1-84150-403-2

Printed and bound by Gutenberg Press, Malta.

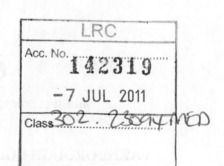

Contents

Contents

Media in Europe Today

Preface

Jönköping, Lugano, Wrocław, Copenhagen, Luxembourg, Hamburg, Braga and Moscow – these were the stops of the Euromedia Research Group on its way to the creation of this book. In all these cities generous hosts enabled the group to discuss the book's concept, the structure of the chapters and indeed the content of each chapter. This opportunity is unique. Group members constantly offer their advice to their fellow authors. This way, the latest developments in scholarly research and in the media industry all over Europe can be incorporated. Irritating or disturbing facts can be put into perspective with the assistance of fellow group members. Over time, the book gained coherence.

The Euromedia Research Group is indeed unique as its members define their own mission and objectives without the presence of external pressures. This high degree of independence allows for flexible ways of working and timely responses.

But the main advantage of working within this network of social science scholars and experts from some twenty European countries is the opportunity to collectively reflect upon changes and developments in the media and communications field. All group members are ready and willing to contribute their specific competencies to the Euromedia Research Group's deliberations.

It is this rich stock of knowledge that allows the group to produce books on the development of European mass media. What unites the group members is their interest in media policy, the changes in the media landscape and their dedication to theorizing on public communication.

Starting from these shared scientific interests, the group decided to write a book for students and scholars in the field of mass communications research. This book builds on the work published in four previous volumes by the group over its 25 years of existence: New Media Politics: Comparative Perspectives in Western Europe (1986), Dynamics of Media Politics: Broadcast and Electronic Media in Western Europe (1992), Media Policy: Convergence, Concentration & Commerce (1998) and Performance & Politics: Media Policy in Europe (2007). Over time, some issues have changed – such as the notion of new media – while others have remained on the agenda through all these years, such as the struggle for legitimacy of public service broadcasting.

The latest book in this series consists of two parts. The first section concentrates on the development of different mass media in Europe. It starts out with the complex task of comparing media systems in Europe, contributing to the scholarly debate of the three media models developed by Hallin and Mancini (2004). The following chapters discuss the development of different media according to the chronology of their emergence: newspapers, radio, television and online media. Questions raised in these chapters concern what determines the success and failure of these media in the light of political, social, cultural and technological change.

The second section of the book explores a range of contemporary issues around public communication which are especially relevant for the development of European media. These include changes in the structure of public spheres; the constantly redefined relationship between media and democracy; developments in media governance and media policy; trends in media industries; the changing position of public service media; the roles and performance of journalism; the relationship between ethnic minorities and the media; and finally, the position of Europe's media in the global context.

The number of chapters corresponds by and large with the number of teaching weeks in the academic year and should provide a comprehensive – but in no way exhaustive – selection of topics for scholarly debate.

This book is written by members of the Euromedia Research Group. Each chapter has its own authors, but the book is a collective effort of the whole group as every chapter has been peer reviewed by two other members of the group. Therefore, the editor of this volume is the group itself. Its members are documented online at www.euromediagroup.org

Josef Trappel and Werner A. Meier
Convenors of the Euromedia Research Group
Salzburg and Zurich, June 2010

Part I

Chapter 1

The Media in Europe Today: Introduction

Denis McQuail

Both the media themselves and the interdisciplinary field of inquiry linked to it have been in a constant state of flux for at least 30 years now, and there is little sign of stabilization. Diverse causal factors are at work and key phenomena can be problematized and defined in quite different ways, as well as from different perspectives. The term 'media' itself, once understood as an identifiable cluster of different means of public communication with a certain institutional identity, is no longer easy to define. Differences between media have become unclear and the overall territory of reference can no longer be clearly demarcated. In the mid-twentieth century, media essentially referred to the newspaper and book press, with broadcasting as a relatively limited but growing novelty (with film, music and advertising as peripheral to the title). Typically, all these media were separate and clearly bounded, identifiable by a known public function, and subject to external and internal regimes of control. The media were – and still are – open to consideration as industry, social and cultural institution or as a key element in democratic (and also undemocratic) politics. Even so, in the second half of the twentieth century, media were not generally considered as in any way central to the main processes of national society and international relations.

Media in a Field of Conflicting Forces

The main forces at work in respect to the relation between the media and society (still the core of the matter) have not changed in general form, but the balance of power between competing forces *has* changed, leading to cross-pressures and conflicts that are still unresolved. The nature of these forces and resulting conflicts are by now well known, but it is useful to be reminded of them at the outset of this book. It is important to bear in mind that they are not blind forces of nature, but rather they are embedded in the projects of identifiable groups, interests or persons, these having unequal degrees of power to affect the course of media development. The main 'forces' in the sense intended can be located under the following headings:

- *Technological Innovation.* The media are fundamentally defined from the start by the particular technologies of reproduction and transmission they employ, and are shaped by the biases of the currently dominant technology of communication. What is done inevitably reflects what is possible to do and what given technologies do best, and the latter expands and changes continuously. But this process is itself driven by a diversity of motives that pertain to other forces.

- *Industry, Business and the Economy in General.* The pursuit of new markets and higher profits harnesses technology to its goals, and the larger media market determines much of the shape of media institutions and provides guiding principles. In the nature of competitive free markets, there is a continued succession of new entrances and exits by major players in various media.
- *Media Politics and Policy.* Governments and politicians give expression and direction to political goals with respect to media that typically require exerting forms of control in order to limit the 'power of media', activate the potential of media for partisan political gains, or simply to advance and protect the interests of the state.

In addition to these three basic factors, the media in Europe have been – and are – driven by a number of other particular dynamics. These include the aspirations of media professionals (such as artists, performers, managers, journalists) to claim and exercise greater autonomy over their work, as well as the efforts of groups in civil society, grassroots organizations, and social or cultural minorities to gain entry to the media for their own communicative purposes. A particular dynamic that is not present in any comparable way outside Europe is the short-term goal of unifying the media market and the (less consensual) long-term aspiration towards developing a European communicative space that would be marked by having a public sphere of its own. Last, but hardly least, is the pressure exerted by popular demand for the products and services of media industries. This form of pressure is diffuse and hardly directed in any specific way, but it is very hard to resist when it comes both with the approval of governments and supported by all the powers of persuasion of media industry publicity.

An Emerging Field for Research

This book is the latest in a series of reports and analyzes of the state of 'media politics' in Europe initiated by the Euromedia Research Group in the early 1980s. At the core of the inquiry were issues specifically relating to all kinds of policies, both at national or international levels, affecting the operation of media as a social and economic institution. Inevitably, this required some attention to the structure and dynamics of media industries, regardless of policy implications. At that time, the study of European media policy was not well developed and related primarily to a few specific issues that had emerged as contentious for European societies as the mass media developed during the twentieth century (particularly after World War II). Public policy for media was largely driven by the self-interests of the state and 'public interest' concerns, with the media themselves having limited autonomy, except for the powers permitted to them under the doctrine of Freedom of the Press. Although the media took rather similar forms across western Europe, the societal contexts and public responses varied quite markedly across states, especially when following lines of political traditions, culture and economic development.

The main issues driving public policy in most countries were (to varying degrees): fears of potentially harmful social and cultural effects from unrestrained popular media forms; concern about a lack of political diversity as a result of market forces (concentration); and the disputed control and financing of television broadcasting, still dominated by various types of public monopoly. Everywhere, vested interests sought to protect themselves from disturbing changes that the media might encourage, as well as advance their own interests via media. Sovereign states clung to their power to harness media to national purposes and to police the boundaries of national culture and language. In varying degrees, the media were regarded as something either in need of supervision or naturally subordinate to higher interests of state and society. But at the core of the debate in most countries, there was a fundamental disagreement about the balance between public and private (market) control, and about the kind, and degree, of any public intervention that might be permitted in media matters. Debates on these issues were conducted at national levels according to domestic circumstances and prevailing political culture and economic possibilities. At the outset, under the 'old media order' of press and broadcasting, wealthier 'northern' states favoured rather more intervention which they could afford, while 'southern' (Mediterranean) states were obliged, perhaps also inclined, to accept what the market had to offer.

Brief History

The initiative taken by the Euromedia Research Group was a response to the widely predicted changes – technological, political and economic – that were about to engulf the media in Europe. With respect to technological changes, the start of the 1980s saw the beginning of an era of satellite television transmission that, in combination with cable systems, was expected to make obsolete the national boundaries of provision and audiences, undermining national political and legal control. In addition, new possibilities for data transmission were being pioneered in forms available to the public, especially as 'viewdata' (forerunner of the Internet), broadcast teletext and even the humble telefax. These developments were mainly based on computerization and digitization, coupled with rapid advances in telecommunications.

Around 1980, political changes were driven by a general shift to the right in European governments, with an accompanying assault on public monopolies and a preference for market-driven media development and governance. Relevant also is that the rise of new communication technologies and media largely undermined the rationale for public monopoly, which had been justified by the wish to fairly allocate the very limited spectrum that terrestrial broadcasting could provide. Public service broadcasting – the centrepiece of public media policy in much of Europe – now came under additional pressure. After 1979, the acceleration of efforts to achieve a unified market for the European Community

(EC) increasingly impinged on the autonomy of national political control of media. This eventually led to the European Television Without Frontiers Directive (TVWF) of 1989, which laid down the ground rules for cross-border television transmission by cable and satellite, essentially opening up all borders. This move, amongst others, made it necessary to consider issues of media policy and industry on a transnational basis. The 'enlargement' and change of the European media sphere following the fall of Communism (after 1990) had a number of important effects, but amongst them was certainly the necessity for reconciling public policies with the realities of market economics.

The possible changes mentioned above took a long time to materialize, since the impulses for change came up against a great deal of resistance in many European states. Resistance stemmed not only from political and economic interests vested in the old order; the challenges posed by changing media were often unwelcome on national cultural grounds, with governments and political parties of all colours being reluctant to give up the potential advantages resulting from their traditional high degree of control exercised over the mass media, especially in broadcasting. In addition, many of the expectations for change were over-hyped, with the reality only slowly becoming available in practice. Before the later 1990s, the truly new electronic media were too limited, uninteresting or expensive to have much impact or attract much attention from policy-makers, despite the utopian and dystopian visions that began to be promulgated.

Nevertheless, by the turn of the century, the media in Europe were in several respects transformed and also on the way towards new and divergent futures. The main changes were:

- A real increase in public availability of many forms of audio and audio-visual media as a result of numerous advances in the recording and transmission of content.
- A significant boost in the volume of content produced and made available for the audience market, either imported or from home production.
- The resulting 'media abundance' was due to a large extent to the opening of the market to commercial operators, the injection of capital, the relaxation of regulatory controls and the opening of frontiers. The media had become a much more significant economic sector in several countries.
- A crisis of legitimacy within the pre-existing regime of public control of media that distinguished between print, broadcasting and electronic media, especially in respect to the degree of control by public regulation. More important was the loss of substantial audience share by public broadcasting in several countries. This 'crisis' was being managed by the relaxation and rewriting of national legislation, usually following some form of public inquiry.
- The phenomenon of 'media convergence' was already in evidence, as the technology and the process of digitization ate away at old boundaries, and old and new media began to compete for the same audience and advertiser markets. Of particular importance was the fate of the newspaper, already weakened and vulnerable, but now directly threatened by

new competing platforms providing nearly all of its traditional services of news, opinion and advertising.

It is worth remarking that the three main issues of early debate surrounding the mass media (fears of harm; media concentration; the broadcasting monopoly) had already been largely sidelined by the processes of change, as already described. There were still some concerns about the possible effects of media, especially as a result of 'commercialization' and the flooding of low-cost entertainment programmes (particularly from the United States), but the debate about the harmful 'effects of television' had largely run out of steam. The issue of press concentration had transmuted into anxieties about the very survival of the newspaper industry, even if in a rather concentrated form. With respect to public broadcasting, by 2000 there was scarcely any monopoly situation to be found, and the issue had changed into a defence of what was left of the institution. The 'Europeanization' of the debate had both weakened it – by favouring a level playing field for market forces in all member states – and given it some potential support by developing and setting some criteria of public benefits that commercial media systems might not reach.

Recent Developments

These brief remarks bring us to the period covered by recent work of the group and this book. We find not so much the emergence of new sources of change, as an acceleration of trends long apparent, especially as represented by the online media sector. What is left of an older media order is now surrounded by rising waters and buffeted by stormier weather. The immediate situation of European media is inevitably influenced by the post-2008 period of recession, which has accelerated economic pressures, although it may also have slowed down the forces for change. But the underlying trends continue. According to almost all indicators, the most immediate problems for media systems and structures stem from the advance of online media, and their growing impact on 'traditional' or 'legacy' media. There is no end in sight to the inroads that online media are making into older media, both in terms of time and money spent by audiences and advertisers. The development of efficient and affordable mobile media platforms, supported by enhanced broadband and WiFi transmission, is an obvious source of increased concern to the established media. Several of this book's early chapters provide a status report on the principal traditional media of radio, press and television.

The largely unpredicted success of 'social media' in its various forms adds a further turn to the screw, since there is really no defensive competition to be offered. The eventual impact on media structures does still depend on how new and old come to be integrated in terms of ownership and production, and it's important to note that 'new' and 'old' media are not fixed entities, but are constantly changing, overlapping and being redefined in the process.

Nevertheless, the mass media – whether new or old – eventually become integrated into society on the basis of definitions of their functions, which in turn give rise to certain structures and forms of governance. Such issues arising under this heading are larger and more difficult to formulate and resolve than matters of economics and new technology, which can usually be handled in media market terms. For political and social life more broadly, change is bringing a good deal of uncertainty and anxiety due to the challenges to established (often unwritten) rules and customs, as well as public expectations. Online media have typically been very lightly and uncertainly regulated, and the possibilities of regulation and intervention seem quite limited. The only exception is where fundamental interests of the state come to be involved (as with organized crime and terrorism, which are peripheral to the main purposes of the media).

We are faced with a broader set of issues than ever before, issues that cannot, as in earlier times, be settled by reference to a political ideology or a national political system. Nor can they be dealt with by the administrative and regulatory apparatus of individual nation states, in which Europe is quite rich. Most solutions will need to encompass the unstoppable advance and convergence of technology, as well as cross-border relationships that not only involve immediate neighbours but are also global in character.

Contemporary Issues

Most of the contents of the present book, which are the result of the most recent inquiries and reflections of the Euromedia Research Group, deal in one way or another with four interrelated types of concern, as described in the following paragraphs.

Coping with Change

This mainly refers to points previously summarized. The whole spectrum of media has become subject to instability and unpredictability as new forms of organization and new functions have emerged. This instability is sufficient to cast doubt on societies' capacity (their governments and representatives) to oversee media activities in a consistent way, despite efforts to construct new regulatory agents for a range of media at a national level but according to principles agreed at a European level. While the media industry can look after itself, according to established economic principles and business practice, society is not equally positioned to safeguard the public interest, even where some degree of agreement is reached on what that might mean. Concerns about this complex of issues are explored at various points in the book, with a shared conviction that in an era that is arguably defined by informational activities and networks of communication, the extent and the quality of communication systems – whether public or private – deserve a high priority.

Public Purposes of Media and Communication

The view just expressed presumes that media of public communication make indispensable and extensive positive contributions to the life of societies and their polities. This potential public benefit is not confined within the borders of a nation state but rather affects wider international relations of cooperation and conflict. Societies, at least in the 'western' model, have until recently relied on a combination of self-chosen media goals (with professional or idealistic underpinning) and state intervention to ensure that basic standards of information and circulation of ideas are achieved.

The brief history of current media upheavals has shaken confidence in this reliance. The potential commercial rewards from the 'communications revolution', both for entrepreneurs and national economies, have sidelined aspirations towards public benefit. The same commercial forces coupled with the triumph of liberal and anti-statist sentiment have effectively brought a halt to intervention and rolled back elements that were in place (such as the public broadcasting monopoly). Even well intentioned interventionists are at some loss to design convincing instruments for securing positive public benefits. New thinking is needed about the nature of the problems and the means for solving them, leaving aside the question of finding the political will.

Public policy for media, in this respect, has traditionally focused primarily on the wide accessibility and quality of information relevant to citizenship and social participation. The main principles invoked, beside that of freedom of the press and expression, were those of equality and diversity. Both are central in the age of 'new media', as inequality has not gone away and quality is often threatened by the media's exploitation for profitable, rather than educational, purposes. There are new challenges arising from the unequal distribution of the means of participation in wider networks of public communication, for both economic and cultural reasons. The age of media abundance has not meant an abundance of all good things for all people, and new forms of division are becoming institutionalized. The once widely accepted goal of 'universal service' (by broadcasting, mail and telephone) has been discounted as too minimalist and also unattainable. The goal and standard of diversity that originated in the democratic political sphere with a demand for a fair allocation of access to limited channels for opposed or alternative voices has, in the period of decline of interventionist policy, been neglected, with increasing reliance on the audience demand on the one hand and market provision on the other. In more socially fragmented societies, there are too many dimensions of cultural and social diversity to legislate for, but there are still some essential requirements for the way the media should behave in a civilized society towards its various component minorities. Public purposes are thus continually being changed, enlarged and in need of continuous redefinition.

Governance and Accountability

It has already become customary in discussions of media policy to adopt the term 'governance' to apply to the varied forms of law, regulation and control that set directions and boundaries to media activity. The term recognizes the complexity of interests and relations involved in media work and relations with society, and the inappropriateness of hierarchical and firm legal models in this context (Collins 2008). Social control of media has to be flexible and informal in order to both respect essential freedoms, as well as to cope with the real complexities and uncertainties of media operation. There has to be a high degree of indeterminacy because of changing situations. This especially applies to the Internet and online media generally, which are taking up an increasing share of all communication activity. Although attention focuses on these media in particular because they are, so far, very under regulated, it is no longer appropriate to think of them as separate media, each with its own regulatory 'regime'.

The shift from a policy model of regulation and control to that of governance is marked in practice by an increased reliance on media self-regulation, and on voluntary forms of conformity to public and private needs and complaints. Although such a shift can be interpreted as a weakening of society's capacity to make media answerable for alleged harms and failings, yet it is difficult to resist and can actually bring some benefits. It does offer some support for the concept of media freedom, which still needs protection in new, as well as old, media. It also places more onus on media to accept responsibility for what they do. In addition, it promotes the development of standards of practice and new forms of accountability that could be more sensitive than traditional legal instruments of law and regulation. Lastly, it opens a larger role for professionalism and other elements of autonomy within media, at least theoretically.

A focus on the issue of accountability has a wide frame of reference. It covers many of the traditional concerns about harmful media effects, especially on the young and vulnerable, public offence, defamation and libel, matters not really dealt with here. The range of potential private and public harms has been considerably widened by the rising and uncontrolled expansion of online media. Accountability relates to the provision of a stable and supportive environment for the conduct of media industries, the promotion of innovation and the protection of consumers. It also relates to the securing of essential media assistance for public purpose, as noted already, and to the development of adequate means for gaining compliance from the media, with particular reference to self-government.

Relations between Media and Political Power

While research and theory concerning media policy has in some respects become 'de-politicized' compared to the post-World War II era and more pragmatic, technocratic and economic in character, there are also reasons for keeping the relations between media and the state and the political system at the centre of attention. There has been quite a rich tradition of thinking about the relations between media systems and political systems, which is reviewed in the chapter that follows, with particular application to Europe. It is clear from this analysis that media governance, as it has been developed, is hard to divorce from a national political culture and there are strict limits to what any 'Europeanization' might achieve. Views of how media should relate to politics and of what the contribution of media to the public sphere should be, are still quite divergent and likely to remain so, gradually affecting the definitions of online media as well.

It can hardly be doubted that the media are as central as they ever were to the competitive democratic process; perhaps more central than ever, given the decline of traditional party political forms. There is an intense interest on the part of all political and societal actors in having various ways to access the media and in controlling them by whatever means, not always to be found recorded in descriptions of systems of governance. But no amount of convergence of media or 'Europeanization' of standards and regulations will have much immediate impact on this matter, although we can expect some development at a European (thus transnational) level for a new kind of relationship between the media and the developing institutions of the European Union.

Conclusion

This chapter has been written in a very general way so as to indicate the overall agreed framework of the book, and in order to avoid getting into the detail that is better set out later on. Even so, what is at stake in the subject matter is actually very concrete and of immediate relevance to the future of media, and the quality of social and political life. It concerns, firstly, the quality of journalism that is relied on to sustain the day-to-day operation of the democratic political system. There is reliable evidence of, as well as a long-held belief in, a significant informational impact by European media, and of public broadcasting in particular (e.g. Curran et al. 2009). The quality of journalism does not depend only, or even mainly, on the past efforts of public broadcasting, but also on the traditions and professionalism of journalism in the press sector, as well as in all other forms of broadcasting. Much depends on the play of market forces, but these cannot be left entirely outside the scope of public policy.

Secondly, the quality of cultural provision by the media has a large and long-term impact on the cultural life of society as expressed in the arts and sciences, and in conjunction with broader educational provisions. This is not just a matter of concern for a small elite, since the performance and effects of media of all kinds continue to be an active topic of broad public opinion. Newer media have given rise to new concerns and a continued call for policies for media responsibility, as well as for public education.

Issues of public information and culture, as summarized in this way, have focused attention across Europe on the potential for maintaining public influence on media in an era where competitive market forces have been elevated to a dominant status. Active political and regulatory attention is being given to how much public support can be given to the media, and for what purpose. Most specifically, the ambitions of public broadcasters to extend their activities into the online media sector have been hotly disputed, on the grounds of legitimacy as well as alleged unfair competition with the private sector. Such disputes are made even more bitter by the absence of any clear regulatory regime for the Internet and other related media. Much is at stake in the immediate future.

The increased centrality of media in contemporary democracies has been mentioned and it is now a well-documented fact of public life. This means that instruments of government and the arts of governance will continue to be directed towards maintaining a model of political communication in accordance with the traditional party and electoral structure. But alongside this, there are increasingly vocal calls (not only from the excluded base of society) to develop new media as a remedy for the apparent decline of citizens' active participation in social and political life (Blumler and Coleman 2009). All in all, it looks as if the sphere of 'media policy' (once held to be withering away in the wake of the abundance of channels) and of content has fresh winds in its sails. Experience, rather than just theory, of recent and increasing media transformation and expansion has lent support to the view that the unchanged ideals of the good society that Europe as a whole is still trying to encourage – principally freedom, diversity and social and cultural equality (all of which need to be continually redefined and evaluated) – cannot be attained without very close and creative attention to the whole spectrum of public means of communication.

Finally, it is worth reminding readers that although Europe is only one arena of media space in the world, and offers one version of purposes and instruments of governance, it may very well be the most developed example of an attempt at transnational jurisdiction. This especially concerns the many sensitive issues that arise in this case (mainly where rights of property, questions of freedom and control are concerned), as applied to the potentially dominant future medium of the Internet (see Zeno-Zencovich 2008). For this reason, the comparative nature of this book is likely to make it particularly valuable, especially as it is a continuation of a series of studies dating back over more than 25 years of European media development.

References

Coleman, S. and Blumler, J. G. (2009), *The Internet and Democratic Citizenship: Theory, Practice and Policy*, Cambridge: Cambridge University Press.

Collins, R. (2008), 'Hierarchy to homeostasis? Hierarchy, markets and networks in UK media and communications governance', *Media, Culture and Society* 30: 3, pp. 295–317.

Curran, J., Iyengar, S., Lund, A. B. and Salovaara-Moring, I. (2009), 'Media System, Public Knowledge and Democracy: A Comparative Study', *European Journal of Communication*, 24: 1, pp. 5–26.

McQuail, D. and Siune, K. (eds) (1986), *New Media Politics: Comparative Perspectives in Western Europe*, London: Sage.

Zeno-Zencovich, V. (2008), *Freedom of Expression: A Critical and Comparative Analysis*, London: Routledge-Cavendish.

Chapter 2

Comparing Media Systems: The European Dimension

Barbara Thomass and Hans J. Kleinsteuber

Comparative media studies have become a central research area within academic media research. International comparisons of media systems have undergone an impressive development over the last five decades. This chapter is about this classic contribution to the study of comparative media systems and what this means for Europe. The authors present short descriptions of the major contributions to comparative studies and subsequently relate them to the European experience.

Comparison: Analytical Tools and Theoretical Concepts

The starting point of comparative media analyses was the question 'Why is the press as it is?' as Siebert, Peterson and Schramm put it in 1956, when they published their famous comparative study which not only claimed to explain what the press does and why, but also (as the subtitle stated) 'what the press should be and do'.

Media systems are embedded in their social environment which is also culturally – and nationally – shaped. Thus they are best considered in the frame of their territorial borders as marked out by the states. Simply put, media systems of different states differ. Why do they differ, in which aspects do they differ? What are the consequences of these differences? What are the dynamics which make media systems change and develop? These are the questions comparative media analyses consider, as well as the drawing up of a typology of media systems in an effort to set up models, and all these are at the basis of this branch of research.

As a counter trend to the comparative media research which looks at media from a national perspective, we proceed with an analysis of media developments which incorporates concepts such as 'internationalization', 'transnationalization' and 'globalization'. While the first still starts from the assumption of national media systems and looks for processes of transgressing borders, the latter claims that national characteristics become less and less important. The vision of a globalized media system is at the end of these arguments.

Comparative media studies are central to today's academic media research. International comparison of media systems has undergone an impressive development in the last 50 years. This chapter's aim is to draw a line from the fruits of 50 years of comparative media system analysis to the discussion of media systems' globalization. It will identify the analytical tools and theoretical concepts of international comparisons of media systems in order to find out the vital desiderata and perspectives.

The Beginnings in the United States: Media Systems alongside the Iron Curtain

Siebert, Peterson and Schramm started efforts at the classification of media systems with their *Four Theories of the Press* (1956) which is still of some influence today, although it has been criticized for various reasons and eventually superseded by much more refined models. Their central idea was 'that the press always takes on the form and coloration of the social and political structures within which it operates' (Siebert et al. 1956: 1f). They identified four types of media systems according to their appearance in history. The main categories they found to describe these types were: the philosophical foundations; the type of relationship between the state and the individual; the aims media pursue in their performance; the forms of control they are subject to; and the forms of ownership.

Based on these categories, they first came up with the authoritarian model, dating back to the sixteenth and seventeenth centuries, a model which is mainly characterized by an understanding of the media during that time (i.e. the press, which had to promote and support the politics of the authoritarian sovereign). The second model emerged in opposition to the previous one and was based on the philosophy of enlightenment. This is the liberal model which mainly turns the previous model's logic of control on its head, meaning that control of the media is now carried out by the market, and the media themselves have the task of controlling the government.

The concepts of the third and fourth models are strongly influenced by the political conflicts of the 1950s. Some years before, the Hutchins Commission on the Freedom of the Press in the United States had criticized the performance of mass media and claimed that the media should show more responsibility. Based on these ideas, Siebert, Peterson and Schramm identified a social responsibility model of the press, whose main characteristic is that the media should be accountable to society and that the state is entitled to interfere when they do not fulfil this prerequisite. Interestingly enough, this model was never put into practice in the United States, but European academics claim that it had been implemented in western Europe with the creation of public service broadcasting – an organizational form for radio and television – which states missions and structures serving the public and being accountable to them.

The peak of the Cold War led to the identification of a fourth model, which is the communist model. This is marked by the media which are firmly in the grip of the state and controlled by it to serve the communist ideology.

This form of classification had a strong normative approach. By looking at the rationales and theories behind the press and describing these normative rationales, the description of the models ended up having a normative bias itself as it was founded on an ethnocentrically grounded philosophy of freedom. It wanted to explain the differences between media systems and press performance, and yet it ended up measuring the performance of media systems in other countries against the background of the western dominant philosophical mainstream of liberalism. The *Four Theories of the Press* thus compared ideas behind the press, not the empirical state of the press itself, and they confined themselves to a few countries only, namely the United States, the United Kingdom and the Soviet Union.

If we find a central reference to Europe, it is in the first, now historically authoritarian model as it describes the early media history of the 'old' continent. This makes sense, but has little relevance for the understanding of Europe's situation today. The other 'theories' reflect the fact that they had been developed during the days of the Cold War and the related confrontation between East and West. The East is clearly represented by the Communist model that has disappeared with the transformation processes in eastern and central Europe (it might have survived in North Korea). On the western side, the libertarian and the public service models were located, both seemingly somehow reflecting the values of the West. This perspective blurred the central distinctions between the two continents. During the 1950s the public service model was absolutely predominant in Western European broadcasting (only in Britain had the policy of commercialization begun with the founding of ITV), whereas in the United States the commercial model had virtually conquered the country (even the small public radio and TV sector of today did not exist). The Siebert et al. classification reflects the assessment at the time, that the 'West' had more in common and that its differences were minimal. As such, the American authors did not really understand the specifics of Europe.

Developing Systems: The Emergence of the South

This schematic classification of media systems was continued in the concept of Ronneberger (1978), who contrasted North–South and East–West systems. The western model, located in Europe and North America, follows the liberal model of Siebert, Peterson and Schramm, as does the eastern, which follows the communist model. He adds two more models, located in the South, in the developing countries, stating that there is one version with politically active media which are endowed by the government with a guidance function, aside media which do not follow any political issues, and a second version, where the media undertake a developing function out of their own will and autonomy, but still in accordance with the governmental sphere. Once again in this concept the western liberal model is the measure of classification and uses the binary code of 'free' and 'unfree' media (Massmann 2003: 31). It is to Ronneberger's credit that he added to the hitherto bipolar consideration the view on developing countries – modernizing theories are consequently in the background of this concept.

A few years later, Martin and Chaudhary (1983) segmented the world into three ideological systems: the western, the communist and the third world. They described important aspects of the media against this background: the nature and treatment of news; the role of mass media, their significance as vehicles of education, persuasion, opinion formation and entertainment; and looked at mass media economics and press freedom. Thus the scope of elements was enlarged and a functionalist view came into consideration. But the approach was a top down one – given the ideological differences of these world systems, the media existence was analyzed in this frame of mind – and not a bottom up approach, which is able to develop a typology out of empirically found differences.

Clearly the increased importance of the developing world is reflected in these approaches. This goes together with the fact that the so-called Third World became an important and increasingly independent actor on the global stage. This became especially visible in the negotiations of the UNESCO General Assembly during the 1970s that led to the confrontation between the western position of 'Free Flow of Communication' against the 'New World Information and Communication Order' (NWICO) with a more controlled and balanced flow, as it was supported by the Second (Socialist) and the Third World. In the Mass Media Declaration of 1978 the member states of UNESCO overwhelmingly voted in favour of the NWICO, which in turn made the United States and United Kingdom leave the world organization under protest (Preston, Herman and Schiller 1989). The continental western European countries stayed in the organization and successfully changed its workings from within. Only many years later did the United States and the United Kingdom return to UNESCO. After years of inactivity, UNESCO started again – this time with a strong European participation – to devise a new Convention on Cultural Diversity. The General Assembly decided in 2005 to adopt it; the United States together with Israel were the sole dissenters, whereas Britain voted in with the rest of Europe. The convention was especially welcomed by Europe's public service broadcasters as it pointed out the right for state action to protect cultural identities.

The Contingency Model: Comparison and Control Structures

The contingency model of communication of Wiio (1983), ironically published in the very same volume of Martin and Chaudhary (1983), marked the effort to leave this normative grounded approach as it tried to find categories by which media systems could be described empirically. He differentiated between the openness or closed character of the receiver system and the message system; between public and private ownership in combination with centralized and decentralized control of the media; and the right to receive and the right to transmit which can lie either with the individual or with the state. Thus he introduced more categories and tried to avoid the hitherto dominant dichotomies of media classification. Although he ended up identifying two types of communication models, the Marxist models (being sender-centred) and the pluralist models (being receiver-centred), his approach enabled him to look particularly at western media systems not as a monolithic entity but as different types of media systems according to the categories in use. Under the heading of the two types mentioned above, he established twelve models in which western states found themselves at different places: (1) controlled mass communication; (2) open mass communication; (3) private communication; (4) directed mass communication; (5) decentralized public model; (6) centralized public model; (7) decentralized private model; (8) centralized private model; (9) authoritarian model; (10) communist model; (11) libertarian model; (12) social responsibility model. The four latter – known from Siebert, Peterson and Schramm – are yet only identified with the category of the right to send and to receive; looking at media ownership brings up other models. Thus with Wiio's approach one can look at conditions, circumstances and situations which are causative for different combinations of internal and external influences on media and their performance.

Instead of using the traditional dichotomies of 'free' and 'unfree' media as they were developed in the United States, Wiio demonstrated that statements about media systems are dependent on their specific elements and the chosen dimensions of classification. It is also emphasized that a degree of control exists in all media systems (in Europe as well as elsewhere), only the source and degree of control differs.

New Dimensions: The Journalists Enter the Stage

Convergent elements of different media systems show another approach which immediately followed from Wiio. Altschull (1984) looked at the purposes of journalism, views of press freedom and articles of faith as they are described by the representatives of the different media systems themselves. Unlike Siebert, Peterson and Schramm, he does not measure the models he finds according to one overruling value system, but looks at the discrepancy of self-description and reality in different countries. The common characteristic of the market model, the Marxist model and the advancing model in his concept is that in all media systems, 'news media are agents of those who exercise political or economical power' and that for that reason 'the content of the news media reflects the interest of those who finance the press' (Altschull 1984: 298).

Thus, Altschull takes up Ronneberger's idea of integrating developing countries with their special approach to media, considers the ideologies of media systems like those of Siebert, Peterson and Schramm, and also includes – as Wiio does – the empirical reality of media.

His contribution to comparative media system analysis is the idea that media systems' classification in communication science has hitherto reflected the bloc ideology of the Cold War. He believed that notions such as objectivity, press freedom, presentation of the truth, the assumption that the media would serve the public's right to information are not actually sufficient for characterizing media systems (Massmann 2003: 46).

These approaches reflect the European perspectives of the 1970s and 1980s. On one side there was the ongoing experience of the division of Europe, but the continent was also seen as a common geographical space; increasingly, the structural similarities of urbanized and differentiated societies on both sides of the Iron Curtain were emphasized. The theoretical school behind this view is that of convergence of industrial societies, irrespective of being 'capitalist' or 'real socialist' as featured by authors such as John K. Galbraith or Jan Tinbergen (Stommel 1977). These approaches went along with the first steps towards *détente* in Europe (e.g. the Organization for Security and Co-operation in Europe (OSCE) and its media regulations) that finally contributed to the breakdown of the Soviet system. One could describe Altschull's approach as a media related version of this – at that time – quite prominent convergence approach on both sides of the Atlantic. In terms of comparative methodology, it may be seen as a 'most similar'-approach, whereas the earlier classifications, based on an East/West confrontation represented a 'most different'-understanding.

Binary Typologies: Open and Closed Systems

The binary differentiation of open and closed media systems is revived again nearly ten years later by Weischenberg (1998), shortly after the fall of the wall – here referring to the theory of social systems. The debate about the collapse of a world political system and lack of empirical knowledge about the insides of the media systems of the socialist countries is still reflected in his approach, as the categories for describing the closed system of the media in the former socialist countries do not go far beyond the general description that the influence of other social subsystems on the media (except the state) was not existent in these countries. A coherent development of categories to find typologies of media systems, as it was developed by his colleagues, does not take place in this work, which is – admitted for the sake of fairness – presented in a student's textbook.

Again, shortly after the demise of the socialist countries, Kleinsteuber (1994) describes three types of media systems: the eastern real-socialist type, the western liberal one and the third world type, underlining that these are only an ideal type of media systems, which do not exist with all the described characteristics in the given countries, but which are abstract models showing collective singularities of a greater number of states. Although he takes the mixed system of public service broadcasting and commercial broadcasting as one important characteristic of the western liberal type, he marks the commercialization of the media system as a central element of this type, and thus introduces an element of dynamics in the so far static description of media systems. He describes the eastern real-socialist system as a historic type which tends to develop into the direction of the western liberal type, thus looking again at the dynamics of media systems. We will return to this idea of dynamization of comparative media analysis later.

The Western Approach: Comparative Media Systems around the Northern Atlantic

An important step in the comparison of media systems was the publication of the book *Comparing Media Systems: Three Models of Media and Politics* (2004) by Hallin and Mancini who took over the intriguing idea of Siebert et al. to use only a small number of simple discreet models, but who claimed to have developed better empirically grounded models. Indeed, they developed a very comprehensive scheme to describe the environment of politics and political culture which is shaping a media system. With this idea they could built upon and

Gurevitch and Blumler (1990) who looked for criteria to describe the political and media systems. Hallin and Mancini's approach follows a very similar scheme, as they include in their analysis only countries of developed capitalist democracies, i.e. countries from western Europe and North America.

They looked for the character of political pluralism in these countries, for ways of parting political power, for the role of interest groups and the role of the state. Concerning the media, historical development of alphabetization and the role of the press, the parallelism of media and political parties, the degree of professionalization of journalists and the degree of state control over the media were the decisive dimensions.

In combination of different occurrences of these dimensions, their analysis resulted in three models:

- *The liberal model* being found in Britain, Ireland and North America, characterized 'by a relative dominance of market mechanisms and of commercial media'.
- *The democratic corporatist model* prevailing across northern continental Europe, characterized 'by historical coexistence of commercial media and media tied to organized social and political groups'.
- *The polarized pluralist model* prevailing in the Mediterranean countries of southern Europe, being characterized by 'integration of the media into party politics, weaker historical development of commercial media, and a strong role of the state' (Hallin and Mancini 2004: 11).

Thus, Hallin and Mancini fulfilled what many scholars before them were seeking to achieve (or were at least mentioning in their critiques of the forerunners): that comparative media system analysis has to start from empirically grounded categories and not from ideologies, and that it must then develop a comprehensive differentiated type of model. The weak point of this approach becomes evident and is not denied by the two authors: it is an enormous problem of economies of research to gather all the required data from different countries in order to draw a precise picture for the models. This is also the reason as to why they developed a typology which is appropriate only for a restricted political system and for a part of the globe, and unable to describe the media systems in eastern Europe, the Arab countries, Asia or Africa.

Hallin and Mancini seemingly reflect the transatlantic perspective of the early theories of Siebert et al. (to which they also refer), but in fact they move away from it. Different to the earlier, highly normative approaches, they base their analysis on a careful consideration of all available material and strictly base their description on empirical materials. In the meantime, methods of comparative research had been developed and led to a much more downsized typology. Siebert et al. had mainly developed ideal types in the definition of Max Weber's, i.e. abstract generalizations that do not reflect individual systems. Hallin and Mancini instead refer to descriptions of single systems and then look for regional similarities, as such creating real systems, based on empirical analysis.

If one wants to dispute Hallin and Mancini's approach it would be for two reasons: (1) the placing of the United States with its near purely commercial system in one group with Britain and its dual media structure is problematic (see above); (2) the strictly geographical approach, based on coherent regions in Europe (North–West–South). This argument applies especially to the northern European model with such different systems like those of Iceland and Germany, Switzerland and the Netherlands. In a study that combines the Hallin and Mancini approach with descriptions of European national media systems, the concrete outcome of the Hallin and Mancini approach is that just two liberal systems are being described (Britain and Ireland), whereas we count eleven systems described for the northern democratic corporatist model (Terzis 2007).

Mentalities and Cultures: The Other Side of Media Systems

The surprising finding of Hallin and Mancini's analysis is that territorial entities generate similar media systems. World regions have common features in their mediascape. This idea is also at the basis of Blum's concept (2005), which aimed to complete the Hallin and Mancini models. He took the similarities of mentalities and cultures in a given world region as an explanation for similar media systems in such a region. Therefore, he introduced further categories into the analysis in order to be able to describe not only the political system but also the cultural features as explanatory variables for different types of media systems. He looked at dimensions such as media freedom, media ownership, funding of media, media culture and orientation of media, and combined these dimensions with some of Hallin and Mancini's into one synthesis. Thus he integrated media-centred and policy-centred elements into his model. Each of the dimensions can follow either a liberal line, or a regulated line or a line in between.

Table 1: Categories for Media Systems.

	A: Liberal	B: Middle	C: Regulated
1. Government system	Democratic	Authoritarian	Totalitarian
2. Political culture	Polarized	Ambivalent	Concurring
3. Media freedom	No censorship	Cases of censorship	Permanent censorship
4. Media ownership	Private	Private and public	Public
5. Funding of media	Market	Market and state	State
6. Parallelism of media and political parties	Low	Moderate	High
7. State control of media	Low	Moderate	High
8. Media culture	Investigative	Ambivalent	Concurring
9. Media orientation	Commercial	Divergent	Public service

Source: Blum 2005.

Combining these dimensions and their occurrences he found that there are six types of media systems which can be described as follows:

- *The Atlantic–Pacific liberal model* – with A grades in every dimension – has a media system which is orientated to commerce, is autonomous and investigative. A typical example is the United States; Australia and New Zealand may also belong to this model.
- *The southern European clientelism model* – with a domination of B grades, which is typical of ambivalence – has a commercial-populist orientation in TV and an elitist public-service orientated print sector. Blum finds it in Portugal, Spain, Greece, Malta and Cyprus, and possibly in eastern Europe.
- *The northern European public service model* – with a strong mixture of A and B grades – has a public service orientation in broadcasting and the print sector. It includes Germany, Scandinavia, the Benelux states and France, as well as modernized eastern European countries such as Estonia.
- *The eastern European shock model* – with dominating B grades – includes a strong state control of the media within a formal democratic frame, which represents a media system where the government often interferes and breaches media freedom, as it is the case in Russia, Ukraine, Belarus, Iran and Turkey.
- *The Arab–Asian patriot model* – located between the B and C grades – postulates that the media are obliged to support development aims and are subject to censorship. Blum names Egypt as typical for this model, as well as Syria, Tunisia, Morocco and Asian countries like Indonesia.
- *The Asian–Caribbean command model* – with a majority of C grades – represents countries where the government has an absolute control of the media, except that the market is used for funding them. China is representative for this model, which also fits North Korea, Vietnam, Burma and Cuba.

With these dimensions and the above typology, Blum created a classification for media systems which allows an integration for the majority of the countries in the world. The main question concerns the adequacy of the affiliation of many countries to the typology. The judgments on the specifications are not adequately explained in the model, and it creates the impression of being rather tentative. Furthermore, it is debatable whether another combination of the dimensions' specification might create further types. Blum did not express how he created the models and why no other combination of specification was necessary.

This points to a problem, which was already discussed with the Hallin and Mancini model: comparing the media systems of the world and explaining their differences by means of the underlying political culture needs an intimate knowledge of many details of the analyzed countries. They will never be concerned with a single scholar or research group but will necessitate international joint efforts in order to apply an agreed set of dimensions and operationalization of their specifications in the analyzed countries. Obviously, Blum's contribution is interesting concerning the landscape of world media systems; it has only limited relevance to European classifications.

Europe is More: Big and Small, Homogeneous or Multicultural

Europe is made of big and small countries (Germany vs. Monte Carlo), nation states and states of multicultural systems (Denmark vs. Switzerland), cultures well protected by their unique languages (Finland, Hungary), or even an economically strong state situated in the centre of a larger language space which could also include smaller states that are in fact partially dominated by larger states (Austria vis-à-vis Germany, Ireland vis-à-vis Britain). Based on the unique experience of Europe and its mixture of many states, the model system of Hallin and Mancini seems to be blind towards the resulting massive differences in the relations between media and politics. Size definitely matters in Europe and a special focus should be placed on small states: small countries like Ireland or Austria tend to keep their public service broadcasters strong, as they are concerned about uncontrollable cross-border influences. As they act under the influence of neighbouring commercial actors, they are less attractive for local commercial media activities. As such, quite another comparative classification could arise, were we to base a comparison on the size of countries, e.g. placing Austria and Ireland in one model or comparing language spaces (the German language including German-speaking Switzerland or Austria, the French space including parts of Belgium and Switzerland). We find strong differences in media policy – especially among small countries – and though some countries place special emphasis on a nationally oriented media policy, others have instead chosen to give that up and tolerate a much more commercialized and internationalized system (like Greece).

While most of the authors, quoted so far, presented classifications of media systems that tended to reduce their typology to a few models, the impressive diversity of media systems across Europe is not well reflected and makes it necessary to find more flexible modes of description in the future. Basically this leads to the central question of all model building, namely that a balance has to be kept between a degree of abstraction which legitimizes the model and a degree of refinement which is adequate for the variety of cases. A lot of further empirical data gathering and modelling will be necessary in this perspective.

Change to Democracy: Transformation of Media Systems

One reason for the problem of finding adequate affiliation of the existing countries to the models, is that media systems are subject to a strong dynamic and that they influence each other a lot. The transformation of the media systems in eastern Europe is a blatant example for this dynamic. Although – according to the hitherto existing models – they belonged until the collapse of the socialist political system to the same types, yet they adopted very different paths. The transformation of media systems has been clarified in different studies (see Thomass and Tzankoff 2001), but the reason for changes of media systems had not been modelled theoretically up until now.

Comparative transformation studies started in the discipline of political science where they describe the phenomenon of change from dictatorships to democracies, as seen in different phases (the simple version: before–during–after). (Kleinsteuber 2010) Transformation research always takes into consideration the time dimension; systems are seen to change along a time axis, whereas most other comparative work looks at systems at a specific time. The focus is usually on the interrelationship between media and politics, including the introduction of press freedom, reorganization of state-owned media, the changing role of journalists, the advent of international media actors, etc. The earliest focus of transformation research was about the end of authoritarian rule in southern Europe in the 1970s (Greece, Portugal, Spain), where some common features may be found, e.g. the survival of media that had been flourishing under the dictatorship, as well as the founding of new post-authoritarian media as genuine products of democratization. One finds a similar situation during the transformation of the Latin American military dictatorships in the 1980s.

The situation turned out to be quite different during the break-up of the Communist regimes in central and eastern Europe. (Dobek-Ostrowska et. al. : 2010) The state-controlled media had little chance for survival and were either sold to investors (often foreign), re-established as public broadcasters or simply disappeared. Therefore the post-Communist democracies passed through a much more thorough process of transformation with change in ownership and often foreign investors moving in. Following a long tradition of state dominance, some of the public-service broadcasters are still suffering from strong pressure from the political majority (Hungary), while others enjoy more autonomy (Czech Republic). Additionally, the behaviour of journalists is an interesting object of research. Sometimes they were among the avant-garde of political liberalization (as in Poland) or lagged behind (as in Romania). So far the resulting cluster of systems is strongly shaped by the authoritarian past, the transformation period, a relatively strong governmental role and a strong influence from European media conglomerates. To give this cluster of media systems a name, one could call them the 'Eastern European/Post-Communist Media Model Countries' (Terzis 2007: 303ff).

The Wider Europe: Beyond the European Union

We can say that all countries of the European Union (EU) follow (more or less) the liberal/public service type of media system (as described by many scholars, starting with Siebert et al.) with a general tendency towards commercialization, following the thesis of commercial convergence by Hallin and Mancini. This general picture applies to the European Union but has to be modified if we consider the much larger Europe of the Council of Europe with its 47 member states, including the independent states that belonged to the former Soviet Union that extend deeply into Asia (Uzbekistan, Armenia and many others). The same goes for the Organization for Security and Co-operation in Europe (OSCE) with a similar number of members. Most of these states in wider Europe are far away from being democracies, as they maintain media systems that are under strong state censorship and practice tremendous repression over journalists. This also applies to Belarus on the eastern border of the European Union. Some of these countries might be seen as a variation of the authoritarian model of Siebert et al. mixed in with the communist model. But this is just a guess.

The transformation process in Europe is not over. In Ukraine it started in 2004 with the Orange Revolution that brought substantial improvements to the media system, but the new system is still fragile. For many other countries in wider Europe, as well as in the rest of the world, media repression is the rule and transformation is a hope for the future; comparative research can show them though, demonstrate to them what has been achieved and where the main actors, supportive of change, may be found. All in all, the comparative research of media and transformation is still in its infancy.

Media Systems beyond National Borders: Interactions and Dependencies

Kleinsteuber presented an approach which concerns some of the central causes of dynamics – those which derive from influences of one media system over another one. While comparison of media systems mostly follows a most similar or most different system design, which is marked by the two comparative methods of concordance or difference, he proposes four further dimensions in order to describe results of comparisons (Kleinsteuber 2004: 86):

- *Diffusion* describes the voluntary transfer of models or ideas which have proved to be successful, e.g. the model of public service broadcasting which was developed in Great Britain and taken over by many countries in Europe and the Commonwealth.
- *Dependence* is given, if a model emerged in dependence on another state, as had been the case with the media systems in former socialist countries.
- *Temporance* is a notion Kleinsteuber creates for the phenomenon, that a similar development occurs, but with a time lag. Thus, the future of multi-channel TV in Europe could be studied in the United States.
- *Performance* describes the phenomenon that similar systems take over positive elements from each other after having evaluated them thoroughly: within the European Union anti-concentration regulation is analyzed in order to come to a harmonization of the respective laws within the membership.

Again, the transformation of media systems in eastern Europe could be better explained by these types of dynamics. Some countries followed a performance path looking at the media laws of western European countries. Others showed temporance in the sense that they had a booming media market (mostly in print), which was sooner or later confined by media concentration processes. Dependence might still be given, e.g. in the relation of economically strong Russia to vassal states like Belarus.

Is the Comparison of National Media Systems Obsolete?

Apart from national media systems influencing one another, we are experiencing processes of media systems transgressing borders, which have made the use of notions like internationalization, transnationalization, globalization or glocalization, as they are common in communication studies. The question arises as to whether it is still legitimate, to carry on with media system classifications in a purely national perspective?

Changes which are characterized by a dissolution of borders regarding the national framing of media communication are obvious and numerous. The global significance of the Internet and the impossibility of regulating it – from a national perspective – are the most apparent signs for this development.

This dissolution of borders can be considered with regard to economic, legal, political, technical and cultural aspects. Economically spoken, globally operating media conglomerates have for a long time had a powerful influence on national media markets. This is true for the US-American entertainment majors (Compaine and Gomery 2000), as well as for global news agencies (Wilke 1997). Media concentration is crossing national boundaries and it has gained a high degree of leverage (Kleinsteuber and Thomass 2004). Entertainment formats are sold worldwide on the global TV markets and advertising for branded products experiences a tendency to standardization in an international scope (Dmoch 1996).

In Europe at least, media law has been passed over to a supranational organization. The European Union has obtained the power for legislation which stands above the possibilities for formation of the national state. And communication politics – even if it does not dispose of institutions which have powers to enforce anything on a supranational level beyond the European Union – has gained within the UNESCO international dimensions (Offenhäußer 1999).

Regarding media technology worldwide, communication streams had already been generated with satellites which eroded the cultural self-determination of national states. Above all it is the Internet which globalizes communication. Digital information overruns any national border; distances are irrelevant for the perception of world affairs. It seems as if geographical borders and barriers are shrinking more and more because of the media, and that the world is becoming a global village with a unitary arena. With regard to the Internet national claims can no longer be upheld. In fact, international networks try to decide on standards and on how to implement them, which are sometimes labelled as a world government (Kleinwächter 2005).

The rapid diffusion of communication technologies raises fears that a commercially motivated cultural unification of the world will take place; that consumers' ideas, audiences' preferences and images of the world will come close to a 'McDonaldization'. Even if processes of globalization are again and again thwarted by attempts at regionalization, this trend is highly visible (Kleinsteuber and Thomass 2002: 189). Furthermore, journalistic cultures are approaching to a degree – at least in the western and industrialized world – that national specifics seem to disappear beyond this trend (Weaver et al. 2006).

In the light of these developments, does it make sense to identify national media systems, analyze and compare them, and work on their classification?

Media system classification, as it was presented in the tradition of communication scholars until now, starts from the idea, that law, geography, linguistic cultures, the political system, the economic constitution and a given state of media technology and its diffusion are formative factors for the media system, which on their side developed historically within a national frame. This legitimizes the analysis of media systems as national ones. Media are embedded within a cultural context, which have national as well as international dimensions, and only the beginnings of global ones. In fact, media law and media politics, even if their reach is reduced because of globalization, make it possible to identify national media systems. Language and cultural spaces as well – not as clearly as media law and media politics – are dominantly bound to national borders. Nevertheless these statements must not obstruct the view that dissolution of borders of the media systems in a global perspective is in full swing.

It is the knowledge of existing national media systems and their tangible performance, tendencies and problems which permits an empirical observation of such statements as internationalization, globalization, as well as deregulation and commercialization. It is the comparison of specific phenomena in given media systems which makes it possible to ask for general tendencies that come into view, crossing borders. National media systems are a clear-cut object of analysis which is subject to long-term changes caused by globalization. This can be made perceptible with the aid of comparison of media systems. To the degree that processes of globalization influence the national media systems, the above mentioned dimensions of *diffusion*, *dependence*, *temporance* and *performance* gain importance as categories of analysis, as they allow with their inherent descriptions to make statements about the interdependence of media systems.

Increasingly though, the unit of analysis will move away from the nation state and – following the logic of "glocalization" – will either move into the small space of the local level, or into the extended space of the continental or global range. An example for the first type of comparative analysis is a study of small-scale television performance (local, regional, small countries) in twelve European countries. The variety of solutions on the continent is impressive (de Moragas Spá and Garitaonandia 1995). Another study applies the comparative methodology to continental spaces, this time the units of comparison are the communication spaces of Europe and Latin America. In which space is the common public sphere further developed? A comparative content analysis supports the thesis that in spite of the multilingual environment the European public sphere is stronger than the one in (the more or less) monolingual Latin America (Mono 2008).

The integration of dynamics into the criteria of analyzing media systems will be able to explain the globalization of media in a systematic way. This is the frame in which comparative media analysis has to develop next.

Conclusion

If we resume to the development of 50 years of media system classification, typologies and their meanings for Europe, we can state the following main trends:

- Comparative media system analysis has been bound for a long time to the approach of measuring the media practice of systems in other countries against the background of their own socio-philosophical foundations, but not to consider the discrepancy between such ideological foundations and empirical practice.
- Media system typologies developed from normative- to empirically-based approaches.
- The first classifications came from the United States and showed only a limited understanding of the specifics of Europe.
- The number of categories used to describe the media systems grew slightly.
- An intensified view on the political system – as being the characteristic environment – has been developed.
- Underlying theories reflect the theoretical achievements of social sciences and communication studies.
- The models have not, in perspective, been able to describe change in media systems – they are relatively static – with the exception of the transformation models.
- Media system analysis, having started from a static description, becomes more dynamic.
- Online media had not been considered until now.
- Comparative media system analysis is a key approach to understanding globalization.
- The comparative study of national media systems stood at the beginning of a European media policy as can be seen in the country chapters of the first important document: *Green Paper Television without Frontiers* (European Communities 1984).
- Comparative analysis in Europe is the starting point for the beginning of harmonization processes.
- Comparative studies are also central to the future of the European project, as it is the best way to gain an understanding of the continent and its ongoing diversity in media systems.

The further development of comparative media system analysis will have to encompass a refinement of specifications of dimensions. In many cases it will have to engage in the empirical testing of the dimensions and must therefore develop international cooperative research structures.

References

Altschull, J. H. (1984), *Agents of Power. The Role of the news Media in Human Affairs*, New York: Longman.

Blum, R. (2005), 'Bausteine zu einer Theorie der Mediensysteme', *Medienwissenschaft Schweiz*, 2, pp. 5–11.

Blumler, J. G., McLeod, J. M. and Rosengren, K. E. (eds) (1992), *Comparatively Speaking: Communication and Culture across Space and Time*, Newbury Park: Sage.

Compaine, B. and Gomery, D. (2000), *Who Owns the Media? Competition and Concentration in the Mass Media Industry*, 3rd edn, Mahwah and New Jersey: Routledge, pp. 359–435.

de Moragas Spá, M. and Garitaonandia, C. (eds) (1995), *Decentralization in the Global Era: Television in the Regions, Nationalities and Small Countries of the European Union*, London: John Libbey.

Dmoch, T., 'Internationale Werbung. Standardisierung in Grenzen', in Meckel, M. and Kriener, M. (eds) (1996), *Internationale Kommunikation: Eine Einführung*, Opladen: Westdeutscher Verlag, pp. 179–200.

Dobek-Ostrowska, B. et. al. (eds) (2010), *Comparative Media Systems. European and Global Perspectives*, Budapest: CEU Press.

European Communities (1984), *Television Without Frontiers. Green Paper on the Establishment of the Common Market for Broadcasting*, Brussels, June.

Gurevitch, M. and Blumler, J. G., 'Comparative Research: The Extending Frontier', in Swanson, D. L. and Nimmo, D. (eds) (1990), *New Directions in Political Communication: A Resource Book*, Newbury Park: Sage, pp. 305–325.

Hallin, D. C. and Mancini, P. (2004), *Comparing Media Systems: Three Models of Media and Politics*, Cambridge: Cambridge University Press.

Kleinsteuber, H. J., 'Comparing West and East: A Comparative Approach of Transformation', in Dobek-Ostrowska, B. et. al. (eds) (2010), *Comparative Media Systems. European and Global Perspectives*, Budapest: CEU Press, pp. 23–41.

Kleinsteuber, H. J., 'Comparing Mass Communication Systems: Media Formats, Media Contents and Media Processes', in Pfetsch, B. and Esser, F. (eds) (2004), *Comparing Political Communication: Theories, Cases, Challenges*, Cambridge: Cambridge University Press, pp. 64–86.

—— 'Nationale und internationale Mediensysteme', in Merten, K., Schmidt, S. J. and Weischenberg, S. (eds.) (1994), *Die Wirklichkeit der Medien. Eine Einführung in die Kommunikationswissenschaft*, Opladen: Westdeutscher, pp. 544–569.

Kleinsteuber, H. and Thomass, B., 'Medienökonomie, Medienkonzerne und Konzentrationskontrolle', in Altmeppen, K. D. and Karmasin, M. (eds) (2004), *Medien und Ökonomie. Band 2: Problemfelder der Medienökonomie*, Wiesbaden: VS Verlag, pp. 123–58.

Kleinsteuber, H. and Thomass, B., 'Kommunikationspolitik international – ein Vergleich nationaler Entwicklungen', in Hans-Bredow-Institut (ed.) (2002), *Internationales Handbuch für Hörfunk und Fernsehen 2002/2003*, Baden-Baden: Nomos, pp. 88–107.

Kleinwächter, W., 'Internet Co-Governance. Towards a Multilayer Multiplayer Mechanism of Consultation, Coordination and Cooperation (M3C3)', in Ahrweiler, P. and Thomass, B. (eds) (2005), *Internationale partizipatorische Kommunikationspolitik – Strukturen und Visionen*, Münster: LIT, pp. 75–98.

Martin, J. L. and Chaudhary, A. G. (1983), *Comparative Mass Media Systems*, New York: Longman.

Massmann, A. (2003), *Kuba: Globalisierung, Medien, Macht. Eine Indikatorenanalyse zur Klassifkation von Mediensystemen im Zeitalter der Globalen Netzwerkgesellschaft*, Frankfurt: IKO Verlag für Interkulturelle Kommunikation.

Mono, R. (2008), *Ein Politikraum, viele Sprachen, welche Öffentlichkeit?*, Münster: LIT.

Offenhäußer, D., 'Die UNESCO und die globale Informationsgesellschaft', in Donges, P., Jarren, O. and Schatz, H. (eds) (1999), *Globalisierung der Medien? Medienpolitik in der Informationsgesellschaft*, Wiesbaden and Opladen: Westdeutscher Verlag, pp. 73–88.

Preston, W., Herman, E. S., and Schiller, H. I. (1989), *Hope and Folly: The United States and UNESCO 1945–1985*, Minneapolis: University of Minnesota Press.

Ronneberger, F. (1978), *Kommunikationspolitik: Institutionen, Prozesse, Ziele*, Mainz: v. Hase & Koehler.

Siebert, F. S., Peterson, T. and Schramm, W. (1956), *Four Theories of the Press: The Authoritarian, Libertarian, Social Responsibility and Soviet Communist Concepts of What the Press Should Be and Do*, Urbana: University of Illinois Press.

Stommel, A. (1977), *Die Sozialwissenschaft und die Konvergenztheorie. Eine Methoden- und ideologiekritische Untersuchung*, Ph.D. thesis, Free University of Berlin.

Terzis, G. (ed.) (2007), *European Media Governance: The National and Regional Dimensions*, Bristol and Chicago: Intellect.

Thomass, B. and Tzankoff, M. (eds) (2001), *Medien und Transformation in Osteuropa*, Wiesbaden: Westdeutscher Verlag.

Tunstall, J. (2008), *The Media Were American: U.S. Mass Media in Decline*, New York and Oxford: Oxford University Press.

Tunstall, J. and Machin, D. (1999), *The Anglo-American Media Connection*, New York and Oxford: Oxford University Press.

Weaver, D. H. et al. (2006), *The American Journalist in the 21st Century: U.S. News People at the Dawn of a New Millennium*, Mahwah and New Jersey: Lawrence Erlbaum.

Weischenberg, S. (1992), *Journalistik. Theorie und Praxis der Medienkommunikation. Mediensysteme, Medienethik, Medieninstitutionen*, vol. 1, 1. edn. Opladen: Westdeutscher Verlag.

Wiio, O., 'The Mass Media Role in the Western World', in Martin, J. L. and Chaudhary, A. G. (eds) (1983), *Comparative Mass Media Systems*, New York: Longman, pp. 85–94.

Wilke, J. (1997), *Nachrichtenagenturen im Wettbewerb*, Konstanz: UVK-Medien.

Chapter 3

Newspapers: Adapting and Experimenting

Anker Brink Lund, Karin Raeymaeckers and Josef Trappel

P rint media markets in Europe are confronted with challenging changes that threaten to destabilize the relationship between newspapers, the advertisers and their publics. Those changes are occurring fast, thus granting the management of print media actors only a limited time to adopt new strategies to reach the vanishing public and to find innovative solutions to attract advertisers. The factors of change are related to societal developments, to shifts in audience and advertising preferences, but also to the appearance of new media competitors; these factors apply more specifically to the newspaper market where free sheets and online media are turning the traditional business model upside down. This may call for experiments, e.g. synergies with online media, mobile platforms and e-readers. It also poses new challenges to decision makers – not only at the national level, but also in the European Union (EU) and the European Free Trade Association (EFTA) – who are habitually more willing to regulate broadcasting than matters concerning the print media.

Digital technology enables media firms to become part of the convergence process that transforms individual media companies into integrated media corporations that offer new possibilities, but also new threats for media content and distribution (Picard 2004). The adoption of technological innovation has implications not only on news gathering and news processing but also on media concentration and the development of political systems (Hallin and Mancini 2004).

European newspaper publishers are struggling to find a new market position facing Google and other non-journalistic media appropriating their traditional income from classified ads, and readers preferring free media to print-based media on subscription. Newspapers do not only face the Internet as a technological challenge. More fundamentally, the very business model of subscription and single copy sale supplemented by classified advertising is in jeopardy. New payment models such as micropayments have failed so far, and cutbacks in staff only temporarily provide relief from the major challenge: how to sell less of more (Anderson 2006) and still make enough money to offer high quality journalism.

In this chapter we will discuss characteristics and current development trends in the print industry, identify strategic responses by the print media industry and spot patterns of print media policy in Europe. We illustrate these processes by taking a closer look to the print media in selected areas: Scandinavian countries (Denmark, Norway and Sweden), the German speaking countries (Germany, Switzerland and Austria) and the Benelux countries (Belgium, Luxembourg and the Netherlands). We also include information from eastern European print markets.

Decline in Circulation and Advertising

In her critical analysis of the printing press as an agent of change, Elizabeth Eisenstein (1980) demonstrates how most historians have failed to make proper sense of the transition from the era before and after the seminal Gutenberg innovation. In order to understand Europe before and after the spread of such a disruptive technology, we should not only consider the progressive changes but also the establishment's struggles to maintain continuity. This was an important lesson from the fifteenth century, which is often forgotten in the current online revolution of the twenty-first century.

In both instances, media analyses tend to overestimate specific changes in the short run and underestimate general changes in the long run. But European newspapers are 'firmly-rooted in history, culture, and politics', as Els de Bens (2007: 141) put it in her overview of the developments and opportunities of the press industry. Newspapers are expected to inform citizens on news and current affairs, they set the agenda for the people but also for many other forms of mass communication and they are considered relevant agents for political success by institutions and politicians. The degree of relevance varies according to different political and media systems in Europe. While the leading role of newspapers for public communication in general is well accepted in most of the northern and central parts of Europe, newspaper consumption – and therefore newspaper relevance – for the political discourse is lower in large parts of southern and eastern Europe.

In Europe, print media is still the backbone of public debate and the production of news (Lund and Willig 2010). What is common to most European print markets, however, is the continuous decline in circulation for subscribed and sold copies. Figure 1 displays the circulation of paid daily newspapers in eight European countries representing Denmark, Sweden, Norway, Belgium, the Netherlands, Germany, Ireland and Switzerland. For all these countries the statistical models based on simple linear regression shows the future development trend in paid daily circulation, assuming trends from 1995 to 2008 will continue.

Since the mid-1990s this decline in newspaper circulation has been fastened and may in part be explained by the steady rise of television and the development of new digital media distributed on the Internet. For example, Germany and Switzerland lost some 15 per cent each of the total newspaper circulation between 2002 and 2008, amounting to a loss of 3 million copies in Germany and 400,000 copies daily in Switzerland. The Netherlands experienced a loss of 400,000 copies between 2004 and 2008; Sweden lost more than 300,000 copies during the same years. Austria had a temporary increase in 2006 when a new high-circulation daily was launched. However, this paper had to rapidly cut down on circulation and so its overall number of copies decreased to 2.3 million by 2008 (see Table 1).

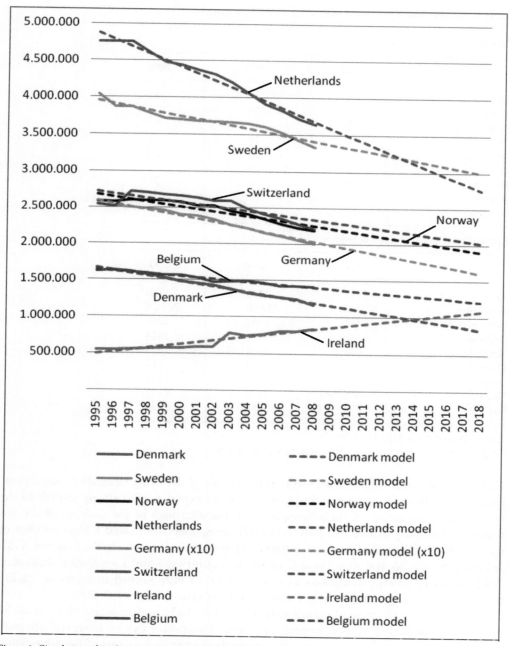

Figure 1: Circulation of Paid Newspapers, Development and Trend.
Source: Based on data from the World Press Trends, various years (http://www.wan-press.org/worldpresstrends/home.php).

Table 1: Number and Circulation of Paid for Daily Newspapers.

Number of paid for daily newspapers

	2004	2006	2008
Austria	16	17	16
Germany	371	370	358
Switzerland	93	91	87
Belgium	28	28	21
Netherlands	35	29	29
Luxembourg	6	6	6
Denmark	30	30	32
Norway	78	77	74
Sweden	90	85	84

Circulation of paid for daily newspapers in thousands

	2004	2006	2008
Austria	2144	2356	2340
Germany	22,095	21,090	20,079
Switzerland	2486	2344	2205
Belgium	1486	1424	1414
Netherlands	4062	3831	3638
Luxembourg	115	114	117
Denmark	1325	1268	1164
Norway	2405	2270	2185
Sweden	3652	3554	3334

Source: World Press Trends (2009)
(http: //www.wan-press.org/worldpresstrends/home.php).

There is, however, an important exception to the rule of declining circulation: most post-Communist countries in central and eastern Europe experienced a strong growth in the number and circulation of their newspapers in the aftermath of the collapse of the old regimes. The newly gained freedom to publish newspapers stimulated a high number of start-ups but in most cases these newly founded papers did not survive in the long run. With reference to Poland and other post-Communist countries, Karol Jakubowicz concludes: 'Tabloidization, falling circulations and the survival of only limited numbers of quality newspapers now appear to be the norm in all of them' (Jakubowicz 2007: 305).

Despite the loss of circulation, newspapers continue to be an important element of the mass media landscape in all European countries. Differences can be observed not only in the market power of newspapers (such as readership figures, shares of the advertising market), but also with regard to their role in political debates. Over the decades, daily newspapers in Europe changed their role considerably. During the peak circulation years, the newspaper landscape was characterized by a press closely affiliated with political parties. In the 1980s and thereafter, the party press retreated in most European countries; titles were closed or had their editorial line changed towards a more forum style press (de Bens and Østbye 1998: 14f). Thus, a smaller number of newspapers managed to enlarge their daily reach and thereby increase their profitability. This emerging dominant type of newspapers brought with it the requirement to redefine the relation between social and political holders of power in society on the one hand, and newspaper owners on the other hand (who in some cases became powerful both horizontally and vertically, and concentrated multi-media corporations with stakes not only in newspapers, but also in television, radio and online media).

Scandinavia, one of the regions with strong newspaper reading traditions, can serve as an example of how these relations are redefined. Denmark, Norway and Sweden invite comparative research because these regional media markets share a number of common features with a long tradition for self-regulation on business terms, combined with politically negotiated and culturally legitimized subsidies. Market-driven competition combined with state subsidies have led to a relatively uniform coverage of news and views.

The homogeneous perspective and weighting in the editorial process rests to a great extent upon the fact that the journalistic actors are dependent upon collective norms and a mutual dependency in a mediated field of strategically conflicting sources in geographically enclosed newspaper markets. Over time, an institutional practice based on professional norms has emerged in which journalists negotiate the news agenda through a constant give-and-take. In doing so, newspapers still deliver the lion's share of news production and public debate. Advertisers, however, do not necessarily honour these efforts, leaving newspapers with growing deficits in revenues.

Ownership Concentration and Line Extension

Change of the newspaper industry all over Europe is motivated by the search for economically viable ways to combat the slow but steady decline in readership. Two dominant options – though often combined – can be observed: corporate expansion and the launch of new products in print markets.

The former strategy is observed since several decades ago and results in a high, or very high, degree of ownership concentration at the national level. The number of newspaper publishers has decreased in almost all countries covered by the compilation of national media systems (Terzis 2007). In the Netherlands, for instance, the three dominating publishers control up to 90 per cent of the newspaper market (Bakker and Vasterman 2007). High levels of press ownership concentration are also evident in the German speaking countries. Austria had only 16 newspapers for its population of 8.5 million in 2008, while Switzerland still had 87 dailies, many of which were very small and published only three or four times a week. Germany had 358 dailies during that year and ranks between the two other countries in relation to the population.

In many European print markets, closure of secondary regional newspapers and the emergence of relatively large media conglomerates led to paradigm change from partisan press to forum press. In Germany, the Axel Springer publishing group and a few other former newspaper publishers developed into integrated media conglomerates with strategic interests not only in the press but also in the online business. The Axel Springer group, for example, took over majority control in Stepstone, one of the largest online job portals in Europe. In a similar move, Swiss publishing companies acquired, or founded, regional radio and television companies in addition to their expansion in regional newspaper markets. The most aggressive example is the Tamedia publishing group in Zurich, who acquired the Swiss capital's leading newspaper, Berner Zeitung, within only two years (2007 to 2009), and also obtained the dominating press group in the French speaking part of Switzerland, Edipresse. Outside Zurich, there is almost no region left where more than one sizeable newspaper exists.

In Austria, the most radical wave of press concentration happened in the 1980s when newspaper competition outside the capital, Vienna, virtually ceased. There are functional newspaper monopolies in all provinces of Austria. These regional monopolies are challenged only by the omnipresent national daily Neue Kronen Zeitung and its regional editions.

In Belgium, the fall of the number of newspaper titles was spectacular. Since 1950 dozens of newspaper titles disappeared in the concentration process and the number of independent media companies shrank from 34 to only five. In Flanders (5.8 million inhabitants), the market is controlled by three groups: Corelio Media, De Persgroep and Concentra. In Wallonia (3.1 million inhabitants), the French-language press is dominated by two groups: Rossel and IPM.

Media ownership in Belgium was until recently determined by language interests. Only a few years ago did the Flemish newspaper group Corelio took an interest in and eventually bought out the Walloon media group, Mediabel. Other recent developments include joint investment procedures in which Flemish and Walloon media firms teamed up to buy newspaper titles. The former independent titles, De Tijd and L'Echo, both financial newspapers, were taken over by a consortium of Rossel and De Persgroep. There are also other joint ventures in media ownership. Concentra and Rossel publish together the free daily, Metro (133,000 copies in Flanders; 122,000 in the French speaking part of Belgium).

Ownership concentration at the national level has expanded significantly across national borders since the early 1990s. Large media (print) corporations – some of them limited by national media concentration rules – realized the opportunity to invest in the post-Communist countries in central and eastern Europe. By 2010, the newspaper market in most of these countries was under control of non-national, mostly West European media companies. Table 2 displays a choice of foreign press ownership in these countries.

Table 2: Foreign Investment of Publishers in Central and Eastern Europe (Selection).

	Media Companies
Bulgaria	• Westdeutsche Allgemeine Zeitung WAZ (Germany): largest and second largest newspaper, largest weekly
Croatia	• WAZ (Germany): interests in daily newspapers • Styria (Austria): tabloid daily, interests in broadsheets
Czech Republic	• Ringier (Switzerland): largest tabloid daily, free sheets and other newspapers • Rheinisch Bergische Verlagsgesellschaft (Germany): second daily, free sheet • Georg von Holtzbrinck / Handelsblatt (Germany): economic newspaper • Verlagsgruppe Passau (Germany): regional newspapers • Modern Times Group (Sweden): free sheet Metro
Estonia	• Schibsted (Norway): first daily newspaper • Marieberg / Bonnier (Sweden): second daily newspaper
Hungary	• Ringier (Switzerland): largest tabloid daily Blick, interests in broadsheets • WAZ (Germany): several regional daily newspapers, news magazines • Springer (Germany): several regional daily newspapers, magazines • Vorarlberger Medienhaus (Austria): several regional daily newspapers • Modern Times Group MTG (Sweden): free sheet Metro
Latvia	• Bonnier (Sweden): largest daily newspaper (shares)
Lithuania	• Orkla (Norway): daily newspaper • Schibsted (Norway): free sheet
Poland	• Springer (Germany): largest tabloid daily Fact, interests in broadsheets • Marieberg / Bonnier (Sweden): national daily Super Express (shares) • Orkla (Norway): economic newspaper (shares)
Serbia	• WAZ (Germany): interests in daily newspapers and magazines • Ringier (Switzerland): tabloid daily, free sheet
Slovenia	• Styria (Austria): largest daily newspaper, free sheets

Sources: Company information and Tabakova, Buric, Smid, Loit, Kaposi, Sulmane, Nugaraité, Lara, Milosavljević (2007).

In the 1990s such investments were conceived by the target countries as welcome opportunities to profit from know-how and financial resources. Without temporary investments from German publishers – such as Axel Springer, Westdeutsche Allgemeine Zeitung (WAZ), Süddeutsche Zeitung and Bertelsmann (Gruner + Jahr) – several newspaper and magazine launches in Austria would not have happened in the 1980s and 1990s. Some of these German publishers have since pulled out of Austria while others (in particular the WAZ group which still holds 50 per cent each of Neue Kronen Zeitung and Kurier, and Gruner + Jahr which controls the News-Group) still hold important shares in the Austrian press.

But foreign domination of the core newspaper markets is rarely considered as acceptable in the long run. The British Mecom Group, for example, ran into trouble when expanding into Norway, Denmark, Poland, Germany and the Netherlands. In the latter market, similar criticism was raised during the takeover of the large Dutch media group PCM, de Volkskrant, NRC Handelsblad, Trouw and Algemeen Dagblad, by the Belgium family trust De Persgroep in 2009. The Dutch media regulator allowed this acquisition only on the condition that De Persgroep sells NRC Media, the company behind NRC Handelsblad and NRC.next.

While the rather long experience in Austria shows that foreign ownership does not necessarily alter the products as long as they are profitable, cases have been reported from central and eastern Europe were publishers unduly used their market power. In several cases, newspapers in central and eastern Europe were bought by western companies only to close them down in order to strengthen another title of the same press group. In Hungary, for example, Ringier (Switzerland) was sharply accused of such practices when it closed down the long standing daily Magyar Hirlap in 2004, only to increase the circulation and market shares of Népszabadság. The former editor-in-chief of Magyar Hirlap publicly called this behaviour 'a catastrophic defeat for press freedom in Central Europe' (Der Standard 2004).

More generally, a driving force for press concentration is commercialization. Since the 1980s commercialization became a dominating trend in media markets, both for broadcast and print media. This commercialization paved the way for growing concentration and the emergence of large media corporations with monopoly aspirations. Bagdikian (2004), Baker (2007) and McChesney (1999) describe how ownership of media firms is concentrated in the hands of a very small number of entrepreneurs who strive for a monopoly market position. McChesney warns explicitly for the manipulation potential of these large media conglomerates and argues that they have an impact on public opinion, selfishly directing the information flow in accordance to their economic and financial interests.

Counteracting forces are weak, however. Newspaper markets are characterized by strong economies of scale and scope, making new market entries very costly, risky and difficult. Successful launches of new newspapers – apart from free sheets – are rare. Again, post-Communist central and eastern European countries are the exception to the rule, but market consolidation and the economic recession have also played part in cooling down ambitions to launch new titles in these countries.

Experiments with Free Sheets

It is general textbook knowledge that a commercially sound newspaper should aim at a split budget of 50 per cent from advertising revenue and 50 per cent income generated by readers (either from subscription or by single copy sales). As of lately, the latter way is the more lucrative because home delivery costs increased far beyond other newspaper related costs.

In 1995, this was one of the reasons why the Swedish Modern Times Group (MTG) decided to offer a newspaper called Metro free of charge to commuters of metropolitan Stockholm. Distribution cost was cut and advertisers were offered comprehensive readership, including a young people audience who had been dropping newspaper reading over the previous decades. From the readers' point of view, the paper was 'free' (at no cost for consumption), i.e. entirely financed by advertisements.

Free weekly and monthly papers based on this business model were well established in many European print markets long before the launch of the free daily papers. But the free daily concept was met with contempt by publishers. No professionals – including most newspaper journalists – seriously imagined that one could make a sustainable business case by giving editorial content away for free on a day-to-day basis. The concept of a free daily newspaper – invented by the two journalists Robert Braunerhielm and Pelle Anderson – was rejected by all major newspaper publishers in Scandinavia. When they finally found financial backing, it came from a company making its money from television and mobile phone services.

This was hardly incidental. Electronic media, in contrast to print media, has a long tradition of delivering free content. In most media markets, radio and television are substantially (or entirely) financed by advertising. In this sector of the media business free-to-air content has been the rule rather than the exception. Only recently has electronic content been provided by subscription (based on satellite and cable distribution) or sold on pay-per-view terms.

Fuelled by their almost instant Swedish success, Metro International exported the concept of free dailies to the Czech Republic (1996), Hungary (1998), Holland and Finland (1999), Chile, United States, Italy, Canada, Poland, Greece, Argentina, Switzerland, the United Kingdom (all 2000) and Denmark (2001).

News about the Metro-concept also reached Iceland. Because in Iceland metropolitan areas are small and public transportation is of little importance, an Icelandic company called Dagsbrún, amended the free paper business model by testing a home delivery model called Frettabladid. The experiment failed in its first attempt. But supported by capital from the Baugur Group, Frettabladid gradually became a commercial success. By 2006, some 95,000 copies were delivered in a country with 105,000 households seven days a week. This gave the paper a share of readership of 70 per cent coverage and an impressive grip on younger readers. Based on their domestic success, Dagsbrún decided to go international in 2006. They chose Denmark and regional markets in the United States as testing grounds because the potentials in terms of readership and advertising were promising. Denmark has a long tradition for newspaper literacy, but the drop in daily use among young readers has been among the highest in Europe. After two years of heavy losses, however, the Icelandic experiment abroad was ended. At the same time several free commuter papers were closed down as well.

These examples illustrate how newspapers adapt and experiment with new business models. Not always successfully, it should be noted. The loss of advertising revenues following the economic recession that hit Europe in the second semester of 2008 is a major concern for all media, but it is far more urgent for those media that fully depend on advertising income. In Switzerland, for example, from seven free newspapers only the three survived the first wave of the economic recession in 2008–09.

The introduction of free newspapers, however, provoked a major shift in the business models of traditional newspaper editors. For example, the Metro and 20 Minutes newspapers (originally launched by the Norwegian Schibsted) were exported to a wide range of European countries and the national newspaper groups had quite different patterns of reaction to those new competitors. In some countries the traditional newspaper groups copied the model and edited their own free newspaper brand, thus competing directly within their national markets with the Scandinavian competitors. In other countries (e.g. Germany) the traditional newspaper groups started legal procedures to stop the publication of free newspapers, and in France the resistance against the free competitors was organized through the Labour Unions who fiercely fought against this new phenomenon. Again in other countries, the Scandinavian brand was acquired by national publishers (e.g. Switzerland).

One way of reacting to the challenge of free newspaper competition was the introduction of compact newspapers. Light versions of existing newspapers addressed the niche of young readers, and readers with limited time and attention. This concept has been introduced in Germany and the Netherlands where Die Welt Kompakt and NCR.next managed to attract a new audience. In Belgium, however, the copycat of this idea was a financial disaster for the newspaper group Corelio who introduced the title Espresso as the light version of its quality newspaper De Standaard. In Switzerland, Ringier first changed the format of its tabloid newspaper Blick to small size, only to return two years later to its former larger format in 2009.

Another major route to escape decreasing advertising income and losses in newspaper circulation is the launch of online media distributed exclusively in the Internet to various reception devices (see also Chapter 6 on online media in this volume). Newspapers were in many countries latecomers when online media were established in the early 1990s. Some newspaper publishers were hesitant to lose their paying readers to the online editions. Lately, newspapers have realized that there is no alternative to an extensive online representation in the Internet. By this move, younger readers can be reached and some circulation losses compensated. However, the need to establish a viable business model with sufficient revenue creation became a pressing need when the economic recession hit the media business in the years 2008 and 2009. In fact, in many European countries only very few – if not only one single, dominant information portal – manage to cover their cost through advertising income alone. Paid content, however, is highly unpopular among Internet users who are accustomed to free access to information.

How this may affect the newspaper business is hard to forecast. But it will probably encourage experiments with micropayments and the so-called 'walled garden' technology in order to regain some of the losses on the printed editions. We shall probably also see newspaper publishers going into e-reader publishing and mobile media to a much larger extent than has been the case in the first decade after the turn of the millennium.

Subsidies and Regulation

European newspapers have been heavily supported by state subsidies since the 1960s. Scandinavian media enterprises, for example, enjoy VAT abatements, distribution benefits and state support for innovative experiments. The crucial question is whether this political tradition, based upon national regulation of the media derived from statutory powers and professional autonomy, can preserve content diversity and a political economy under global convergence and increasing ownership concentration.

Aside from press subsidies, the national governments of Europe and the European Union regulatory authorities tend to keep a low profile in mingling with the print media business. Media regulation at the national, as well as at the pan-European, level is much more explicit on the broadcasting market. Consequently, newspapers enjoy comparatively far reaching freedom with regard to content regulation. Their content autonomy is firmly rooted in the nineteenth century at a time when censorship was abandoned and the proclaimed 'free press' emerged. However, contemporary media markets raise concerns about pluralism and opinion diversity.

Media ownership concentration poses the question whether newspapers (and media in general) guided entirely or predominantly by market forces and competition rules can deliver the optimum result for contemporary democracies (Trappel and Maniglio 2009). Democratic virtues critically depend on the public discourse displayed by newspapers and other news media. Therefore, print media regulation concentrates on measures to maintain (or establish) pluralism with little or no interference in editorial matters. In cases where competition rules are ineffective to maintain pluralism, other forms of intervention, such as direct or indirect subsidies, are executed in various European countries.

As shown above, most European national print media markets are divided between only a few business actors. In the United Kingdom, two publishers control 55 per cent of the print market; in Italy there are five dominant press groups; in Spain six media groups control 90 per cent of the market (two of them account for 50 per cent); and in small countries, very few publishing groups divide the markets among them: five in Belgium and only four in the Netherlands, three in Norway and one dominant publisher in Ireland. Regulation at the national level to prevent press concentration was not successful or was implemented too late, when the concentration process was already too far spread (like in the Austrian case).

Some countries developed specific media policy measures to regulate the national newspaper market. Selected European countries implemented national anti-trust legislation, as well as regulation on cross-ownership. Big media corporations regard these national regulation measures as obstacles for their expansion and seek support for their position with the European Commission. The Commission, however, tends to direct such complaints back to the national legislative framework. Only major concentration cases meet the requirements (such as a minimum turnover of 2 billion Euros) and have to be decided at the European level. These requirements normally do not apply to European newspaper companies which are of considerably smaller size.

Some media regulation is based on specific numeric indicators. In Germany the Bundeskartellamt (Germany's national competition regulator) argues that no newspaper group can acquire more than 25 per cent of the shares of another German newspaper group. As a result, German newspaper editors who had intended to expand their activities, ended up seeking growth opportunities across the national borders (in central and eastern Europe), or they diversified into the magazine or broadcasting markets. A similar development can be seen in Norway, where the major player Schibsted was forced into a globalized strategy rather than a national market consolidation.

In France, there is a highly elaborated set of rules in place including indicators such as market shares and geographical penetration. The French anti-trust regulation stipulates that no group can acquire more than 30 per cent of the overall circulation of national newspapers. This measure was criticized as the 'Hersant-standard', since this 30 per cent was very well tailored to the then existing market situation where media mogul Robert Hersant indeed controlled the market to that extent.

Scandinavian countries have developed relatively sophisticated media policy regimes covering the press. These nations have a long tradition of parliamentary control of the mass media as a cultural-political supplement to market-based self-regulation under free trade conditions. Government intervenes in media business with the intent of securing diversity and national identity. The official political goal has usually been to create and preserve the basis for free speech and fair competition on the media market. But tools and methods utilized for political regulations vary from nation to nation (Kelly et al. 2004).

In order to mitigate inequalities in opinion making and access to public debate, all the Scandinavian nations have some form of politically defined subsidies for the printed mass media, ranging from direct funding over tax relief to cheap rates for delivery by the postal services. Norway, however, is the only Scandinavian country in which formal limits of ownership have been politically regulated. This may be an incentive for national media houses to expand internationally to a greater extent than other Scandinavian players. While Norway and Sweden offer direct support to selected newspapers to varying degrees, the representatives of the press, supported by a political majority, have rejected similar proposals in Denmark. The consequences of these differences in press subsidies are disputed and invite future research (Rambøll 2009).

The past 100 years of interaction among media businesses and political regulators has created institutional conditions that, to a great degree, have preserved home markets for national and regional newspapers in Europe. It has been difficult and risky for foreign players to penetrate the print market, and the promise of success was limited. These barriers of entry, however, have decreased, e.g. free sheets from Metro International and Schibsted penetrate a growing number of European newspaper markets.

At the European level, media policy developed and implemented by the European Commission has not addressed newspapers specifically. Media policy is directed towards free competition and regulation on the European level and is tailored to the largest players in the market. Press subsidy schemes as effective as the ones in Austria, France, the Netherlands and some Scandinavian countries are as a matter of principle suspected to be incompatible with the rules of the common market (state aid rules) but they are tolerated as exceptional practices of long national tradition if proper notification takes place. Audio-visual policy and print media policy overlap in the area of online media. The 2009

Broadcasting Communication by the European Commission stipulates that online media markets should become the domain of private companies with strict rules for public service media companies.

Another way of supporting newspapers that are still important for public deliberations and for keeping the public informed is their use in the educational system. This introduces the medium to the younger generations who are more literate in terms of the Internet and other electronic channels of communication. In Belgium, editors and policy makers have joined forces in a long term effort aiming at the preservation of the future readers' market. Since 2003, Flemish newspaper publishers distribute almost 1 million copies to schools every year. Within each school year, approximately 100,000 students participate in the Newspapers in Education Project. Research-based results (Raeymaeckers et al. 2009) indicate that the project is successful: participants have a more positive attitude towards newspapers and newspaper reading, and subsequent participation suggests a cumulative positive impact.

Conclusion

Loss of revenue requires publishers to reconsider their business model and look for innovative ways to cope with digital convergence. Online media are an essential market segment where publishers compete with broadcasters and genuine web-only content providers. It is, however, doubtful whether the implemented model of free access to information and entertainment can be developed into a sustainable business proposition of 'selling less of more' in a profitable fashion.

Advertising markets are sensitive to economics and have started to migrate towards new media. Over time, the free sheet business model, which is currently very successful in the reader market, may translate well into the advertising market. But newspaper publishers have already lost much of their classified business to online media (e.g. Google), and they are on their way to lose considerable amounts of display advertising as well.

Currently it is difficult to see a strictly market-based solution to these challenges – unless the quality of newspaper journalism suffers severely. Optimists comfort the European print media business that waning newspapers have sustained competition from new media for more than half a millennium (Dimmick 2003). This has been achieved by constantly adapting to new communications technology in an experimental fashion (Achtenhagen 2008).

Pessimists, though, suggest that the current crisis of print media calls for 'thinking the unthinkable', as Clay Shirky (2009) has eloquently put it: 'The newspaper people often note that newspapers benefit society as a whole. This is true, but irrelevant to the problem at hand; "You're gonna miss us when we're gone!" has never been much of a business model. So who covers all that news if significant fractions of the currently employed newspaper people lose their jobs?'

References

Achtenhagen, L. (2008), 'Understanding Entrepreneurship in Traditional Media', *Journal of Media Business Studies*, 5: 1, pp. 123–42.

Anderson, C. (2006), *The Long Tail: Why the Future of Business Is Selling Less of More*, New York: Brockman.

Anon (2004), *Der Standard* newspaper, 7 November.

Bagdikian, B. H. (2004), *The New Media Monopoly*, revised and updated edn, Boston: Beacon.

Baker, E. C. (2007), *Media Concentration and Democracy: Why Ownership Matters*, New York: Cambridge University Press.

Bakker, P. and Vasterman P., 'The Dutch Media Landscape', in Terzis, G. (ed.) (2007), *European Media Governance: National and Regional Dimensions*, Bristol and Chicago: Intellect, pp. 145–55.

Bromley, M., 'The United Kingdom Media Landscape', in Terzis, G. (ed.) (2007), *European Media Governance: National and Regional Dimensions*, Bristol and Chicago: Intellect, pp. 43–54.

Buric, N., 'The Croatian Media Landscape', in Terzis, G. (ed.) (2007), *European Media Governance: National and Regional Dimensions*, Bristol and Chicago: Intellect, pp. 327–37.

de Bens, E., 'Developments and Opportunities of the European Press Industry', in Meier, W. A. and Trappel, J. (eds) (2007), *Power, Performance and Politics: Media Policy in Europe*, Baden-Baden: Nomos, pp. 142–70.

de Bens, E. and Østbye, H., 'The European Newspaper Market', in McQuail, D. and Siune, K. (eds) (1998), *Media Policy: Convergence, Concentration and Commerce*, London, Thousand Oaks and New Delhi: Sage, pp. 7–22.

Dimmick, J. (2003), *Media Competition and Coexistence: The Theory of the Niche*, Mahwah: Lawrence Erlbaum.

Eisenstein, E. (1980), *The Printing Press as an Agent of Change*, Cambridge: Cambridge University Press.

Hallin, D. C. and Mancini, P. (2004), *Comparing Media Systems: Three Models of Media and Politics*, Cambridge: Cambridge University Press.

Jakubowicz, K., 'The Eastern European/Post-Communist Media Model Countries', in Terzis, G. (ed.) (2007), *European Media Governance: National and Regional Dimensions*, Bristol and Chicago: Intellect, pp. 303–13.

Jyrkiäinen, J., 'The Finnish Media Landscape', in Terzis, G. (ed.) (2007), *European Media Governance: National and Regional Dimensions*, Bristol and Chicago: Intellect, pp. 97–109.

Kaposi, I., 'The Hungarian Media Landscape', in Terzis, G. (ed.) (2007), *European Media Governance: National and Regional Dimensions*, Bristol and Chicago: Intellect, pp. 363–74.

Kelly, M., Mazzoleni, G. and McQuail, D. (eds) (2004), *The Media in Europe: The Euromedia Handbook*, London: Sage.

Lara, A., 'The Polish Media Landscape', in Terzis, G. (ed.) (2007), *European Media Governance: National and Regional Dimensions*, Bristol and Chicago: Intellect, pp. 399–410.

Loit, U., 'The Estonian Media Landscape', in Terzis, G. (ed.) (2007), *European Media Governance: National and Regional Dimensions*, Bristol and Chicago: Intellect, pp. 351–62.

Lund, A. B. (2007), 'Media Markets in Scandinavia: Political Economy Aspects of Convergence and Divergence', *Nordicom Review*, 28: 1, pp. 121–34.

Lund, A. B. and Willig, I. (2010), *One Week of News 1999–2008*, Aarhus: Ajour.

McChesney, R. W. (1999), *Rich Media, Poor Democracy: Communication Politics in Dubious Times*, New York: The New Press.

Milosavljević, M., 'The Slovenian Media Landscape', in Terzis, G. (ed.) (2007), *European Media Governance: National and Regional Dimensions*, Bristol and Chicago: Intellect, pp. 433–44.

Nugaraité, A., 'The Lithuanian Media Landscape', in Terzis, G. (ed.) (2007), *European Media Governance: National and Regional Dimensions*, Bristol and Chicago: Intellect, pp. 387–97.

Picard, R., 'Environmental and Market Changes Driving Strategic Planning in Media Firms', in Picard, R. (ed.) (2004), *Strategic Responses to Media Market Change*, Jönköping: JIBS Research Reports, pp. 1–17.

Raeymaeckers, K., Hoebeke, T. and Hauttekeete, L., (2008), 'Newspapers in Education in Flanders: A Case in Point of a Successful Media Policy Aimed at Qualitatively Supporting the Future Readership Market', *Journalism Practice*, 2: 3, pp. 414–26.

_____ 'Newspapers in Education in Flanders: A Press Policy to Support the Future Readership Market for Newspapers', in Franklin, B. (ed.) (2009), *The Future of Newspapers*, London: Routledge, pp. 290–302.

Raeymaeckers, K., Hauttekeete, L. and Deprez, A. (2007), 'To Read or not to Read: Can Policy Support the Future Reader Market? A Flemish Case Study', *European Journal of Communication*, 22: 1, pp. 89–107.

Rambøll (2009), *Udredning af den fremtidige offentlig mediestøtte*, København: Styrelsen for Bibliotek and Medier.

Shirky, C. (2009), 'Newspapers and Thinking the Unthinkable'. Available at: http: //www.shirky.com/ weblog/2009/03/newspapers-and-thinking-the-unthinkable. Accessed 23 February 2010.

Smid, M., 'The Czech Media Landscape', in Terzis, G. (ed.) (2007), *European Media Governance: National and Regional Dimensions*, Bristol and Chicago: Intellect, pp. 339–50.

Sulmane, I., 'The Latvian Media Landscape', in Terzis, G. (ed.) (2007), *European Media Governance: National and Regional Dimensions*, Bristol and Chicago: Intellect, pp. 375–86.

Tabakova, V., 'The Bulgarian Media Landscape', in Terzis, G. (ed.) (2007), *European Media Governance: National and Regional Dimensions*, Bristol and Chicago: Intellect, pp. 315–25.

Terzis, G. (ed.) (2007), *European Media Governance: National and Regional Dimensions*, Bristol and Chicago: Intellect.

Trappel, J. and Maniglio T. (2009), 'On Media Monitoring – the Media for Democracy Monitor (MDM)', *Communications*, 34: 2, pp. 169–201.

Chapter 4

Radio: A Resilient Medium

Hans J. Kleinsteuber

One might say that radio is the quintessential European technology. American observer Ithiel de Sola Pool argued that in Europe the tradition of the centralized rule is well reflected in the one-way dissemination technology of radio (and later television), whereas in North America interactive technologies (telegraph and telephone, Internet) had a better chance to evolve because of the more horizontal tradition in politics and culture (de Sola Pool 1983). Hence, some of the elementary inventions concerning radio technology have been first realized in Europe (by Heinrich Rudolf Hertz, Guglielmo Marconi, Alexander Stepanovich Popov), whereas the first applications of the new wireless communication technology were first implemented in North America (by Reginald Fessenden, etc.). There is no doubt that a more playful application of the new technology was attempted there. Radio as a medium started earlier and in a more decentralized, individualized fashion (during 1919–20 in the United States and Canada). In most European countries the development started slightly later (e.g. in the United Kingdom in 1922, in Germany in 1923).

If one compares radio developments in North America with those in large parts of Europe, one finds significant differences. In the United States, radio emerged from a coalition between the electrical industries and the radio amateurs, the state being largely absent. Radio started at the local level and was later connected into nationwide networks. In this environment commercial interests could take over the new medium at an early stage (Hilliard and Keith 2005). In Europe the national state took the lead, usually in alliance with the electrical industry. Central actors were large companies (BBC during the early days) or the state postal and telephone administration (in Germany). In Germany there was a fear of 'rebels' taking over the new means of communication and using it against the government. Also many of the European states were unstable because of the presence of ethnic minorities, class tensions and demands from extremist organizations (Fascist and Communist) to take over radio as a propaganda tool. The German development was radically different from the one in the United States: radio was established by the state and put under strict bureaucratic supervision, with any independent activity, even by radio amateurs, being strictly forbidden (Lersch and Schanze 2004). The centrality of the system made it easy for the Nazis to take over on the day of seizure of power in January 1933 and convert it into their leading propaganda tool.

Steps in European Radio History

Radio stations started in Europe in the early 1920s: they were established by the national government, that kept them under tight control even though some started as private corporations (like the BBC) and were made public later on. Usually one programme in Amplitude Modulation (AM) technology (on long or middle wave) was offered with a long reach of signals. Services were seen as a means to keep the nation together, and radio became a source of national identity; radio programming was centralized, connecting the country with the capital. Already in the early years the signal travelled across borders; early radio receivers offered programmes from stations like Radio Monte Carlo, Hilversum, Radio Vatican, etc. Programming was mostly financed by a monthly licence fee and there was no, or only little, advertisement. Programming usually included a broad spectrum of news, education, classical and light music, all under governmental supervision. In many countries there were grassroots radio movements by citizens, some demanding access to the new medium, others just experimenting with the exciting new technology. Usually the audience was excluded from influencing any decision-making; only in the Netherlands did the different 'pillars' (constituent groups in society) jointly establish a unique decentralized radio system that survived for many decades.

Radio was soon recognized by governments as a central tool that could influence audiences. This basically led towards two directions:

- Securing independence of the radio broadcaster from the state through special statutes such as the ones in Britain (the BBC Royal Charter) that led to the shaping of public service radio; in this tradition free access to foreign radio programmes was part of an understanding of radio freedom.
- Placing radio under strict government supervision as in Nazi Germany, where radio became the central tool of propaganda. Receivers were produced that were too weak to receive foreign stations, and reception of foreign stations was banned.

This early European radio regime lasted until 1945, when the dictatorial regimes collapsed and the public service model took over in western Europe.

Radio in Europe developed in three phases:

Phase 1 – until the end of World War II: Amplitude Modulation (AM) technology; state broadcasters with one programme; governmental control; continental reach of programmes; state models rule in Europe.

Phase 2 – until today: Frequency Modulation (FM) technology; public service broadcasters with several programmes under (more or less) pluralistic control, with local and national reach; at times Cold War confrontations ('radio wars'); in the 1980s commercial stations were launched; dual radio system; emergence of community radio.

Phase 3 – started around 2000: digital technology and different platforms (terrestrial, satellite and cable, Internet and mobile phone); diversity of broadcasters (public, commercial, community); range of global and local stations; little external regulation; rediscovery of radio in Europe.

Already at the end of the 1920s, radio was seen as an ideal instrument to reach audiences beyond national borders. The first station was Radio Moscow, offering programmes in other European languages as of 1929, and propagating the achievements of the Bolshevik Revolution (1917) to the rest of the capitalist continent. Germany started to transmit programmes to the many German-speaking people living beyond its borders. Britain established its BBC Empire Service in 1932 to provide information to listeners at the outposts of the Commonwealth (Anduaga 2009). The communication channels were either long wave or increasingly short wave, as it was recognized that signals could travel around the world without using much energy. Only a few stations could operate on long wave; on short wave there was unlimited access.

After World War II the second phase in the development of radio started. In political terms it was defined by a number of factors including:

- The end of most of the Fascist dictatorships
- The beginning of the Cold War
- The general introduction of the public service model in western Europe

The public service model for radio had evolved first in Britain and in Scandinavia during the years between the wars. Central elements were (and still are):

- An independent organization, created by the state
- Totally (in the United Kingdom) or mostly (in Germany and elsewhere) financed by a monthly or annual licence fee; financed with some advertisement, full financing by advertisement being exceptional
- Service has to be comprehensive, covering the entire territory, serving the nation and different segments in society
- Remit for programming is defined by the state (usually parliament); it includes information, education, culture, entertainment
- High probability of some political influence, as parliament or government have a say in its management (Lewis 1999)

The breakdown of dictatorships in western Europe meant that the former state activities in radio were replaced by public service models, e.g. in Germany, Austria and Italy so as to make the countries fit for democracy. The development in Communist eastern Europe was different: here radio was defined as a central element of agitation and propaganda under the guidance of the ruling Communist Party, with central control of news dissemination, and censorship and rejection of western influences (e.g. in popular music) being part of this policy.

These political factors were accompanied by important technological change: the introduction of Frequency Modulation (FM), first complementary to, later on as a substitute for Amplitude Modulation (AM) technology. After the war, frequencies were redistributed in Europe in the so-called Radio Administration Conferences, where the then occupied countries lost some of their AM frequencies to neighbouring countries and allied military forces. A country like Germany was therefore interested in the prompt use of a new range of FM frequencies. This required the development of new radio receivers, but FM also offered a much higher sound quality, allowed (later) stereo and specific services, like additional data via the Radio Data System (RDS). The most important change was related to the number and range of frequencies. FM allowed the introduction of multi-channel radio across Europe. Public service organizations extended their programme supplies and introduced new, more specialized content with emphasis on popular music, culture, news, a regional focus, etc. Another element of FM was that the transmission space, which was much smaller, could provide just one city agglomeration with content. As public service organizations usually did not have the resources to introduce local radio throughout the country, the pressure for the admission of additional non-public radio stations increased.

In general, radio suffered from the increasing competition of television which became the leader among all mass media. Radio withdrew and became a medium for complementary listening activities and started to serve special audiences interested in local affairs, pop music aimed at youth and young adults, classical music aimed at the more highbrow listeners, etc.

The emerging Cold War was clearly reflected in the development of radio: especially the vast range of long and short wave stations which were attributed a new mission. Both sides of the divided continent rebuilt their existing international radio systems to transmit programming across the Iron Curtain to the other side of Europe. This included western and eastern broadcasters who offered programming in languages that were spoken 'on the other side'. BBC World Service, Deutsche Welle and Radio France Internationale were active on the western side; Radio Moscow on the Communist side. In addition, practically every European state offered some kind of international radio. The eastern side, especially the Soviet Union, attempted to jam signals from the West and made reception in their region impossible, although with limited success.

A very special station was Radio Free Europe/Radio Liberty (RFE/RL) because it was run mainly by former citizens of Communist countries who had in-depth knowledge of the situation there. The station played a significant role during the Cold War years broadcasting from the 'free' side of the divided Continent to the 'unfree' audiences beyond the Iron Curtain (Critchlow 1995). At times RFE/RL was supported by the CIA and saw itself in the role of breaking information barriers. At the end of the European division, the station moved to Prague and continued its activities, still reporting the news to twenty countries (mainly states on the territory of the former Soviet Union) in 28 languages, emphasizing the fight for media freedom in these countries (www.rferl.org).

In western Germany regular stations of the public system broadcasting on AM and FM frequencies reached every spot of Communist East Germany and often reported suppressed information from inside the country. One could say that an electronically created common communication space survived in spite of the division of the country. After the Cold War this system of polarized radio communication throughout Europe came to an end, some of the programmes disappeared, while others moved to online platforms. Some of the remaining broadcasters concentrate on European services; in 2008 they founded the European Radio Network (Euranet) in an effort to provide news focusing on Europe (www.euranet.eu).

Fight over Commercial Radio

The renaissance of the radio after World War II was based on the western public service model, but already in the early days some commercial broadcasting was available in Europe. In 1931, French businessmen established the Compagnie Luxembourgeoise de Radiodiffusion (later RTL), starting AM transmissions from Luxembourg and covering large parts of Europe with entertainment that was financed through advertisements. After World War II, the RTL station – transmitting through middle and short wave – became the leading commercial broadcaster in Europe using English, French and German, offering a programme that combined popular music, disc jockey announcements and advertisement spots. Also around France a ring of so-called *radios périphériques* including stations in Germany, Andorra and Monte Carlo, was tolerated. In Spain, on the fringe of Europe, non-state radio was accepted provided it strictly followed the rules of dictator Franco. A network of Catholic stations (COPE) was already established in 1957 which still exists today. Also, commercial radio could operate after the war.

The 1970s were the years when the still dominant public service model was seriously challenged. Public radio emphasized news, culture and educational programming, and transmitted limited musical entertainment. This led to a movement in a number of countries (Netherlands, United Kingdom, Scandinavia) establishing offshore radio stations that circumvented the public monopoly. They transmitted from the High Seas outside of national control and called themselves pirate radios. Quickly, they acquired large audiences and forced media decision makers to open up the market to commercial broadcasters who mainly offered popular music (Harris 1977).

Considering these developments, it became clear that public monopolies could no longer be sustained, and during the 1980s (in most western European countries) the media law was changed and commercial radio, financed through advertising, was introduced under a licence system. A dual system of broadcasting was established, consisting of the old public service system alongside a new commercial one. The commercial model was taken from the United States and during the founding years, US consultants helped to establish the new system. It adopted many features of the well-developed US commercial system, including format radio (i.e. just one type of music, e.g. Easy Listening, Top 40), disc jockeys guiding the listeners through the programme, news limited to short announcements, the branding of stations, radio games to entertain the listener, etc. With this increasing diversification, some classical music stations arose as well as stations for significant migrant groups, e.g. for northern Africans in France, West Indians in Britain, Turks in Germany. In many cases the commercial radio stations were aimed at young audiences who were (and are) of special interest to advertisers, whereas public broadcasters remained prominent among older listeners.

Along with the dual system, a central media authority was established in each country, somehow modelled after the American Federal Communications Commission (FCC) which was established in 1934 to give out commercial licences. By way of an example, in France the Conseil Supérieur de l´Audiovisuel (CSA) was established, in Germany (where broadcasting responsibility rests with the sixteen Länder states) fourteen regional authorities were set up. Although regulation for commercial broadcasters differed from country to country, commercial radio followed a global pattern of formatted programming.

In central and eastern Europe commercial radio did not exist before the breakdown of the Communist system. But already during the phase of transformation, the first advertisement-financed radio stations started to emerge and drew large audiences away from the old state broadcasters. Quickly a dual system emerged that was placed under regulation. Only later on were the state-controlled stations transformed into a public service model, often still with considerable political control and a relatively weak position vis-à-vis commercial competitors. In Russia and other countries of the former Soviet Union, strong state control remained, but a lively commercial sector was established, at times taking up diverging stances in countries with little diversity left.

Today commercial radio in Europe is predominantly in the hands of national owners, meaning that media authorities secured that licences were given to national investors. But the first pan-European networks are emerging. The leading one is Radio NRJ (or Energy) which is offering a music format aimed at young people (hit music only). It started as a pop music station in Paris in 1981 and has become the most successful commercial network in France today. It has since then expanded into about a dozen European countries in western and eastern Europe (www.nrjgroup.com). NRJ follows the commercial logic of the early networks in the United States: those also started as local stations that later on interconnected into a common network.

Whereas NRJ is recognized as a brand for music for the young in large parts of Europe, another pan-European actor, the RTL Group – owned by Europe's largest media conglomerate Bertelsmann (the leading European entertainment group) – keeps a low profile. RTL has invested in 32 stations across Europe (in 2009), most of them in Germany, Belgium, the Netherlands and Portugal (www.rtlgroup.com). The stations cater to different audiences and accept the local flavour of the region.

Since the 1980s a dual radio system has been established in western Europe, which means that there is a more or less balanced competition between the public model (i.e. a genuine product of Europe) and the commercial model (i.e. an import from the United States). The dual model, however, is not a copy of the American radio system (in which the public sector is not state-created and very small). It first emerged in peripheral states like Canada and Australia, where some of its features could already be found in the 1930s.

Community Radio

The idea of non-commercial, non-public stations was first realized in the United States (Pacifica Network) in the late 1940s. Europe took a different route. In those years, when pirate stations attacked the public service system, many illegal stations – usually from the political left – went on air. During the 1970s and 1980s civic actors established a wide variety of stations, some tolerated by the state, others heavily prosecuted. In this founding generation, three types of non-commercial radio could be found in Europe:

- In the South (France, Italy), the stations called themselves *radios libres*: they were seen as a place for alternative information and counterculture.
- In the West (Netherlands, Belgium), the stations followed more the pattern of local community radio and were quickly legalized.
- In the Scandinavian countries, the state established a dense network of a high number of local stations, grounded in civic control and targeting urban neighbourhoods, e.g. Närrradio (near radio) in Sweden (Kleinsteuber and Sonnenberg 1990).

Commercial and community stations started during those years; in some European countries they enjoyed the same legal status, in others they had to comply with different rules and regulations. Today the landscape of non-commercial radio is extremely diverse. This diversity is reflected in their labelling as they include community, free, independent, local, ethnic, campus, public access radio, etc.

Models of Community Radio in Europe

Britain has a long history of fighting for community stations, but only the Community Act of 2003 established the legal foundations for such stations. More than 100 stations are active (more are licensed). A portion of the broadcasting licence fee goes into a Community Radio Fund, which is administered by the Ofcom communications regulatory agency that provides stations with some financing (for country studies, see Peissl and Tremetzberger 2008).

Ireland has a small market that suffers from strong media influences from neighbouring United Kingdom. Besides four nationwide public and two commercial stations, there are nearly 50 regional and local stations active, both commercial and community ones. Already existing stations were legalized through the Radio and Television Act of 1988, controlled by the Broadcasting Commission of Ireland (BCI) that has licensed nineteen community radios. A small share of the broadcasting licence fee is reserved for the support of such stations (Day 2008).

In the Netherlands, the public radio system came under hard pressure through pirate stations and very early a local broadcasting system was established. The legal basis is the Media Act of 1987. The particular policy goal is that each local community should rely on some media structure, in most cases FM radio, but also cable TV, videotext, etc. In 2007, 292 such licences had been delivered to 385 of the 443 local communities, over 90 per cent of which provide for terrestrial radio. As this type of local radio is seen as part of the public system, it is well regulated, receives some public funding and is strictly separated from the commercial sector. Very early on, the Association of Local Broadcasters (OLON) started to defend the interests of this sector. Today the Netherlands has a uniquely dense network of local radio stations in Europe.

In Austria the community sector started in 1998; by 2008, fourteen stations were active, all located in urban centres. They see themselves as 'free' stations and defend their interests through an influential Association of Free Radios. The stations get some funding from various institutions, including national, regional and local governments, and the media regulatory agency (Purkarthofer, Pfisterer and Busch 2008).

The situation is most complicated in Germany, as the sixteen federal Länder states of the Republic have the final word over radio regulation, and all states have created legislation and supervisory bodies. They created different environments for what is called 'citizen media'. As a result, there is one state without any community activity (Saarland) while in others there are traditionally free, educational or public access radio stations (on a first come, first served principle). In the largest land of North Rhine-Westphalia, 46 local stations have been created by law with a commercial format and a local community window. Because of this decentralized structure, representation of common interests is difficult for stations and political interference remains high. In general, the community radio sector in Germany is not well developed.

In central and eastern Europe, during the phase of transformation, many community stations were established as a voice of dissent and civil society participation. Sometimes they played an important role in the process of democratization. Starting in 1991, Tilos Rádió ('Forbidden Radio') in Hungary presented itself as a platform for freedom of speech and independent, commercial free radio programming. Everywhere in central and eastern Europe, radio turned out to be an important tool for change from an authoritarian to a more democratic regime, as it is easy to handle, very cost-effective and offers low entrance barriers. Some of these early stations survived, while others changed into commercial stations or disappeared.

Digital Radio in Europe

Since the 1980s, digital technologies are deeply changing the environment of audio services, starting with storage technologies (CDs, etc.). Digital studio equipment also became common. It seemed like a logical extension of this trend to introduce digital radio transmission technology to substitute the old FM system. Developments were started at the European Union level, based on the EUREKA-147 project launched in 1987 in a number of European Union countries. (O'Neill et. al. 2010) The specification designed by engineers was called Digital Audio Broadcasting (DAB) and was ready to be introduced in 1999; the United Kingdom and Germany were among the first to start regular service (Hoeg and Lauterbach 2003). The advantages of DAB seem to be rather obvious: a more robust signal (especially at high car speed) providing better sound (CD quality), the use of a different band (outside of FM) freeing frequency space, making significantly more programmes available and it is also more energy efficient. The European Union recommends a switch to digital radio by 2015 in order to free FM frequencies.

The introduction of DAB in many European countries proved to be a failure in parts of the Continent with notable exceptions in Britain and Denmark. A comparative study of DAB developments in four European states found very different situations, including success in the United Kingdom, whereas neighbouring Ireland is still waiting at the starting gate. The study states: 'The differences result from the varied policy decisions taken by the governments and broadcasters in those countries, policies that both reflected and also reinforced differences in the existing organizations and structures of radio in each country' (Lax et al. 2008: 162).

In most European countries public broadcasters felt obliged to use the new service, but often just through simulcasting (repeating FM programmes). Commercial broadcasters often rejected the technology as they saw no business model in it, and had no interest in opening up the market for competitors. In general, DAB was too much a product of engineers, not sufficiently recognizing the specific demands of radio listeners (e.g. only a small share of listening is actually done in cars). Moreover, the technology proved to be quite expensive and not always reliable. In order to revitalize the DAB norm, DAB Plus was introduced in 2009 (first in Switzerland), with more features and better use of the frequency band, but some of the old problems remain.

In addition, the international broadcasters of Europe (BBC World Service, Deutsche Welle, etc.) developed the Digital Radio Mondiale (DRM) norm, digitizing AM broadcasts on short, middle and long wave. DRM may even be used to substitute FM services. International broadcasters started transmission in DRM, but again the response is minimal. DRM has a special European quality, as a DRM short wave signal from a single antenna is able to reach the whole of the European continent. Hence, actors with an interest in the European audio space are experimenting with DRM, like Radio Vatican and RTL Radio (in memory of its earlier success in Europe).

In sum, radio developments *de facto* follow different directions. By 2010, radio transmission is possible via a variety of platforms and channels. Hundreds of European radio stations are available for European audiences via satellite. More promising is the audio streaming of existing radio stations (offline), as well as stations exclusively available online. Advanced Internet radio sets offer thousands of radio stations from Europe alone:

accessing a reggae station from London or a turbo-folk station from the Balkans is easy to manage. The Internet helps to navigate through Europe's diversified radio landscape by offering a nation-by-nation list of live radio stations (www.live-radio.net). A specially designed website assists anyone interested in learning languages through radio services and in getting to know more about neighbouring European countries (www.youngcivicradio. wordpress.com).

Mobile reception today is possible via a transistor radio which costs very little. Nowadays, FM receivers are installed in many mobile phones. With any Internet-equipped phone it is also possible to receive radio programmes online. With these possibilities in mind, DAB and DRM will not be given too much of a chance in Europe. In other words, it remains highly unlikely that FM services will be switched off by 2015.

Radio in Europe Today

The best material on the European radio scene is available from the *European Broadcasting Union* (EBU), the multinational organization of Europe's public broadcasters. It claims that in 2007 radio was the most used medium per week: 17.12 hours as opposed to TV (16.50 hrs), Internet (10.78 hrs) and newspapers (5.16 hrs), but use is declining, especially among young audiences who increasingly use other digital devices (EBU 2007). The EBU notices a 'great diversity' in terms of current audience shares and overall radio listening. Looking at the five large western European countries, one comes across market shares for public broadcasters (2005) in Germany (around 55%) and the United Kingdom (53%) on the one hand, and France (20%), Italy (19%) and Spain (8%) on the other. In the small countries on the continent, the gap is even larger, reaching from Flanders (68%) and Switzerland (67%) to Portugal (12%). In sum, in the Nordic countries, listening to public service radio is relatively high (63 to 81%); the score is lower in eastern Europe (6 to 49%) and quite low in the Mediterranean area (Greece: 16%) (EBU 2006: 3–18).

The same diversity may be found in radio listening time (but some of the differences may also be due to varying measuring techniques): it is highest in northern and western Europe (Germany: 193 min per day, United Kingdom: 185 min) and lower in the South (Spain: 110 min). Again diversity is strong between Poland (302 min) and Romania (269 min) on the one hand, and Croatia (95 min) and French-speaking Switzerland (99 min) on the other (EBU 2006: 19–21). It is not easy to explain these differences, even among otherwise similar countries. It might have to do with competition from television, the relative strength of the public system, political restrictions or subsidies for radio, influences from neighbouring countries sharing the same language, etc. Comparison of the financial basis of radio also shows considerable differences.

Table 1: Share of Radio Advertisement, Seen from a Cross-Country Perspective, 2005 (in per cent).

United Kingdom	3.8
Germany	4.4
Italy	4.6
France	7.7
Spain	9.4
United States	11.5

Source: World Advertising Trends (www.vprt.de, accessed 31. 05. 2010).

European Radio Policy

In the US context, William A. Richter emphasized that radio in the history of this country was the first national medium (different from the localized press). 'Radio gave Americans something that they had never had before: the ability to experience one special moment as a country' (Richter 2006: 2). This element was certainly also present in Europe, where, very much for the same reason, governments took control of the new medium to secure political stability and loyalty. Different from the United States, radio in Europe soon became a cross-border medium with radio waves reaching citizens with a broad spectrum of different messages, coming from democracies, but also from Fascist and Bolshevist dictatorships. Radio was a medium for nation building in both the United States and Europe. In addition, in Europe it was a medium of public responsibility, transcultural messages and at times propaganda or subversion.

For many years the European Union showed little interest in radio, considering it small-scale and 'backward-looking'. In the 1980s, when a unified European media policy was first designed, the focus was on television as it was seen as the ideal pan-European instrument to create a common audio-visual space. This approach is reflected in the Television Without Frontiers Directive (TVWF) of 1989. It ignored radio as a medium of European significance. The European Union's attempts to digitize radio transmission through DAB were mainly driven by technology considerations, and the idea to digitize Europe with a unified standard. The unique qualities of radio played no role.

This stance changed over the recent years. On the one hand, the policy of a televized audio-visual space showed little results as television remained a national medium. On the other hand, radio was discovered as a low-cost local medium counter weighing some of the shortcomings of the dominant media television and print outlets. Modern radio pretty much reflects the European idea of diversity and allows the reception of practically all stations that are active in Europe. Moreover, networking and programme exchange are easy to accomplish.

Hence, radio was finally discovered at the level of European politics. The European Parliament adopted a resolution in support of community media in Europe. It 'stresses that community media are an effective means of strengthening cultural and linguistic diversity, social cohesion and local identity, which explains the diversity of the sector' (Resolution of 25 September 2008). A declaration by the Committee of Ministers of the Council of Europe on the role of community media promoting social cohesion and intercultural dialogue points in quite the same direction (Declaration of 11 February 2009).

As a consequence, radio policy has somehow left the nation-state level and moved to the European level. In media politics, public radio services are represented by the Radio Department of the European Broadcasting Union (EBU) and the commercial sector is represented by the Association Européenne des Radios (AER) that claims to speak on behalf of 4,500 stations in all 27 European Union member states and Switzerland. In 2004 the 'third media sector' also became active in Brussels and established the Community Media Forum Europe (CMFE), promoting the idea of community radio on the continent, and to a lesser extent also TV and online media.

Radio Theory and Research

Radio as the first electronic mass medium was widely discussed during its birth years in Europe. In the late 1920s, German author Bertolt Brecht (who also wrote radio dramas) envisioned 'radio as an apparatus of communication', as opposed to the distribution of programmes. He emphasized that radio could be much more a medium of participation and feedback, only the existing structures did not allow this (Brecht 1979: 24; first 1927). In the 1930s, German-American Rudolf Arnheim was the first to look at the characteristics of radio as a specific sound medium. He considered radio to be an instrument of art and studied its aesthetics of sound. Working in different parts of Europe (e.g. he wrote his book in Italy and published it in London), he also underlined its potential as an international medium that could link people from different cultures in Europe (Arnheim 1936).

It is difficult to state whether there was a 'European idea' of what radio stands for. During the first years there were commercial (Marconi, Telefunken) as well as state activities. Usually after a few years, the state took over and used the newly discovered tool for influencing public opinion. Looking at it more closely, one realizes that Europe became a laboratory for experimenting with a wide variety of models that shaped the media landscape of the continent up to the present day (Lersch and Schanze 2004). Canadian media guru Marshall McLuhan described radio as the 'tribal drum'. By comparing the Anglo-American and the European developments of radio, he saw a link with the rising movement of Fascism on the continent. 'The more earthy and less visual European cultures were not immune to radio. Its tribal magic was not lost on them, and the old web of kinship began to resonate once more with the note of Fascism' (McLuhan 1964: 259). In the 1970s, French Philosopher Jean Baudrillard complained about the fact that the media are unable to connect producers and consumers. Media, he claimed, are anti-mediatory and can only produce non-communication. He even rejected the idea of the (then new) *radio libre*, arguing that perhaps speech is free, but public space is so saturated that nobody can make him- or herself be heard any longer (Baudrillard 1988; first 1972).

In general, the experience of radio inspired different thinkers with far reaching ideas, but most of the approaches described radio as such, as a medium of unchangeable nature, even at times when its dynamics could clearly be seen. For many years radio suffered under the hegemony of television services; it was described as the 'invisible' (Lewis and Booth 1989) or the 'forgotten' medium (Pease and Dennis 1995). It suffered from marginalization and was seen as the 'Cinderella of communication studies' (Lacey 2008: 21).

But during these years it also underwent a deep change and was rediscovered as a medium of variety, at low access cost and able to reflect high diversity in Europe (Antoine 2006). The redefinition started in the 1990s, accompanying the founding of many stations in the community sector. Universities now routinely operate campus stations, and a new connection between empirical radio research and university radio stations has been established (Starkey 2004). A Radio Studies Network was founded in the United Kingdom in 1998 that also edits the Radio Journal. The European Communication Research and Education Association (ECREA) established a 'Radio Research Section' in 2007 (www. ecrea.eu). The DRACE Group of researchers looks at digital radio cultures in Europe (www.drace.org).

The present discussion is centred on questions like where radio comes from, what it means today and where it is heading. Research work is not just about traditional radio but also about 'radioness', as the edges of the medium begin to blur thanks to new digital technologies. Radio in the digital age will include audio services like podcasts, MP3 players, etc. (Menduni 2007). New insights inspire renewed thinking: 'Radio is always both an abstracted idea…and a material reality' (Lacey 2008: 29). In sum, there is no doubt that it will, one way or the other, survive in Europe.

Conclusion

Radio is still a central mass medium in Europe as user figures show. As such it is interesting to see how variable the organizational structures and user patterns across Europe are. In the North there is more radio listening, in the South television fills much of radio's space. Also, in the North the use of public service programming is stronger than in the South or East of Europe.

Radio in western Europe just after World War II meant public service, a model that embodied 'Europeanness'. It was exported to other parts of the world, especially to the British Commonwealth and Japan. In Latin America one finds citizen movements that strive to introduce a public alternative to the powerful commercial conglomerates. The European public service system was never free from political interference, but thanks to the victory of television political influences diminished. Demands for 'free' radio sometimes turned out to be demands for commercial radio, as it was introduced on a large scale in Europe in the 1980s. Copying the US model led to some 'Americanization' in European radio, but the invested capital remained (as opposed to television) in European hands.

For different reasons, radio enjoyed a comeback since the beginning of the 'dual' system that in fact evolved into a formidable three-headed radio structure (i.e. public, commercial and community). This change did not just introduce thousands of additional commercial stations but it also opened the continent for thousands of community stations. Whereas the commercial sector follows a global pattern, the community scene is extremely diverse, including stations with political, educational, cultural, ethnic orientations or just a place to enjoy the fun of radio production, becoming a participant in Brecht's vision. After many years of ignoring the 'outdated' radio medium, the European Union has now recognized its renewed role and supports the lively landscape of community media.

References

Anduaga, A. (2009), *Wireless and Empire: Geopolitics, Radio, Industry and Ionosphere in the British Empire 1918–1939*, Oxford: Oxford University Press.

Antoine, F. (ed.), (2006), 'Nouvelles voies de la radio' (The Way Ahead for Radio Research), *Recherches en Communication*, 26.

Arnheim, R. (1936), *Radio: The Art of Sound*, London: Faber and Faber.

Baudrillard, J. (1988; first 1972), *The Ecstasy of Communication*, Cambridge, MA: Semiotext(e).

Brecht, B. (1979), 'Radio as a Means of Communication: A Talk on the Function of Radio', *Screen*, 20: 3/4, pp. 24–28.

Critchlow, J. (1995), *Radio Hole-in-the-Head/Radio Liberty: An Insider's Story of Cold War Broadcasting*, Washington, DC: BookSurge Publishing.

Day, R. (2008), *Community Radio in Ireland: Participation and Multi-flows of Communication*, Cresskill, NY: Hampton Press.

de Sola Pool, I. (1983), *Technologies of Freedom*, Cambridge, MA: MIT University Press.

EBU (European Broadcasting Union) (2006), *European Public Radio: Recent Trends and Audience Results*, Geneva: EBU Strategic Information Service.

EBU Radio Assembly Dublin (2007), *Radio in Europe: Trends and Audiences.* Available at: http://www.rte.ie/ebu/english/speaches/day1/alex_shulzycki/shulzycki_radio_dublin.ppt#372,1,The. Accessed 17 February 2010.

Hagen, W. (2005), *Das Radio. Zur Geschichte und Theorie des Hörfunks – Deutschland/USA*, München: Fink.

Harris, P. (1977), *Broadcasting from the High Seas. The History of Offshore Radio in Europe 1958–1976*, Edinburgh: Paul Harris Publishing.

Hilliard, R. and Keith, M. C. (2005), *The Quieted Voice: The Rise and Demise of Localism in American Radio*, Carbondale: Southern Illinois University Press.

Hoeg, W. and Lauterbach, T. (eds) (2003), *Digital Audio Broadcasting: Principles and Applications of Digital Radio*, San Francisco, CA: John Wiley & Sons.

Kleinsteuber, H. J. (2006), 'A Great Future? Digital Radio in Europe', *Recherches en Communication*, 26, pp. 135–46.

Kleinsteuber, H. J. and Sonnenberg, U. (1990), 'Beyond Public Service and Private Profit: International Experiences with Non-Commercial Local Radio', *European Journal of Communication*, 5: 1, pp. 87–106.

Lacey, K. (2008), 'Ten Years of Radio Studies: The Very Idea', *The Radio Journal*, 6: 1, pp. 21–32.

Lax, S., Ala-Fossi, M., Jauert, P. and Shaw H. (2008), 'DAB: The Future of Radio? The Development of Digital Radio in Four European Countries', *Media, Culture and Society*, 30: 2, pp. 151–66.

Lersch, E. and Schanze, H. (eds) (2004), *Die Idee des Radios. Von den Anfängen in Europa und den USA bis 1933*, Konstanz: UVK.

Lewis, P. M. (1999): 'Ears and Memories: European Public Service Radio in the 1990s', *Communications* 24: 2, pp. 209–227.

Lewis, P. M. and Booth, J. (1989), *The Invisible Medium: Public, Commercial and Community Radio*, Houndmills: Palgrave Macmillan.

McLuhan, M. (1964), *Understanding Media: The Extensions of Man*, New York: Mentor Books.

Menduni, E. (2007), 'Four Steps in Innovative Radio Broadcasting: From Quick Time to Podcasting', *The Radio Journal*, 5: 1, pp. 9–18.

O´Neill, B. et. al. (eds.) (2010): Digital Radio jn Europe. Technologies, Industries and Cultures. Bristol: Intellect.

Pease, E. C. and Dennis, E. E. (eds) (1995), *Radio – the Forgotten Medium*, New Brunswick, NJ: Transaction.

Peissl, H. and Tremetzberger O., 'Community Medien in Europa', Rundfunk und Telekom Regulierungs-GmbH (ed.) (2008), pp. 137–228.

Purkarthofer, J., Pfisterer, P. and Busch B., '10 Jahre Freies Radio in Österreich', Rundfunk und Telekom Regulierungs-GmbH (ed.) (2008), pp. 13–116.

Richter, W. A. (2006), *Radio: A Complete Guide to the Industry*, New York: Lang.

Rundfunk und Telekom Regulierungs-GmbH (ed.) (2008), *Nichtkommerzieller Rundfunk in Österreich und Europa*, Wien: Rundfunk und Telekom Regulierungs-GmbH.

Starkey, G. (2004), *Radio in Context*, Houndmills: Palgrave Macmillan.

Völkner, T. (ed.) (2006), *Internationales Radio in Europa: Situation und Zukunftsperspektiven*, Remscheid: Gardez.

Chapter 5

Commercial Television: Business in Transition

Laura Bergés Saura and Gunn Sara Enli

From the 1980s onwards, the rise of neo-liberalism, the fall of Communism and the expansion of the European Union (EU), as well as digitization and convergence imposed changes on the broadcast sector in Europe. In addition to demands for pluralism from the public and changes in social structures, these trends worked together to create a new model for European television characterized by multiple TV channels, segmentation of massive audiences, increase of global flow of TV content and of global audiences, deregulation of the TV sector, as well as some degree of re-regulation of the public service broadcasting. Thus, although it is still necessary to consider state regulation and political-cultural intentions in order to understand the developments of television in Europe, industrial and economic aspects have become increasingly important factors in the European television systems.

By 2010, it is no longer scarcity but availability that best describes the European TV market: in December 2008, there were 6200 private commercial channels out of 6500 channels in the European Union – local, regional, national and international channels, through terrestrial, satellite and cable transmission networks. A key question is nevertheless whether the increase in channels and the growth of the commercial TV sector in particular, has resulted in more diversity (McQuail 2001). In the following discussion, we will focus on the key principles upon which European TV systems are based.

Rights, Culture and Economy in the European Television Policies

Until the 1980s the dominant approach in television policy was based on cultural or ideological objectives and considerations, such as the universal right to be informed and to have access to culture, to contribute to public opinion and the public sphere. Television was also used to build identity or, especially in authoritarian countries, to ideologically control society and disseminate official propaganda. Public monopolies, justified by the scarcity of the spectrum and the economic barriers to broadcasting, were the main instrument for the communication of public policies.

Audio-visual policy has since the 1980s been increasingly influenced by a framework of economic and industrial objectives, reflected in national re-regulation of television and telecommunications; the EU strategies described in the *White Paper on Growth, Competitiveness, and Employment* (European Commission 1993); and the international discussions and agreements on the liberalization of services (General Agreement on Trade in Services, and later agreements inside the World Trade Organization).

The European audio-visual policies – reflected in the Audiovisual Media Services Directive (AVMSD), the support programme for audio-visual works and the European Union treaties, followed up by national legislation – start from an acknowledgement of the specific economic and cultural duality in the function of television and audio-visual services. For this reason, besides the policies to promote growth of the European audio-visual industry, the EU television policies also include measures to guarantee cultural and linguistic diversity, promote cultural activities, protect certain communities and secure public service objectives (see Chapter 11 in this book).

The cultural and industrial motivations for media regulations are closely connected in a global world of trade and competitions: the political intention is not only protection of the European culture, but also of the European audio-visual industry. Particularly, the predominance of US companies in the international market is regarded as a threat to European cultural industries. The efforts to strengthen the European market for culture has succeeded to a certain degree: the number of productions and programme exchanges in the European internal market has grown. In spite of the increase in European cultural production, however, the trade deficit

---

Culturally Motivated Regulations of the TV Industry

Cultural Diversity
The European Union, encouraged especially by France, defended the cultural exception clause in the General Agreement on Trade in Services (GATS) negotiations for the liberalization of services, which was agreed in 1994, and maintained this position in the following World Trade Organization (WTO) negotiations in Doha. Thanks to this clause, protectionist measures in audio-visual and cultural services can be kept.

The European Union supported the UNESCO convention on the Protection and Promotion of the Diversity of Cultural Expressions, adopted in 2007, which states that cultural goods and services, television among them, must not be treated as having only commercial value.

The European Union and national programmes to protect European and national cultural creation and cultural diversity: MEDIA programme, national and sub-national programmes, quotas for European audio-visual works (national productions and co-productions, productions in minority languages).

The Social Responsibility of Media
The European Union Audiovisual Media Services Directive (former Television Without Frontiers Directive): includes measures for the protection of minors and restrictions on the advertising of certain products: tobacco, alcohol, medicinal products and medical treatment.

Pluralism
National restrictions on ownership concentration, based on the principle of pluralism, have been increasingly reduced in the last twenty years (Østergaard 1992, 1997; Kelly et al. 2004). The European Union has not yet adopted any measure that guarantees pluralism, despite several studies on this subject (European Commission 1994, 2007).

with the United States in this field has not been reduced (Graham and Associates 2005). The introduction of new audio-visual technologies has boosted the European media industries, but also improved the presence of US products and companies in Europe.

Despite the policies to support the private audio-visual industry (in most countries), public service broadcasting continues to be the main tool to protect national productions and diversity of programmes. Especially in small- and medium-sized countries, whose private sectors cannot compete in the global market, public service broadcasting is usually the main customer for national productions and content in minority languages (see Chapter 11 in this book).

Structure and Dynamics in the Expansion of European Private Commercial Television

The process of privatization of television in Europe has resulted in an increase in players in the audio-visual industry. Media groups and companies in related business took the opportunity to expand their activities in the field of television, both geographically and technologically from western to eastern Europe; from analogue to digital, satellite, cable and terrestrial television; from consecutive scheduling to on-demand services. The expansion is thus both a process of privatization and of internationalization. The number of small- and medium-sized companies has also grown significantly, but the large players in the market have benefited from their size to remove competition through mergers and acquisitions, to acquire a dominant position in the new digital market. Key factors explaining this 'winner-takes-it-all' logic in the industry are the media firms' distribution, promotional and financial capacity, advertising multimedia sales capacity and control over great content stocks, accompanied by a favourable regulatory framework (McChesney 2004).

Access to attractive media content and copyright have become a key battleground in the television market, especially in the genres of popular cinema and sports, with football as a particularly popular content (see Chapter 10). High prices paid for football rights and popular fiction films – as strategic content for pay-TV – have favoured concentration in television industries[1] and are making it difficult for public service broadcasters to compete on equal footing. This ownership of content by the big media groups has also placed them in a good position with the development of digital terrestrial, and Digital Subscriber (Line DSL) and Internet Protocol (IP) television.

The largest television companies have in turn benefited from their position in the advertising markets. All large media groups have subsidiaries that concentrate their advertising sales, offering advertisers and agencies a wide range of media for different target markets. They also take advantage of their relations with the main advertising agencies. The launch of the first private channels and the later consolidation of the big audio-visual companies have also relied on the financial support of large companies from outside the media industry (refer to the box below), bearing up the first few years of losses that are unsustainable for smaller companies which, in many cases, are forced to close.

The support of investment and other financial entities also helps to explain the expansion of major European audio-visual groups, and their ability to compete and cooperate with US media groups. In this sense, it is important to highlight the relation between the liberalization of television and telecommunications, and the liberalization of financial markets and international investments. In parallel to the measures attempting to protect national and European culture and markets against the hegemony of US products and companies, the liberalization of the financial markets has allowed international – and especially Anglo-Saxon companies – to enter the European market. Thus, US investment arrived through private equity firms, operating in financial liberalized markets (see box).

The actual influence of these groups on media production is empirically hard to prove (see Schulz et al. 2008), but their presence affects the general strategy of the companies. External capital:

- Reinforces the interests of non-communication companies in the media industry
- Favours concentration of ownership, instead of competition, to assure profitability for shareholders
- Allows for competitive strategies based on debt, which reduce competition
- Makes media more dependant on economic or financial cycles, and on the volatility of financial markets
- Reduces the diversity in the television and digital systems, in terms of property, organizational models and contents

---

Non-Media Firms in European Television: Energy, Real Estate and Consumption Good Companies

France
Bouygues: building, energy and real estate company that acquired the privatized TF1, later acquired Eurosport, launched Le Chaîne Info and the pay-TV platform TPS – merged with Canal+/Vivendi in 2007 – and offers video-on-demand services.

Compagnie Générale des Eaux (GDE): founded Canal+ in 1983 and began its expansion on the audio-visual and telecommunications industries, under the name of Vivendi. The expansive strategy of the group in the 1990s, dependent on high levels of debt, led the group to financial problems and a restructuring: progressive reduction of its participation in the non-media activities (water, waste, transport) from 2000 on, and merger of Vivendi Universal Entertainment with NBC in 2003, to create NBC Universal, 80 per cent owned by General Electrics (GE) and 20 per cent owned by Vivendi. In 2010, Vivendi left NBC Universal (the latter bought by Comcast), and keeps its interests in the Canal+ group and in other telecommunications activities.

Bolloré Group: invests in plastics and packaging, transportation and international logistics, as well as television (DTT, production and technical services), free sheets and advertising companies (Havas, Aegis).

Lagardère Group: formed from the merger of magazine publisher Hachette and defence aeronautics company Matra, it has launched five new thematic digital channels and provides production services for television.

Italy
Mediaset: The Italian Prime Minister Silvio Berlusconi's company coming from the building and real estate businesses, among others, expanded from its first investment in local TV to the present multimedia group.

Greece
Shipping, real estate and refinery companies in Greece feature among the stakeholders of private television.

Russia
Gazprom, Alfa Group, Severstal and Nafta: emerged after the privatization of the Russian economy in the 1990s, are the main owners of Russian media, including television.

Sweden
Kinnevik: from the paper industry, began to invest in audio-visual and other media from the 1990s onwards and now manages the Modern Times Group (MTG).

Financial Investors
Permira and KKR (Kohlberg Kravis Roberts): financial investors with headquarters in London and New York. Bought the Scandinavian Broadcasting System (SBS) in 2005, present in nine European countries. In 2007, acquired the second largest private commercial television company in Germany, ProSiebenSat.1, and merged both companies in 2009.

Central European Media Enterprises (CME): investment society with headquarters in Bermuda and capital linked to the big US media groups. Most successful beneficiary of the privatization of television in central and eastern Europe in the 1990s.

Rothschild, Merrill Lynch, JP Morgan and other investment societies, are also present in the European broadcasting sector (stakeholders in Vivendi, in cable providers, among others).

A second key characteristic in the expansion of private television and audio-visual networks in Europe has been the entrepreneurial and technological convergence with telecommunication, and information and communication technologies (ICT) companies. The telecommunication sector – also subject to the liberalization and privatization in the 1980s – and ICT companies, whose promotion has been one of the objectives in the construction of the Information Society (European Commission 1993), have developed products and audio-visual services that break the monopoly of television as the unique audio-visual medium (see Figure 1).

Telecom companies first began to compete with private broadcasters in the European television market launching cable and satellite television channels, and from 2006 onwards they started to develop DSL and mobile audio-visual services. Competition among audio-visual services is often bypassed by entrepreneurial convergence, through mergers and alliances, adding value to the telecom networks and allowing media firms to exploit their content in new different windows. In the television-Internet convergence, competitive and

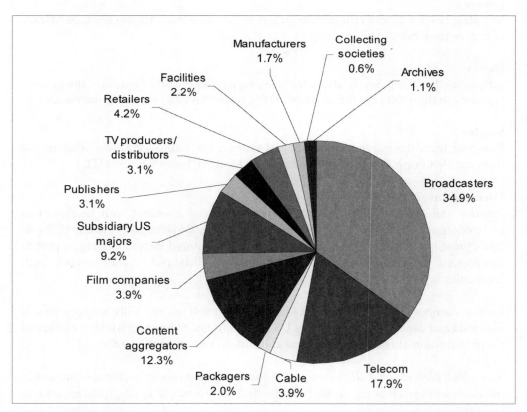

Figure 1: Breakdown of Providers of On-Demand Audio-Visual Services by Primary Activity (December 2008).
Source: European Audiovisual Observatory (EAO) (2008): G.6.2.

cooperative relations can also be found between audio-visual and ICT companies. The three largest US ICT enterprises – Windows, Apple and Google – are present in all European audio-visual markets and, together with the public service broadcasting organizations, dominate this sector with lead positions in the audio-visual broadband services market, both in terms of use rankings and income share (see Chapters 6 and 10).

The expansion of private commercial television and audio-visual services has leant on external financial resources (from shareholders and debt) and on the increase of operating revenues, generated from advertising as well as from viewers. The introduction and expansion of private television gave rise to a redistribution of total adspend among all the media, thereby increasing competition between entertainment and drama –with more commercial value for advertisers – and information. However, viewers' subscriptions have become an increasingly important resource for television companies, expanding the concept of television from mass mediated national broadcasting to new forms of audio-visual content distributed to specific markets (channel platforms, premium services, pay-per-view, video-on-demand, online services), where the economic and cultural segmentation of the audiences gains importance. This transformation in the mode of television reception has important implications on the social construction of sense, the composition of the public spheres and the role of mass television in contemporary democracies (Wolton 1992, 1995; Dayan 1997; also see Chapters 7 and 8 in this book).

After years of losing ground, public service television funding stabilizes or even increases in some countries (de Mateo and Bergés 2009), representing almost 30% of the total audio-visual revenues in EU-27. The market share of advertising-financed television slightly increased in the 2000s, reaching about 25% of the market total, until the advertising crisis at the end of the decade. But during the 2000s the growth is higher in revenue from viewers, especially for broadcasting pay-services and online distribution. Pay-TV packages, premium services and thematic channels account for about 25% of the market, more than four points above the market share in the early 2000s. In contrast, retail audio-visual sales and rentals (cinema, DVD) are slowly declining (EAO 2008: T.2.3 / G.2.4).

In addition, the processes described above – privatization, concentration, internation-alization, digitalization and commercialization – have imposed significant changes in the organization and governance of television. Television performance in the traditional model of public service broadcasting was based on different kinds of political control (see Chapter 11) and the production was basically done in-house. In the new scenario, TV governance depends to a great extent on private corporate control and on marketing and financial determining factors. Also, as a result of the substitution of centralized models by decentralized production and organizational models, the operation of television has now changed.

These strategies of outsourcing and decentralization of the production process helps TV channels to fulfil their quotas on national and independent production, but have also undermined the position of trade unions and of the workforce in general. Within industrial communication groups, television is now a division assigned to scheduling and (some) production – mostly news production – while other responsibilities such as advertising sale and marketing, production of different genres for different national and international audiences, transmission and investments are allocated to other divisions, all under a general multimedia strategy within multi-sector groups. Therefore, decisions on programming need to take into account the diverse interests of the different media and non-media activities of the entire group.

Besides the common characteristics in the expansion of private television across Europe, there are also significant national differences. Key factors of variations are related to the size of the national markets, the strenght of related industries, the political, cultural, linguistic and economic conditions, international relations and audio-visual policies. The first countries that opened television to private ownership adopted regulations that, in most cases, protected national television from foreign investment. Moreover, in western Europe the prior existence of national media and advertising industries assisted the launch and expansion of national private television networks. In western Europe, the five larger countries – Germany, the United Kingdom, France, Italy and Spain – account for about 80 per cent of the total revenues of EU-27 TV companies (EAO 2008: T.3.4).

The Largest European TV Markets

Among the larger countries, the United Kingdom has the most prominent position. This is both because of its linguistic and trade related close ties with the United States, and its long history with the mixed model of public and private television since the adoption of the Television Act in 1954. Along with a strong public service, the mixed model allowed the consolidation of a private national industry composed of channels and independent producers with a considerable economic strength and leading positions in audience rankings. The United Kingdom has the highest production level in Europe: in 2007, European channels (EU-20) broadcasted 21,247 hours of British contents. This is in fact far below the figures for the United States (303,107 hours) which remains the main provider for both big and small channels, but it is above the amount of the second European country, Germany, with 14,025 hours (EAO 2008: T.8.5). The United Kingdom is also a significant player in the production of new formats (such as video games) and retail distribution, with four of the 40 biggest production companies in Europe. But besides this national industry, the News Corporation stands out as the major actor playing in the United Kingdom audio-visual market, with its majority share in BSkyB, and its production and import capacity, being the fourth biggest media group in the world (see Table 1).

In Germany, the liberalization of television and the growth of the private audio-visual industry were initially led by German media companies: the press and book publisher Bertelsmann, the Kirch Group and the German company RTL, based in Luxembourg. After 25 years of private television, the situation today is characterized by ownership concentration. In 2001, Bertelsmann and RTL merged, turning into a multinational group with TV channels and production companies in many countries. After the bankruptcy of

Table 1: The Big Groups in the European TV Systems.

Group	Group Revenues* (Million €)**		TV Channels in European Countries
	2008	2007	
News Corporation	22,434	20,908	• United Kingdom (BSkyB), Italy (Sky Italia), Germany and Austria (Premiere). • All countries: channels and programmes included in pay-TV platforms (Fox, National Geographic, Twentieth Century Fox). • Others: TV channels, audio-visual production, magazines, newspapers, books in America, Asia, Oceania and Europe.
Vivendi	25,392	21,657	• France (Canal +), Poland (Cyfra+). • Others: Universal Music Group, SFR-Telecom, Telecom Morocco, Zaoza-mobile entertainment, 20 per cent of NBC Universal (until 2010).
Bertelsmann-RTL	16,118	16,191	• Germany (RTL TV), France (M6), United Kingdom (Five), Netherlands, Belgium, Luxembourg, Croatia and Hungary (RTL channels), Greece (Alpha TV), Russia (Ren TV), Spain (Antena 3 TV). • Others: press, magazines, books, production, services.
Lagardère	8214	8582	• France (Gulli, Canal J, TiJi, Filles TV, Virgin 17). • Others: press, magazines, books, production, services.
Mediaset	4252	4082	• Italy (Canale 5, Italia 1, Rete 4, Premium services, DTT channels), Spain (Telecinco, DTT channels).
ProSiebenSat.1 Media + SBS	3054	2298	• Germany (ProSieben, Sat1, Kabel 1, N24, subscription TV), Austria (Sat 1, Kabel 1), Belgium (VT4, Vijf TV), Bulgaria (The Voice), Denmark (Kanal 4, Kanal 5, The Voice, 6'eren), Finland (The Voice, TV Viisi), Hungary (TV2), Norway (TV Norge, FEM, The Voice), Romania (Prisama TV, Kiss TV), Sweden (Kanal 5, Kanal 9), Switzerland (Sat 1, ProSieben), the Netherlands (SBS6, Net5, Veronica).
Modern Times Group	1.369	1.164	• Scandinavia and the Baltic (Viasat Broadcasting, free-TV and satellite premium pay-TV), Czech Republic, Hungary, Slovenia, Bulgaria and Macedonia, (free-TV channels), Ukraine (satellite premium pay-TV platform), Russia (shareholder in CTC Media).
CME	n.a.	613	• Czech Republic (TV Nova, Nova Cinema, Galaxie Sport), Slovakia (TV Markíza), Slovenia (Pop TV, Kanal A), Ukraine (Studi 1+1, Kino, Citi); Croatia (Nova TV).

* This includes all the revenues of the groups, not only European TV.
** Exchange rates for News Corporation and CME figures: €1 = $1.4708 (2008), $1.3705 (2007); for Modern Times Group: €1 = SEK9.6152 (2008), SEK9.2501 (2007) (ECB reference exchange rate).
Source: News Corporation Annual Report http://www.newscorp.com/Report2008/AR2008.pdf
Vivendi Annual Report 2008 http://www.vivendi.com/vivendi/IMG/pdf/20090408_annual_report_en_080409.pdf
Bertelsnmann Annual Report 2008 http://www.bertelsmann.com/bertelsmann_corp/wms41/customers/bmir/pdf/Bertelsmann_Annual_Report_2008.pdf
Lagardère Annual Financial Report 2008 http://www.lagardere.com/fichiers/fckeditor/File/actionnaires%20individuels/assemblee_generale/2009/doc_de_ref_2008_en.pdf
Mediaset Annual Report 2008 http://www.mediaset.it/gruppomediaset/bin/59.$plit/Mediaset+Group+-+2008+Annual+Report.pdf
ProSieben Sat1 Media Annual Financial Report http://en.prosiebensat1.com/imperia/md/content/investor_relations/2009/Kennzahlen_final_GB2008/englisch_GB_2008.pdf
Modern Times Groups Annual Report 2008 http://www.mtg.se/en/Annual-Report-2008/
Central European Media (CME) Annual Report 2008 http://www.cetv-net.com/file/u/filings/form_10k_2008_12_31.pdf

Leo Kirch, the News Corporation gained control of the main pay-TV platform, Premiere, and renamed it Sky Deutschland (Germany) in 2009. In 2006, ProSiebenSat.1 – successor of the Kirch Group after its bankruptcy in 2002 – was acquired by financial investors. In addition to these three companies, demand for commissioned programmes generated by strong public service addressing the large German-speaking market of 100 million people, have enabled the creation of an important production industry, with ten companies among the 40 biggest producers in Europe (EAO 2008: T.9.2).

In France, the two main media groups are backed by industrial capital. Vivendi and TF1 are followed by Lagardère, which has less investment in audio-visual activities. Determined and continued policies to support national audio-visual production have been adopted by different French governments, resulting in the consolidation of the sector, with the highest share of national production in TV programming, but with low international circulation.

The Italian and Spanish television systems have been conditioned by a socio-politic and economic tradition defined by some authors as the 'family or Mediterranean welfare state' (Bandrés et al. 1997), determined by 40 years of dictatorship in the Spanish case. Smaller industrial structures in these two countries, together with the political decisions, lead to a weaker public service broadcasting and a greater presence of foreign capital in the TV systems and – especially in Italy – to higher ownership concentration. Silvio Berlusconi, the Italian Prime Minister and owner of Mediaset, enjoys almost a monopoly of free-to-air television, composed of RAI and Mediaset channels. In the Italian pay-TV market, the main player is News Corporation with its Sky platform, following the bankruptcy of Telepiu and Stream.

Compared to the other larger nations, Spain is recognized as the nation most open to foreign investment. Since the launch of the first private TV channels through to the new digital audio-visual services, foreign media groups have played an active role in the Spanish market. Mediaset, Bertelsmann, Vivendi, Televisa, WPP and RCS have stakes in free-to-air analogue and digital television, while cable and DSL-TV counts are in the hands of international telecommunications and investment firms. National press groups and banks also invest in Spanish television, taking advantage of the alliances with bigger foreign groups in order to improve their position in the press markets.

In Russia, the television system is determined by the country's large territory and population which is composed of 146 million inhabitants, eight different time zones, 70 languages and a complex administration system composed of federations, republics, regions, provinces and autonomous districts. This complexity is reflected in a TV model where satellite is a fundamental technology in building national channels, and where regional television plays a key role, particularly in more prosperous regions. Nine channels reach more than 50 per cent of the population, in a mixed model of state television (more than public service television) and private commercial channels, operating – in most of the cases – with alliances with regional and local channels. Private television in Russia is closely tied to the large firms that emerged from the privatization of the economy, giving these oligarchs a powerful communication tool. There is also some foreign capital, with MTG and RTL involved in free-to-air television (Groteck 2008; Kachkaeva et al. 2006).

The Small- and Medium-Sized European Markets

In the smaller western countries, the socio-economic and technical transformation of the 1980s challenged the national systems in a different way. With a population between half a million, such as Luxembourg, and 16 million, such as the Netherlands, the home market for advertisement and media content is considerably smaller.

The eleven small- and medium-sized countries of western Europe account for nearly 15 per cent of the EU-27 TV revenues (EAO 2008: T.3.4). The economic and cultural ties among the Scandinavian countries have defined a regional audio-visual market where, above national differences, there are some common elements: the strength of PSB, which has generated demand for producers who have a very limited linguistic market; the significant presence of editorial, industrial and telecom companies in the three Scandinavian markets (Modern Times Group MTG, Telenor, Schibsted); and the internationalization of television, first with satellite broadcasts from London and later through investment companies (Kinnevik, SBS). The strength of the telecom and electronics companies in the Nordic countries (with Telenor and Nokia) is reflected in their alliances with television companies and producers to develop new audio-visual services, first through satellite and cable, then through mobile telephony and IP television.

In other small- and medium-sized countries, protectionist measures favoured the investment of national press groups in the launch of private television. In the Netherlands, Belgium, Ireland, Switzerland, Austria and Greece, press owners had shares in the first private channels, but they counted on other allies in their expansion to television activities. In the case of Greece, shipping companies, real estate firms and refineries have played a significant role. In Austria, the influence of the German market stands out, with the investment of German groups in free-to-air channels (ATV) and pay-TV (Sky Germany). Austria also represents an important additional audience for German channels. In Switzerland, the high audience market shares for channels from the neighbouring linguistic zones (Germany, Italy, France) have limited the interest of foreign groups to launch TV channels in this country. The unfavourable market structure also affected Swiss private commercial broadcasting such as TV3 and Tele24, which were closed down only two years after their launch in 1999. Private television now consists of a few local and low-budget channels. In Ireland, the influence comes from the United Kingdom and North America, with the presence of Granada, Liberty Media, CanWest Global Communications and United Pan Europe Communications (UPC). In the Netherlands, the private television system is mostly in the hands of big multinational groups, particularly Bertelsmann and SBS. Cable systems (penetration of nearly 100 per cent of households) are by majority owned by US capital, following the acquisition of Casema by UPC in 2002.

In central and eastern Europe, the adoption of the new television model started from a very different point of departure. On the one hand, these countries could not rely on private media industries capable of leading the introduction of private television. The old legacy determined weak consumption markets, and therefore weak national advertising industries. On the other hand, television's privatization took place when the liberalization of international trade, investments and financial markets was already adopted at the international level in Europe. In sum, these forces worked together and thus explain the high level of TV internationalization in those countries, and the importance of private equity firms in financing private television. MTG runs terrestrial free-to-air channels and pay-TV platforms in ten central and eastern European countries; CME is present in six countries; SBS, as well as Bertelsmann-RTL, in three. The central and eastern European countries account for a mere 5 per cent of the EU-27 television market (EAO 2008: T.3.4), with Poland (38 million inhabitants) as the main market. Limits on foreign investment in television make Poland the country with the most national capital in television.

TV Content in Transition

Research has documented that the television channels' schedules are related to structural factors such as ownership and financing models (Kops 2007; de Mateo and Bergés 2009). Publicly funded channels tend to offer more information and cultural programmes, and have a more diverse scheduling for different target groups than commercial channels. Channels funded by advertising tend to concentrate on entertainment, sports and some news, targeted at an audience younger, more urban, and more segmented than that of public service broadcasting. This implies that small- and medium-sized countries particularly depend on public broadcasting to provide for original first-run drama and children's programming.

Regarding the origin of the TV productions, there is still a general US market domination, but there is a considerable proportion of national production and intra-EU exchange of content as well: 50 per cent of drama broadcasted in EU-15 in 2007 was of American origin. The highest percentage of US drama was seen in Luxembourg, Denmark, Norway and Sweden, all with more than 60 per cent. On the contrary, the determined policies supporting national production in France are reflected in the lowest percentage of US broadcast productions of only 30 per cent of drama in 2007 – although this is still higher than national fiction. France is also the country that provides for the most co-productions, both with other European and with its US partners.

National fiction accounts for 15 per cent of all fiction broadcasted in EU-15 in 2007, with higher percentages in France (28 per cent), the United Kingdom (19 per cent) and Spain (18 per cent), followed by Italy (15 per cent) and Germany (13 per cent). The internal EU market has also grown, and non-national European fiction accounts for 10 per cent of the fiction broadcast. Inter-European co-productions are less important with just about 5 per cent of broadcast drama, but European co-productions with third countries (particularly the United States) are growing, accounting for nearly 10 per cent (see EAO 2008: T.8.4 / G.8.5). The geography of these intra-EU exchanges suggests the existence of clear-cut regional markets. Fiction from France, Germany and the United Kingdom has a significant presence in neighbouring countries: German production in Austria and the Czech Republic; UK drama in Ireland, Finland and Norway; French drama in French-speaking Belgium.

Even though the national production does not make up a high percentage, the programmes in national languages are as a rule situated in prime time slots, achieving high audience rankings, corresponding to the preference of the public (Waisbord 2004). The relevance of language in the audio-visual markets is also reflected in the higher percentage of co-productions and imports from the United States and Australia in the United Kingdom and Ireland, and likewise with Latin American productions in Spain.

While national and European content has gained space on the primary channels, particularly in public service channels, secondary channels resort to US content stocks to a greater extent, both for drama and documentary (Graham and Associates 2005). For new and niche channels, US imports are an efficient way of entering the market without the investments and risks involved in TV production, though they might not always connect with the domestic audiences, their national culture and identity.

The format industry fuelled by the growth in reality TV productions across Europe and worldwide is an interesting counter-force to the US dominance in the canned fiction trade. Format production is a strategy for compensating the need for attachment to the viewers' national culture and language environment, while at the same time reducing innovation costs. Among the European countries, the United Kingdom stands out as the main global player in the format trade market as the number one exporter of formats in 2009 (see Chapter 14). In addition, small- and medium-sized countries have entered the global TV market, e.g. the Netherlands and Sweden through the international format trade. Reality TV is thus a strong driver in the international trade with TV content, and it's also one of the factors that has increased Europe's shares in the market.

Reality TV is also a result of blurring boundaries between fiction-based genres and factual genres. This hybridization means a combination of conventions from fiction production – such as casting, manuscripts, narrative editing, etc. – and production methods used in factual TV – such as the focus on ordinary people, observational filming and documentary-style voice over. Cost reduction needs and innovations to attract audiences bring out other new hybrid genres such as *infotainment* (information + entertainment) or *infotising* (information + advertising). These blurring boundaries have resulted in criticism of decay, and discussions about television's role as a provider of information in democratic societies.

Additionally, TV companies have explored the new feedback opportunities provided by digital technology through phone-ins, text messages and the TV-Internet convergence. Classic show entertainment such as *The Eurovision Song Contest* has for example been successfully renewed in recent years by including televoting as a key element in the competition. The use of digital return channels in television production is a strategy to strengthen the relationship with the viewers at a time when there's increasing competition from a variety of new TV channels, as well as new media platforms, though the real improvement in citizen participation is disputed (Jackson 2008).

In order to compete in this convergent media landscape, branding is becoming an increasingly important part of the TV companies' activities, for niche channels in particular and on-demand services. The economic value of an established brand is evident in the big channels' increasing launch of small linked channels or spin-off channels.

Predictions of television's death have been flourishing since the early 1990s, and the future of broadcast TV in an era of the Internet as an expanding media platform is debated among academics and industry representatives. But an indicator of the persistence of TV is the viewing time devoted to it in Europe: over 140 minutes per day in Austria, Switzerland, Norway and Sweden, and more than 250 minutes in Hungary and Croatia. (EAO 2008: T7–01). These figures demonstrate the dominance of television, even in a fragmented and digital media landscape, and point to a conclusion that the rumours of TV's death are highly exaggerated. Television has taken on new forms and is present on new platforms, such as the Internet and the mobile phone. Television transmission is no longer dependent on broadcast airways or frequencies, and is thus more accessible to independent producers who publish their TV content online. Nevertheless, TV has adapted to changes in the media landscape and incorporated trends of interactivity and multi-platform activities (Enli 2007). Television is thus still a medium of highly relevance in today's digital age.

Conclusion

The evolution of the European television systems during the last three decades has been marked by the end of two monopolies: first, the end of the public broadcasting monopolies, which were common in almost all European countries; and second, the end of the monopoly of television as the unique audio-visual window of homes to the world, with the introduction of new audio-visual digital services. Nevertheless, the market rationale has resulted in an oligopolic model, where the main actors in the socio-economic transformation – known as neo-liberal globalization – are also leading actors in the television landscape.

The commercialization of television has meant cost reduction in content – such as news for mass audiences – in order to compensate the high expenditure on popular content serving mass preferences, or on high value contents for exclusive audiences. As a result, one can talk about the trivialization and de-politization of the public spheres represented and built by television, and a progressive socio-economic segmentation in the contents available for different social groups.

The digitalization of television also introduces innovations in content and new possibilities for television audience activities, particularly in multi-platform formats. On the one hand, these activities serve as additional sources of revenue and clearly represent a welcome supplement to advertising and viewers' licence fee (two financing models that are under increasing pressure in the digital age). On the other hand, these new interactive services have the potential of renewing television, and offer producers the possibility to re-connect with the viewing public at a time when television is increasingly regarded as an old fashioned medium when compared to new online social media and search-based media platforms.

Note

1. This was one of the reasons why ITV Digital in the United Kingdom and the Kirch Group in Germany were declared bankrupt in 2002; why two pay-TV platforms, Stream and Telepiu, were merged in Italy in 2003; and why Vía Digital and Canal Satélite Digital were merged in Spain in 2003. These changes left the News Corporation with a monopoly over pay-TV satellite platforms in the United Kingdom and Italy, as well as a monopoly over Digital Plus in Spain.

References

Bandrés, E., Cuenca, A., Gadea, M. D. and Sánchez, A., 'El desarrollo del estado del bienestar moderno en el sur de Europa', in Maravall Herrero, J. M. (ed.) (1997), *III Simposio sobre Igualdad y Distribución de la Renta y la Riqueza. Políticas de bienestar y desempleo*, Madrid: Fundación Argentaria, pp. 89–149.

Dayan, D. (1997), *En busca del público*, Barcelona: Gedisa.

de Mateo, R. and Bergés, L. (2009), *Los retos de las televisiones públicas*, Sevilla and Zamora: Comunicación Social.

EAO (European Audiovisual Observatory) (2008), *Yearbook Online Premium Service 2008*. Available at: http://www.obs.coe.int/yb_premium/public/. Accessed 15 February 2010.

EC (European Commission) (1993), *White Paper on Growth, Competitiveness, and Employment. The Challenges and Ways Forward into the 21st Century*, COM (93) 700 final, Brussels: European Commission.

—— (1994), *Green Book on Pluralism*, COM (94) 353 final, Brussels: European Commission.

—— (2007), *Media Pluralism in the Member States of the European Union*, SEC (2007) 32, Brussels: European Commission.

Enli, G. S. (2007), 'The Participatory Turn in Broadcast Television: Institutional, Editorial, and Textual Challenges and Strategies', Ph.D. thesis, Oslo: University of Oslo.

Graham and Associates Limited (2005), *Impact Study of Measures (Community and National) Concerning the Promotion of Distribution and Production of TV Programmes Provided for Under Article 25(a) of the TV Without Frontiers Directive. Final Report*. Available at: http://ec.europa.eu/avpolicy/docs/library/studies/finalised/4-5/27_03_finalrep.pdf. Accessed 15 February 2010.

Groteck Co. Ltd (ed.) (2008), *Digital Television in Russia*, in European Audiovisual Observatory. Available at: http://www.obs.coe.int/online_publication/reports/digitaltv_groteck.pdf.en. Accessed 15 February 2010.

Jackson, J. D. (2008), 'Broadcasting and Public Spaces: A Normative Essay', in RIPE 2008 Conference, *Public Service Media in the 21st Century: Participation, Partnership and Media Development*. Available at: http://www.uta.fi/jour/ripe/2008/papers/Jackson_John.pdf. Accessed 15 February 2010.

Kachkaeva, A., Kiriya, I. and Libergal, G. (2006), *Television in the Russian Federation: Organisational Structure, Programme Production and Audience*, in European Audiovisual Observatory. Available at: http://www.obs.coe.int/online_publication/reports/tv_russia_internews2006.pdf. Accessed 15 February 2010.

Kelly, M., Mazzoleni, G. and McQuail, D. (eds) (2004), *The Media in Europe. The Euromedia Handbook*, London: Sage.

Kops, M. (2007), 'A Revenue-Based Methodology for the Classification and Comparison of Broadcasting Systems', working papers of the Institute for Broadcasting Economics, no. 223e, Cologne: University of Cologne.

McChesney, R. (2004), *The Problem of the Media: US Communication Politics in the Twenty-First Century*, New York: Monthly Review Press.

McQuail, D., 'The Consequences of European Media Policies and Organisational Structures for Cultural Diversity', in Bennett, T. (ed.) (2001), *Differing Diversities: Cultural Policy and Cultural Diversity*, Strasbourg: Council of Europe, pp. 73–92.

Østergaard, Bernt Stubbe (ed.) (1992, 1997), *The Media in Western Europe – The Euromedia Handbook. Euromedia Research Group*, London: Sage.

Schulz, W., Kaserer, C. and Trappel, J. (eds) (2008), *Finanzinvestoren im Medienbereich* (Financial Investors in the Media Field), Berlin: Vistas.

Waisbord, S. (2004), 'McTV: Understanding the Global Popularity of Television Formats', *Television & New Media*, 5: 4, pp. 359–83.

Wolton, D. (1992), *El nuevo espacio público*, Barcelona: Gedisa.

—— (1995), *Elogio del gran público*, Barcelona: Gedisa.

Chapter 6

Online Media: Changing Provision of News

Josef Trappel and Gunn Sara Enli

News of the assassination of Archduke Franz Ferdinand of Austria and his wife Sophie in Sarajevo in June 1914 (an event that was later to be considered as the starting point of World War I) was brought to people's attention through the special editions of newspapers. The surrender of the German forces that ended World War II in 1945 was first reported on radio. The collapse of the World Trade Center twin towers in New York on September 11, 2001, was simultaneously reported on TV and on news sites on the Internet. And when pop star Michael Jackson died in June 2009, Twitter was reportedly the first medium to circulate the news globally.

Breaking news needs to travel fast and its history is that of mass media's immediacy. Since the mid-1990s, there are good reasons to include digital media distributed and circulated primarily via the Internet as a relevant complement to the range of news media. Digitization and the circulation opportunities provided by the Internet have prompted newspapers, radio and television to reconsider their role and position in the provision of news (Ala-Fossi et al. 2008). Moreover, online news has developed its own and specific characteristics in news production and news distribution, resulting in changing news consumption habits of a growing part of the online population worldwide. This chapter looks into the processes of online news production, its implications on content, journalism and media policy (regulation). It also deals with the recent phenomenon of user-generated content (UGC) and its implications on news. Finally, some thoughts on the future perspectives of online news are provided.

Changing News Provision

The status and the commercial value of news have changed considerably over the last two decades. In the early 1980s news was collected, selected, processed and distributed by mostly large media organizations in Europe. Public service broadcasters and large publishing houses provided global, national and regional news to the public at large. News agencies played a central role at the global and national level and provided abundant news to the editorial staff within media companies. Printed and broadcast news were the result of a multi-step selection and the editing process was conducted by professional journalists all along the production chain, from the selection of any event considered relevant to the delivery to homes. Since the turn of the century this production chain became much more diversified and news became a commodity of a large and increasing number of media outlets. Not only has the number of television stations multiplied following the licensing of private competitors, but the advent

Table 1: Use of Online Content in Germany.

Frequently Used Online Content in Per Cent of Online Users (Age 14+)

	2004	2005	2006	2007	2008	2009
News (national, international)	46	47	45	46	52	59
Information on science, research, education	44	44	42	46	44	45
Information on leisure time activities, events	42	44	40	45	50	43
Service information (weather, traffic)	38	43	37	42	47	47
Information on culture	31	33	36	35	34	35
Information on sports	31	29	29	32	34	37
Information on economics and stock exchange	26	24	21	25	24	32

Source: ARD/ZDF-Onlinestudie (2004–2009); van Eimeren and Frees (2009).

of the World Wide Web and the mass access to the Internet has also stimulated many more actors to become news providers.

What became known as 'online media' (Trappel 2007: 126) increased in public popularity. The longitudinal survey of Internet use in Germany clearly demonstrates the increasing relevance of online news. Fifty nine per cent of the German online population frequently searches for news on the Internet (see Table 1).

News is made available online almost immediately after the arrival of the news at the respective news-desk. Speed in news processing and distribution reigns over journalistic accuracy and investigation. Easy access to news material facilitated the arrival of a large – and further growing – number of complementary news outlets: this spectrum contains large corporate online media with well-equipped journalistic newsrooms, as well as smallish news offices with little more than automatic news feeds provided by news agencies and presented online on a specific website. For the first time in media history, news is provided to the general public by actors with little or no professional background.

This growth in the number of actors providing news could be misinterpreted as growing news diversity. In order to better understand the process of online news provision, a closer look at the business structure is required.

Corporate Online Media

News provision is a costly business. Short-term events or long-term developments need to be identified, reported and processed by skilled and experienced personnel. Such qualified journalists are normally employed by large media corporations or news agencies. Building on the strength of corporate media organizations, news is generated and distributed via the various media outlets.

Table 2: Top Five Online News Media in Selected European Countries (2009).

Ranking	1	2	3	4	5
Austria	ORF ON	derStandard.at	Krone.at	Kurier.at	News.at
Belgium	hln.be	dhnet.be	nieuwsblad.be	lesoir.be	RTL.info
France	TF1.fr	L'Equipe.fr	Le Monde.fr	Eurosport.fr	France2.fr
Germany	Spiegel online	Bild.de	T-Online.de	RTL.de	Sueddeutsche .de
Hungary	Origo.hu	Index.hu	Lap.hu	Nemzeti Sport Online	Hírkeresö.hu
Italy	La Repubblica	Il Corriere della Sera	La Gazzetta dello Sport	Leonardo.it	Il Sole 24 ORE
Netherlands	nu.nl	Telegraaf.nl	NOS.nl	ad.nl	GeenStijl.nl
Norway	VG Nett	Dagbladet.no	Aftenposten Interaktiv	NRK.no	Nettavisen.no
Spain	El País.com	El Mundo Deportivo	20 minutos.es	Telecinco	RTVE
Sweden	Aftonbladet.se	Expressen.se	Dagens Nyheter (dn.se)	Sveriges Tele-vision (SVT.se)	Dagens Industri (di.se)
Switzerland	Bluewin.ch	20 min.ch	TSR.ch	Tagesanzeiger.ch	SF DRS.ch
United Kingdom	BBC Newsline	The Guardian	Skye	Daily Mail	Telegraph

Source: Alexa (www.alexa.com/topsites). Accessed 1 March 2010

Contrary to the overly optimistic view of early observations (Rheingold 1995) that the Internet would deliberately provide new and alternative views in international and national news, the online media quickly became part of the dominating media companies. It seems that Edward S. Herman's observation of more than ten years ago is still valid, namely that there is no evidence that new communication technologies break the corporate stranglehold on journalism (Herman 1998: 201). In Germany and the United Kingdom, for example, the leading online news providers today are Spiegel.de, a subsidiary of the leading news magazine, and BBC.co.uk, the online division of the public service broadcaster. This pattern can be found in many other European countries thus demonstrating the leading role of the dominating media corporations.

In the overall website popularity rankings in various countries in Europe published by alexa.com,[1] news websites are generally not top of the ranking. Search engines such as Google, Yahoo or Bing, social websites such as Facebook, YouTube or Wikipedia, as well as commercial sites such as Amazon.com and eBay are generally by far more popular than news websites. When the most popular news websites are selected from this overall listing, however, corporate news websites lead the news ranking (Table 2). This is the case in Austria, Belgium, France, Germany, Italy, Norway, Spain, Sweden and the United Kingdom. In Switzerland, the most popular news website is run by the national telecommunication incumbent and Internet service provider Bluewin, which also publishes online news produced by its own newsroom. In the Netherlands, the first and the fifth of the highest ranked websites are from outside the regular media industry. The only real exception in this listing is Hungary, where the first three news websites are not affiliated to any of the dominant national media conglomerates.

Despite the fact that most leading online media are part of large media corporations, online news provision has so far failed to develop a stable business model. The dilemma is the following: on the one hand, large media corporations are interested in a growing level of diversification of their news products (economies of scale and scope; Küng, Picard and Towse 2008: 19f). The Internet and the World Wide Web provide them with an additional channel for distributing news produced for radio, television or print media. Economies of scope could contribute to a better economic performance. Moreover, corporate online news erect high barriers to market entry for potential competitors and help to stabilize their own market position. Therefore, an online media division is indispensable for large media corporations, apart from being further justified by the growing interest by online users.

On the other hand, online news has become free giveaways. The abundance of freely accessible online news outlets decreased the willingness of online users to pay for online news services. More than any other mass medium in history online news became a public (collective) good with little to no opportunity to exclude users who are not willing to pay for the service. Users are not rivals in the consumption of online news. In addition, whenever news is published online, any competitor could – legally or not – take over the news items into any other website at no cost. Automatic news search algorithms enable small websites to constantly update the news on their sites. Therefore, the economic and business incentives to produce exclusive news decrease given the immediate spread of the news within the Internet.

Advertising as the second major source of mass media income shows similar patterns. The price for online advertising per thousand contacts is much lower than for newspapers, television or even radio. Moreover, online advertising tends to focus on those websites with the highest reach, measured in visits or unique users. Secondary websites achieve little advertising flow, while market leading news sites profit. Furthermore, a considerable share of the online advertising spend does not go to online media at all. Search engines like Google, Yahoo (with Bing) and MSN account for large online advertising market shares (Ala-Fossi et al. 2008: 152). Exact figures, however, are not available. Established instruments designed to collect information on advertising flows in print media, radio or television are often not prepared to monitor the flow of online advertising.

The resulting contradiction between the speed necessary to deliver breaking news online and the impossibility to capitalize on such breaking news has serious structural implications. Firstly, and most obviously, the degree of ownership concentration in online media is considerably higher than in any other mass media market (Trappel 2007: 127). As shown in Table 2 above, online media markets are dominated by leading media companies – and not by start-ups or genuine online companies. Secondly, quality in online journalism is far removed from any standards achieved by the press, radio or television. Although Mark

Deuze claims that 'online journalism can also be the stomping ground for exciting, creative and innovative forms of news, where the conventions, roles and cultures of different types of media as well as producers and consumers of information converge' (Deuze 2008: 199); he also admits that 'a picture emerges of an atomized profession, isolated and connected at the same time, yet also blind to each other (and thus itself), and the wider society it operates in' (Deuze 2008: 204).

Various large-scale research projects covering many countries in Europe and beyond report similar findings and can be summarized as follows (van der Wurff 2005; van der Wurff and Lauf 2005; Paterson and Domingo 2008): online newsrooms are understaffed, journalists' working time is overwhelmingly concerned with editing news items delivered by other sources (such as news agencies, the Internet at large, user-generated content, Weblogs, Wikipedia, competing online media, videotext, etc.), own investigations by online journalists are rare and fall prey to speed and immediacy, the social status and reputation of online journalists within the media company is low. Online journalists are often less well trained than other journalists[2] and are paid less. All these factors impede the development of an articulated and distinct field of online journalism. Kees Brants underlines similar threats and problems of online journalism: 'The indolence of "copying and pasting", the difficulties with checking reliability of sources and posts, copyright issues in hyperlinks, the lack of an online culture of correcting mistakes, the lack of a professional sense of social responsibility and accompanying values and codes, and regular updating running the risk of hyping and diminished accuracy' (Brants 2007: 117).

Some media firms have begun to re-integrate online newsrooms into existing newsrooms of newspapers, television or radio. Under the heading 'online first', e.g. newspaper journalists are required to first quickly produce a short version of an article for the website and then to write an extended version for the newspaper (examples include The Guardian in the United Kingdom, Die Welt in Germany and Blick in Switzerland). In this way, more professional competence is delivered to the online news without, however, lifting the pressure exerted by the requirement for immediacy.

In summarizing ethnographic research findings from online newsrooms in selected countries worldwide, Chris Paterson finds that 'there is little indication that online journalism is inherently better journalism for all its interactive and in-depth potential, for the shovelware phenomenon (repackaging content produced for other media) continues unabated, with news agency, print and, to a lesser degree, broadcast journalists setting the agenda for websites' (Paterson 2008: 6f).

The exceptions to this rule are those online newsrooms that profit either from their market leading position (such as Spiegel.de in Germany) with sufficient advertising income to sustain the online operations, or from sources of finance distinct from usage fees (paid content) or advertising revenues. To date, the traditional advertising-based business model does not work well for general news online. Apart from very few exceptions, advertising revenues do not provide sufficient resources for maintaining cost-effective online news services. User-fee-based business models only work in the realm of specialized news, such as financial services or consumer information (such as product tests), where consumers (or businesses) are willing to pay for the additional comfort of receiving specialized news items online.

Online media run by public service broadcasters (such as the BBC) are generally better placed and deliver added value complementary to radio and television (Trappel 2008). The latter imbalances provoked protest among publishers and private commercial broadcasters claiming market distortion by public service online media.

Thirdly, the predominant institutionalization of online media as subsidiaries of integrated large media corporations has important implications on inter-media competition:

- Deficit spending online media intensify the economic pressure on all other media outlets within the respective media conglomerate.
- Losing money online deprives other mass media of investments for innovation.
- Journalistic quality levels are compromised and deteriorate due to the lower level in online media.
- Displaying breaking news in online media first ('online first') suits the inherent logic of online media but devalues print media, radio and television.
- Increasing online news consumption by a growing share of the people forces newspapers, radio and television to adapt their model of news provision (e.g. concentrating on background news, explanation, the 'larger picture', etc.)

Finally, online news potentially modifies fundamental rules and practices of political communication. While corporate online media as such can be expected to reproduce by and large the established journalistic routines of the political process, non-corporate Internet applications run by citizens, as well as intermediary organizations, might impact on political communication in new and divergent ways. Political parties, as well as single politicians, might circumvent traditional mass media channels (including online media) in order to display their messages on their own Internet platform. In times of elections or referenda, such websites gain importance and offer additional communication channels for the electorate. Moreover, such messages are likely to find their way back into online media: online journalism is highly susceptible to easily accessible Internet sources and are likely to adopt such messages. This inroad into mainstream online news media is also available to those Internet users who run Weblogs or use other interactive devices from the family of Web 2.0 applications.

User-Generated Content in the News Process

The rise of the Internet in the 1990s presented new opportunities for ordinary people to respond to media content and to engage in web publishing. The processes of change in media production have traditionally been supported by the introductions of various technological innovations. The telegraph and wireless broadcasting are examples of technologies that have reshaped the working processes of journalism. With the introduction of digital technology and convergence of media platforms, these changes have recently increased.

The boundaries between media professionals and non-professionals have since then been blurring, and by 2005 the term user-generated content (UGC) had entered mainstream usage. The term user-generated content – or consumer-generated media, or user-created content – is fairly self-explanatory, and is defined as content created by the users themselves, as opposed to the corporate media. Included in the category of user-generated content are various forms of online genres, such as discussion groups, social network sites, blogs and wikis. The launch of the video sharing site YouTube in 2005, and the massive popularity of the social networking site Facebook from 2006 onwards, represented a shift from 'passive' to active and interactive media consumption. The users were no longer just receivers of information and stories, but also producers and storytellers. In tandem with these challenges, however, came new opportunities, and traditional mass media increasingly sought ways to tap into the popularity of user-generated online sites, and to transfer successes from non-professional collaborative media to corporative media.

An extensive body of research on online news production has pinpointed that the editors of established mass media increasingly include material generated by ordinary people. This journalistic method is described by Axel Bruns (2005) as 'gatewatching', contrasting the classic 'gatekeeping', in which newspaper editors selected news stories from the in-box in their offices (White 1950). The three key characteristics of user-generated content are collective storytelling, sharing culture and online socializing. Together, these three factors make up a strong force that influences the established mass media, and imposes changes on the relation between the producers and the consumers. Hybrid concepts such as 'prosumers' and 'prousers' have been introduced to describe the new tendencies in the ecology of media production.

Journalistically, the benefits of UGC are particularly valuable in situations in which the newsrooms have difficulties accessing relevant information by means of traditional journalistic methods. User-generated content provides ordinary people with the tools to report from regimes with censorship, and thus inform the external world about the situation in their nation. A recent example is the Iranian censorship on information, and the official attempts to disrupt e-mails and social networking sites by blocking mobile phone networks and confiscating satellite dishes in the aftermath of the presidential election held in 2009. The fact that Iran has not managed to stop the ordinary people from providing a flow of uncensored news pouring out of the country demonstrates how digital technology and new media skills impose a transition in current journalism towards increased globalization and interactivity.

User-generated content includes a range of online presences, which might be summarized in four categories: (1) Professional-institutional actors, including the global news providers BBC, CNN, Al Jazeera (AJE), etc. and the websites of newspapers and national broadcasters. (2) Professional-individual actors such as Andrew Sullivan, the Baghdad Blogger, etc.

(3) Non-professional-institutional actors, including government agencies, non-governmental organizations (NGOs), political parties, etc. (4) Non-professional-individual actors, including private bloggers (McNair 2006: 119). These categories demonstrate that user-generated content comes in many variations and includes a range from the highly institutional to the highly independent.

A European institution that extensively integrates UGC with professionally-generated content is the British BBC. The interactive arm of BBC Online 'Have Your Say' includes eyewitness reports and commentaries; the BBC receives e-mails and digital photographs and videos from users worldwide. User-generated content enables 'ordinary people' in the streets who happen to be eyewitnesses on the spot to report when a supposed newsworthy story evolves. The definition of newsworthiness, however, is not decided by the individual users but by the media institution; the BBC has about twenty staff members administrating the content, moderating online debates and collecting an average of 12,000 e-mails daily. The BBC Interactivity Desk has since 2001 registered individuals who contribute with user-generated content to a contact database. The BBC refers to these users as their 'global network of stringers', who even though they are not professional journalists yet they are capable of providing the BBC with direct access to stories. The systematic development of relationships with their contributing users eventually becomes a part of the overall BBC output (Heinrich 2008: 141). This way of partnering with the audience and enabling non-linear news flows is an example of collaborative journalism enabled by an international media institution.

User-Generated Content – Key Advantages and Disadvantages

The discussions on user-generated content are fairly polarized, and represented by enthusiasts on the one hand, and critics on the other hand. The enthusiasts argue that the usage of contributions from ordinary people in established media companies represents a democratization of the public sphere. Social media such as the social network site Facebook and the microblogging site Twitter have become journalistic tools of importance according to some researchers, while others have condemned them as trendy hype that will have no lasting impact on journalism. The polarized opinions are typical of these new phenomena because of the unpredictability of their future development and the fast-paced changes in user patterns.

Related to Barbie Zelizer's (1993) well-documented point about how journalists share an 'interpretive community', the inclusion of external interpretations of current events in the mainstream media should provide a more diverse and representative news coverage. The critics, on the other hand, argue that the term 'the myth of user-generated content' is more of a hype for the technological savvy few rather than a reality for the majority of ordinary people. Moreover, user-generated content is criticized for being falsified and non-authentic. First, there have been episodes when material produced and circulated as if generated by users, was in reality produced by media professionals. The video series LonelyGirl15 was for example presented as having been created by a 'real' blogger and achieved massive popularity on YouTube, but at the end it turned out to have been produced by people working in the media industry. A second main critique is that user-generated content tends to be opinionated and subjective, compared to the journalistic ideals of balance and objectivity that are emblematic for established news media. The first UGC scoop evolved in 1998, when the Drudge Report first covered the Clinton-Lewinsky scandal. The corporate media was reluctant to cover the story without more evidence, and was less willing than the non-professionals to risk publishing it. This example demonstrates how UGC operates within different norms and guidelines than traditional journalism, and how this might secure the information flow and bottom-up perspectives. Thirdly, user-generated content might challenge editorial standards in terms of trustworthiness. In the process of including user-generated content in mainstream media, a demand for new editorial methods for critically examining the reliability of the incoming material emerges. There are examples of news stories that are based on false information from users, but the fact that the collaborative news production is based on collective intelligence implies that other active users will rapidly correct mistakes and errors (Bruns 2005). For the established companies, the challenges related to this collaborative media production are risks related to the lack of institutional and editorial control. In some cases, the media institutions manipulate user-generated content to be compatible with the editorial standards and journalistic policy. For example, two separate studies of UGC in a Norwegian and a Slovenian news programme have shown that the production teams posted 'user-generated content' themselves as if they were audience members (Enli 2007; Erjavec and Poler Kovacic 2009).

However, the advantages of user-generated content in mainstream media seem to outweigh the disadvantages. For the media companies, UGC's key advantages are related to economy, audiences and innovation. UGC represents a low-expense editorial resource, and an opportunity to generate nearly free content which is a very interesting business model. Furthermore, UGC might build an alliance with the audience, and even serve as a lock-in mechanism because users are more loyal to media products to which they have contributed. UGC, in the context of mainstream media, might also promote the specific media company as innovative and technologically up-to-date.

For journalistic production, the key advantage is the instant access to breaking news. Editorial access to material such as video footage and eyewitness reports, represents valuable resources in news production. A key example for this is the news flow from the Schiphol crash in Amsterdam in February 2009, which was heavily reported by Twitter. Eyewitness news from the plane crash was broadcasted through Twitter postings made by individuals who were situated near the actual accident. Only minutes after the crash, Jonathan Nip had used his mobile phone and posted the following message on Twitter: 'Airplane Crash@ Schipol Airport Amsterdam'. The network of Twitters quickly picked up the news and resent (re-twittered) the news to their networks; thus the news spread fast and very soon new eyewitnesses entered the Twitter dialogue, and subsequently the first pictures from the plane crash were posted on Twitter. Twenty minutes after Nip posted the first message the news

SMS-Based User-Generated Content

The Internet is the main platform for UGC, but the mobile phone is becoming increasingly important for transmitting written messages and digital photographs to other mobile phones, or computers fitted with the required software. SMS-messaging (Short Message Service) is restricted to 160 characters per message, while longer messages, including images and sound, are sent by MMS (Multi Media Service). In other words, the mobile represents a portable, digital and near-instant return channel implemented in digitization's early stage of production and distribution of media content. European television networks started tapping into the market of SMS/MMS-messages from the late 1990s, and from 2002 onwards this practice has grown dramatically. Europe seems to be leading the way in experimenting with combinations of mobile phones/text messages and traditional media, but the trend is currently spreading worldwide.

was being presented on BBC and CNN. CNN eventually credited Twitter as their source in the news story. Consequently, social online media have become an arena for breaking news based on input from amateur journalists, and are clearly in dialogue with mainstream media.

One effect of living on the outskirts of the large media markets may consist of leading in innovation in ways that include user-generated content in mainstream media production. For example, both the Nordic countries and the Baltic region illustrate this argument (see boxed text above). The Nordic counties have been in the forefront of implementing digital technologies and rapidly spreading digital devices such as mobile phones in countries such as Finland, Norway and Sweden. Norway and Finland have been characterized as early adopters in implementing SMS-based television in the early years of the new millennium (Beyer et al. 2007). Similarly, the Balkans region has recently launched 'mobi news' as a participatory genre intended for ordinary people who transmute from viewers into producers and send their real stories by mobile phone directly to the editors (Erjavec and Poler Kovacic 2009). The editorial staff of the Slovenian 'mobi news' programme Svet (World) receive about 60 photographs from users every day, which shows a massive engagement in the bottom-up perspective in the programme. This engagement is partly explained by the historical traditions of surveillance in the former socialist regime (Erjavec and Poler Kovacic 2009: 161). Consequently, rather small countries on the periphery of the large media markets have cultural, technological and economic reasons for experimenting with various forms of user-generated content.

Online News – Business without Regulation?

Online news media as well as UGC benefit from relaxed rules and regulation. Corresponding to the different stages of media regulation (van Cuilenburg and McQuail 2003), online news media clearly fall into the most recent phase. The press was institutionalized in Phase I when '[t]he common assumption was that the medium for overtly political communication should be the printed newspaper, for which there was no policy except freedom from censorship and subjection to the rule of law' (van Cuilenburg and McQuail 2003: 187). Later, television was institutionalized as a public service with clear normative and socio-political strategic concerns. The third phase, commencing in the 1990s and labelled as 'search of a new communications policy paradigm' (van Cuilenburg and McQuail 2003: 197) is characterized by the technological and economic (market) logic as driving force. Although not very clear in its final appearance, this media policy phase has left the initiative for the establishment of governance rules to the economic actors themselves. Internet governance, however, is so far limited to agreements on technology and infrastructure. Rules on conduct or content have not been achieved. Online news media, therefore, may be the least regulated mass media ever in history.

Despite the fact that a growing number of people use the Internet for (political) information purposes with potentially important implications for public deliberations, literally no specific rules apply: contrary to the public service phase, online news media are not requested to fulfill any normative obligations and ownership restriction rules do not apply at all. Jurisdiction is a particular problem given the high degree of flux concerning the establishment location of online media. National rules apply only to those companies established in the respective country but cannot be applied to others. Not even within the European Union do communal provisions exist for online news media. The Audiovisual Services Directive (formerly Television Without Frontiers Directive) does not contain any specific rules for online news media.

The only exception to the virtually non-regulated online media field is the dispute on the legitimacy of public service broadcasters to engage on the Internet in general and in online news in particular. The conflict is rooted in the fundamental question as to whether the remit of public service broadcasters should include the freedom to extend services into the Internet. The public service media organizations of several European Union member states have already been under the Commission's scrutiny, acting on the basis of complaints by private commercial media who claim that extended Internet services provided by public service media organizations would distort competition beyond what is acceptable under the Amsterdam Protocol of 1997 (European Commission 2009).

Germany and the United Kingdom have by now gone the furthest. In an attempt to settle this dispute between private commercial television broadcasters and public service media before the European Commission, the German Länder (responsible for media policy in Germany) accepted the implementation of a so-called three-step-test for all Internet services provided by public service media organizations. The first step is to demonstrate the democratic, social and cultural value of the online services. The subsequent step is to show how the intended online services would contribute to competition in journalistic quality. The third step is to display the financial implications the intended online services would have. In early 2009 the first test results were published (for the Mediathek of one German public service broadcaster). The complicated procedure resulted in a non clear-cut picture. According to this test, there might be some, but only minor market distortions. The final say on the future of this Mediathek is left to one of the bodies of the public service media's board.

In the United Kingdom, the public value test for any additional online service is a complicated procedure as well. Carried out by internal as well as external evaluating bodies, the BBC intends to demonstrate the additional public value its operations generate (BBC 2004; Collins 2007).

In other European states there are formal legal attempts to define the legitimate range of online services provided by the public service media. To draw a clear line between the appropriate services necessary to fulfill the public remit and the online services that go beyond it is often disputed. The 2009 Broadcasting Communication by the European Commission established standards for this procedure based on the principles of the Amsterdam Protocol on public service broadcasting. According to this Broadcasting Communication, public service broadcasters may even use state aid to provide new online services, 'provided that they are addressing the same democratic, social and cultural needs of the society in question, and do not entail disproportionate effects on the market, which are not necessary for the fulfillment of the public service remit' (European Commission 2009: para. 81).

Public service media, however, need to undergo a test procedure, as already implemented on a voluntary basis by Germany and the United Kingdom. This test procedure should be applied by the EU member states. 'To this end, Member States shall consider, by means of a prior evaluation procedure based on an open public consultation, whether significant new audiovisual services envisaged by public service broadcasters meet the requirements of the Amsterdam Protocol, i.e. whether they serve the democratic, social and cultural needs of the society, while duly taking into account its potential effects on trading conditions and competition' (European Commission 2009: para. 84).

Such a procedure, including a public hearing for each intended online service, is a considerable obstacle for public service media to fulfill its 'important role in bringing to the public the benefits of the new audiovisual and information services and the new technologies' and to diversify its activities in the digital age, as proclaimed by the European Council earlier (European Council 1999). The first experience in Germany shows that such a test takes time and costs a considerable amount of money, especially if consultancy services need to be employed to scrutinize the potential effects on trading conditions. The procedure proposed by the Commission will therefore reduce the public service media's online engagement – not on grounds of media policy claims, but because of the additional bureaucratic burden and expenditure.

Online News on the Future Research Agenda

'In short, online or digital journalism is here to stay, but its identity, place, and status are still very much "under construction" – as indeed anything online is.' What Mark Deuze

(2008: 199) notices for online journalism equally holds true for online news at large. High levels of uncertainty are characteristic for the current stage of online news development. The following issues are crucial for the future of online news – and equally for news provision in general:

- *Search for Business Models.* The provision of online news is, in most cases, a loss making business. In 2009, Rupert Murdoch together with various other US media companies announced the intention to introduce paid content on the news websites later in the year in order to stabilize the overall news business. Indeed, the absence of sustainable business models for online news might become the most relevant issue for the future of online news.
- *Crisis to Lower News Quality.* The economic recession triggered by the US sub-prime crises in 2008 strongly affects advertising-based news business. Advertising revenues for news media dropped dramatically by up to 30 per cent in 2009. Several newspapers filed for bankruptcy in the United States. In Europe, many journalists have been dismissed. Although this crisis was not caused by online media, the economic recession puts at risk the survival of purely advertising-funded media. Online media are thus affected strongly and might be subject to budget cuts. But there is an alternative: online news might become the blueprint for lowering journalistic standards for all other news media, thus economizing on expensive journalism. The consequences of such substitution would be severe: a reduction in the quality of journalism means even lower standards in online journalism. UGC would be no viable alternative to professional news.
- *Quality Management.* Online news is subject to various quality hazards. How can online news organizations guarantee journalistic quality in the long run? How can immediacy match accuracy when online news increases in popularity? Economic stability would certainly help. But the establishment of an identity with operating rules is indispensable for sustaining social and political relevance for online media.
- *Ownership Concentration Rules.* The absence of media policy rules for online media resulted in unprecedented corporate control over a new medium. UGC and Web 2.0 might help to balance the dominance of corporate media. Nonetheless, media policy at the national and the European level should scrutinize online news media not only in terms of legitimate online activities of public service media but also in terms of cross ownership control. Why are there rules in most countries to exclude newspaper owners of particular power from owning radio or television – and no such rules apply to online news media?

Conclusion

Online news is changing news provision. UGC as well as newly established professional routines in online newsrooms affect the press, radio and television. After more than ten years since their inception, online news are stuck in new routines with too little resources to speed up innovation. UGC might add to traditional news provision but cannot replace profound journalism. However, closer links to the public, more interactivity, more participation, more links to individuals and groups in society might strengthen the position of online news. Public service media are required to closely observe these developments as they might determine their own future. Therefore, the debate on the future of public service online activities becomes of central importance.

Although online news are often intertwined with other media, their news immediacy and growing popularity set standards for all other news media. In times of economic crisis, online news media might lower the overall journalistic standards by providing free access to basic news at low cost. Further research is needed to better understand what effects such low-cost-journalism has on overall news provision and which business models might enable news organizations – probably by integrating UGC – to maintain high quality news standards.

Notes

1. The website alexa.com generates its country listing automatically. Therefore, the ranking does not necessarily reflect the status provided by more accurate research on visits or unique users. But it does provide a comparative picture based on the same (but maybe not the best available) methodology.
2. Training in online writing and editing has increased in many European countries over the last decade. These skills have now become part of the curricula in most journalism training programmes and might improve the situation in the long run.

References

Ala-Fossi, M., Bakker, P., Ellonen, H. K., Küng, L., Lax, S., Sádaba, C. and van der Wurff, R., 'The Impact of the Internet on Business Models in the Media Industries – A Sector-by-Sector Analysis', in Küng, L., Picard, R. and Towse R. (eds) (2008), *The Internet and the Mass Media*, Los Angeles, London, New Delhi and Singapore: Sage, pp. 149–69.

BBC (2004), *Building Public Value: Renewing the BBC for a Digital World*, London: BBC.

Beyer, Y., Enli, G., Maasø, A. J. and Ytreberg, E. (2007), 'Small Talk Makes a Big Difference', *Television & New Media*, 8: 3, pp. 213–35.

Brants, K., 'Changing Media, Changing Journalism', in Meier, W. A. and Trappel, J. (eds) (2007), *Power, Performance and Politics: Media Policy in Europe*, Baden-Baden: Nomos, pp. 105–21.

Bruns, A. (2005), *Gatewatching: Collaborative Online News Production*, New York: Peter Lang.

Collins, R. (2007), *Public Value and the BBC: A Report Prepared for The Work Foundation's Public Value Consortium*, London: The Work Foundation.

Deuze, M., 'Towards a Sociology of Online News', in Paterson, C. and Domingo, D. (eds) (2008), *Making Online News: The Ethnography of New Media Production*, New York: Peter Lang, pp. 198–209.

Enli, G. S. (2007), 'The Participatory Turn in Broadcast Television: Institutional, Editorial, and Textual Challenges and Strategies', Ph.D. thesis, Department of Media and Communication, Oslo: University of Oslo.

Erjavec, K. and Poler Kovacic, M. (2009), 'A Discursive Approach to Genre: Mobi News', *European Journal of Communication*, 24: 2, pp. 147–64.

European Commission (2009), *Communication from the Commission on the Application of State Aid Rules to Public Service Broadcasting*. Available at: http: //ec.europa.eu/competition/state_aid/legislation/specific_rules.html#broadcasting. Accessed 1 March 2010.

European Council (1999), *Resolution of the Council and of the Representatives of the Governments of the Member States, Meeting within the Council of 25 January 1999 Concerning Public Service Broadcasting*, Official Journal C 30, Brussels: European Council.

Heinrich, A. (2008), 'Network Journalism: Journalist Practice in Interactive Spheres', Ph.D. thesis, Department of Media, Film and Communication, Dunedin: University of Otago.

Herman, E. S., 'The Propaganda Model Revisited', in McChesney, R. W., Wood, E. M. and Foster, J. B. (eds) (1998), *Capitalism and the Information Age: The Political Economy of the Global Communication Revolution*, New York: Monthly Review Press, pp. 191–205.

Küng, L., Picard, R. and Towse, R., 'Theoretical Perspectives on the Impact of the Internet on the Mass Media Industries', in Küng, L., Picard, R. and Towse, R. (eds) (2008), *The Internet and the Mass Media*, Los Angeles, London, New Delhi and Singapore: Sage, pp. 17–44.

McNair, B. (2006), *Cultural Chaos: Journalism, News and Power in a Globalized World*, London: Routledge.

Paterson, C., 'Why Ethnography?', in Paterson, C. and Domingo, D. (eds) (2008), *Making Online News: The Ethnography of New Media Production*, New York: Peter Lang, pp. 1–11.

Paterson, C. and Domingo, D. (eds) (2008), *Making Online News: The Ethnography of New Media Production*, New York: Peter Lang.

Rheingold, H. (1995), *The Virtual Community: Surfing the Internet*, London: Minerva.

Trappel, J. (2008), 'Online Media within the Public Service Realm? Reasons to Include Online into the Public Service Mission', *Convergence*, 14: 3, pp. 313–22.

—— 'Towards the Upper Limit: Structure and Policy of Emerging Online Media in Europe', in Meier, W. A. and Trappel, J. (eds) (2007), *Power, Performance and Politics: Media Policy in Europe*, Baden-Baden: Nomos, pp. 123–40.

van Cuilenburg, J. and McQuail, D. (2003), 'Media Policy Paradigm Shifts: Towards a New Communications Policy Paradigm', *European Journal of Communication*, 18: 2, pp. 181–207.

van der Wurff, R. (2005), 'Impacts of the Internet on Newspapers in Europe', *Gazette: The International Journal for Communication Studies*, 67: 1, pp. 107–20.

van der Wurff, R. and Lauf, E. (eds) (2005), *Print and Online Newspapers in Europe: A Comparative Analysis in 16 Countries*, Amsterdam: Het Spinhuis.

van Eimeren, B. and Frees, B. (2009), 'ARD/ZDF-Online-Studie 2009: Der Internetnutzer 2009 – multimedial und total vernetzt?', *Media Perspektiven*, 7, pp. 334–48.

White, D. M. (1950), 'The Gatekeeper: A Study in the Selection of News', *Journalism Quarterly*, 27, pp. 383–90.

Zelizer, B. (1993), 'Journalists as Interpretive Communities', *Critical Studies in Mass Communication*, 10, pp. 219–37.

Part II

Chapter 7

Deficits and Potentials of the Public Spheres

Barbara Thomass

This chapter will discuss the challenges which have arisen for public spheres and the consequences of the related developments for political communication in Europe. In this chapter, public sphere is understood to mean the public communication that takes place in defined spaces with general access, and with reference to, common subjects that are mainly imparted by the media. It was originally conceptualized for the national frame and has been transferred to transnational levels, as well as to the European level.

Given the ongoing democratic deficit within the European Union (EU), the question stands: what is the quality, the performance and the perspective of European public spheres? Related to this is the challenge of the 'Europeanization' of the public sphere, i.e. the process of developing public spheres at the European level. Therefore, this contribution will look at the process of audience fragmentation and ask if a disintegration of society might be the consequence. On the other hand, the digitization of public spheres can be interpreted as an enhancement of participation. Supra-nationalization (the transfer of decision-making to the European level) and the regionalization of the public sphere (the degree, to which regional public spheres refer to the European level) are developments to be observed as counterparts to multi-layer governance in Europe. The extended commercialization of the mediascape will be discussed with its possible effects on de-politization of the public sphere. The resume will give an evaluation of the communication deficits and potentials in Europe.

Public Sphere(s) in Europe – An Empirical or a Normative Concept?

With the foundation of the European Union the project of European integration has migrated from being primarily an economic project to being a comprehensive political and social one. With the enlargement of the political aims and the increasing dislocation of national competences at the European level, the connection of the European population to the policies of the European Union via a public sphere has become a vital question, which is relevant from a theoretical, as well as from a practical perspective (Bach 2000; Gerhards 1993, 2000; Eder 2000; Schlesinger and Kevin 2000; Semetko et al. 2000; Baerns and Raupp 2001; Javnost-The Public 2001; Hagen 2004; Kevin 2003; Klein et al. 2003; Erbe and Koopmans 2004; Hagen 2004; Tenscher and Schmidt 2004; Trenz 2005; Berkel 2006; Langenbucher and Latzer 2006; Statham 2007; Salovaara-Mooring 2009). This is where the question of the emergence of a European public sphere arises.

Trying to define the complex concept of the European public sphere, the following difference is primarily important: do we conceptualize it empirically or from a normative perspective? When we talk about the existing public sphere which can be empirically described, it is important to state that this is not a holistic sphere, but a diversity of public spheres which are entwined with each other in various complex ways (Hickethier 2000; Nieminen 2009). They can be defined according to the space that they open, to the media that are involved, to the audiences which emerge or are served, to themes, groups, etc. Thus we can understand the public sphere as a network of networks (Trenz 2009).

When we talk about the emergence or development of a European public sphere, usually the normative perspective prevails, where the public sphere is regarded as being an eligible and emphatically desirable construct – as analyzed and theorized by German sociologist and philosopher Jürgen Habermas – and it is then used in the singular form. Even within this tradition at least two different forms of political public sphere are conceived (Gerhards 1997):

- *A representative-liberal model*, which considers the public sphere as a system of observation which delivers information about the political elite to citizens, on the basis of which they can make political choices in elections. The political elite for its part is enabled to receive information about the electorate, so that they can adapt their political programmes to the electorate's perceived needs. Mass media function in this model as agents of mutual observation.
- *A deliberative model*, which takes into account the functions the media should fulfil. It demands the participation of citizens in the public sphere, meaning there's citizen feedback to civil society, rationality and debate; the result of this should not be based on a simple majority decision, but on a real dialogue between the communication partners.

If we lay aground the latter model – and take it as the more normative of the normative concepts – the following prerequisites for communication in the public sphere can be deduced:

- Equality and reciprocity in the integration of those involved in the public sphere
- Openness and an adequate capacity for dealing with issues and contributions in keeping with the high competence of those involved in the public sphere
- A discursive structure: arguments, objections, critique

These are far-reaching requirements, and in the following discussion it is useful to identify and define the contribution of the media to the public sphere. Translating these requirements into the political reality of Europe and taking into account the often-bemoaned democratic deficit of the European Union (see below), it signifies that the European public sphere needs:

- Democratization of the political processes, so that the identification of citizens with Europe through interest and participation is possible

- Coverage of these processes, i.e. the reporting of European policies in the media, in ways which provide a public sphere at the European level, in manifold ways

This raises the question of whether the emergence of a European sphere means that media in the European Union member states are reporting more on European issues, or whether a combination and homogenization of national public spheres is taking place. These offer two possibilities for the emergence of European public spheres (Gerhards 2002: 142):

- A supra-national European public sphere evolves as a homogeneous media system, which circulates content and information to European Union member states. However, this concept is no longer conceivable since many efforts to create pan-European media have failed.
- Instead, we find a Europeanization of national public spheres in the sense that more and more European issues find their way into the national media, and that similar agendas develop including exchanges of views, knowledge and opinions (see van de Steeg 2000).

Comparing these two possibilities, we must admit that the first one is highly unlikely, and that the Europeanization of public spheres has been researched in several empirical studies. Furthermore, we can differentiate between the development of a European mass public sphere and the emergence of a transnational elite public sphere, which is more probable for the time being. While the first involves a great number of citizens in public communication, the latter sees a minority of competent actors who are concerned with only a minimum amount of feedback between the procedures of opinion building in diverse national forums (Kremer 2004). Until now, the European public sphere has been an elite public sphere as it comprises above all of European politicians, experts, journalists in Brussels, lobbyists and representatives of European civil society. Nevertheless, it is worth noting that such elite public spheres contributed to the development of democracy in western countries (Kaelble 2004). An argument for the probability of an elite public sphere possibly emerging is the fact that the public sphere in Europe is multilingual and demands language competence for access. On the other hand, countries like Spain or Switzerland demonstrate that multilingual democracies can also have working public spheres.

The Democratic Deficit in the European Union

The prerequisite for the emergence of a European public sphere – the Europeanization of national public spheres – is that political actors, audiences and the media show interest in European issues, and are prepared and willing to interact. This necessitates a complex concurrence of journalists, audiences and political actors, which is embedded into the democratization of the European Union. It also necessitates that European issues become more relevant to citizens, so that there is an incentive for journalists to cover European issues, resulting in more responsiveness from political representatives.

The existence and state of the European public sphere is closely connected to the performance of democracy within European institutions. It is not yet clear whether a European public sphere is a prerequisite for democracy or whether it is a result of it. Is a vibrant democracy only possible if the democratic institutions of the European Union are developed and work well? Or, are well-functioning democratic institutions the basis on which vibrant democracy can be developed? In either case, coverage of European affairs plays an important role, if we start from the assumption of a triad in the emergence of the European public sphere: stakeholder activities on the European scene are a condition for the media exhibiting an interest in European events and affairs. Media audiences are interested in European issues depending on how the media cover them. And the media cover European topics depending on the interests of their audiences.

The European Union is accused of suffering from a democratic deficit for several reasons. On the one hand, political decision-making has migrated from the national state to the European level. Up to 60 per cent of national laws are predetermined there. This means that the European Union makes more and more decisions with a normative dimension. The abundance of competences that are concentrated within the EU Commission coincides with an increased risk of mistakes and abuse of power (Meyer 2000: 132). On the other hand, the functioning of the European Union and the European Commission are relatively undemocratic; the European Parliament is too weak to provide checks and balances. Decisive power is concentrated within the European Council of Ministers which is responsible for issuing directives and guidelines. Its sessions take place behind closed doors, so that there is a deficit of public access. The Commission, which is responsible for the proposition drafts of directives and guidelines, is an organ of initiative and an organ of execution at the same time, and it has a deficit in democratic control. The Parliament has functions and competences that are not well developed; the rights that have been transferred from national parliaments to the European level have not been given to the European Parliament. This is a democratic deficit as well. All three institutions are inert and cumbersome when modernization and innovation are required. Furthermore there are no European parties; instead, there are only national parties which are aligned in eight rather heterogeneous factions. So we can state that, in general, there is a low transparency in respect to procedures and competences within the European Union. One explanation for this observation is the fact that the European Union started as an economic project before it became a political one, resulting in measures aimed at political integration being neglected for a long time. Instead, politics work in very informal yet opaque networks, which are extremely difficult for journalists to report.

These are the reasons why the development of a European public sphere can be considered to be necessary. Also, the fact that the economic sphere is becoming increasingly transnational means that a public sphere will be required at the European level too.

Digitization of the Public Sphere = Enhancement of Participation?

The developments within the information and communication technologies have brought up new possibilities for media services and media use, which can be interpreted from the perspective of public spheres. The fact that the media function as amplifiers of political information and knowledge is true for old as well as for new media. Beyond this, online technologies serve communication processes that are no longer one-directional.

With digitization and new electronic media, the significance of group communication and interpersonal communication is growing, reinforcing, for instance, the capability of lobbies and other activist groups to inform themselves and intervene in the discussion of public affairs. The Internet also increases opportunities for the international exchange of information. So, more media than before intervene in the construction of public spheres. But the notion of the digital divide is also applicable for different parts of Europe, i.e. eastern Europe is heavily lagging behind in Internet penetration compared with western European and Nordic countries.

There is a growing literature exploring the role of the Internet in influencing levels and styles of political participation. It is above all the technical potential of the Internet which has been the cause of lively debate about new perspectives for political participation in Europe (and in general). The Internet is regarded as an important element for the emergence of new democratic paradigms (Slaton 1998: 338), and it is better than any other medium apt to compact public sphere and provide transboundary arenas of opinion building. This should then give back more legitimacy to the political process. Given the democratic deficit of the European Union (see above), it is obvious that it needs this sort of legitimacy, which is hard to find as online channels for political communication on European issues are rare. The German website Europa Digital is one of these lighthouse projects, which enhances the public sphere by delivering transparency on European politics and by inviting participants to cooperate and discuss various topics on its forum.[1] The Europatermine website is more straightforward still, and by regularly updating the agenda of European events it offers possibilities to its audience to get involved.[2]

Another example of contributing to a transnational public sphere in Europe is cafebabel. com, a website that works on the basis of virtual local newsrooms all over Europe and offers its articles in five languages,[3] guaranteeing that common knowledge on European issues is offered and can trigger debates. Other websites like these add to a growing virtual sphere of communication on European topics.

However the Internet's technological potential does not mean that it *will* be used. Interactivity alone is not enough – the political system has its own logic of communication, which tends to avoid interactivity and exclude non-elites.

However, it is not yet clear why the Internet is perceived as a medium that can – at least potentially – increase participation. The European Union has tried to pursue this route with the project Europe for Citizens (2007–13). This aims to enable citizens to become more active in the democratic life of their community and in shaping the EU project.[4] The European

Urban Knowledge Network (EUKN) provides a site aimed at facilitating the exchange of demand-driven knowledge and experience on urban issues.[5] Another site is Pep-Net, which tries to build a European network of stakeholders active in the field of eParticipation.[6]

Rabia Karakaya Polat points to the fact that the relationship between the Internet and political participation is made up of three different facets: the Internet as an information source, as a communications medium and as a virtual public sphere (Polat 2005). Her main argument is that it is these facets of the Internet that may affect the levels and styles of political participation, and it is for this reason that they are of interest to political communication, as well as to the public sphere.

With respect to political participation via the Internet, online media introduce novelties into the construction of the public sphere, as an unprecedented number of speakers may be active on various channels at the same time. This, though, takes place within the context of a fragmented audience.

Fragmentation of Audiences = Disintegration of Society?

While the concept of the political public sphere started from the supposition of a single space where public communication of relevant issues in society takes place, the reality of media audiences and of multicultural societies is quite different.

Technological and industrial developments occur within an increasingly differentiated media environment and among fragmented audiences. The growing differentiation of media content is accompanied by an increasing differentiation of media use. While specialization of media use patterns has long been common for radio, music devices, film and magazines, it is a rather new development for television which hitherto appeared as the medium of integration per se. The use of newspapers – which once used to give a comprehensive picture of society – is now in decline, and as a whole divides, cleavages between different parts of society are growing. The forums where communication between different parts and groups of society exchange views and interests have diminished.

Fragmentation is visible with respect to social integration and the formation of one coherent identity as European citizens. Identification with the idea of Europe and the European Union is predominantly a perspective of the elite people. It appears that less educated people tend to be more 'Eurosceptic' and less connected to Europe (Herzog 2007).

Fragmentation is further reinforced by differences in access to the media: in northern Europe, newspapers reach up to three quarters of the population. In France, Spain, Greece, Portugal and Italy, less than 40% of the population are newspaper readers (Hasebrink 2007: 156). Radio use shows great differences too: in Switzerland and Ireland, about 90% of the population use the radio daily, but this sinks to 60% in Romania, Portugal and Spain. Daily TV use ranges in Europe from two and a half hours a day in the Nordic countries to more than four hours a day in Eastern Europe (Hasebrink 2007: 156).

Much more serious are the differences that exist in European societies with respect to Internet access and use. Elderly people, those who are less educated and those living in rural areas are at risk of being cut off from the so-called information society. Furthermore, European societies differ with respect to diffusion paths, meaning the ways in which new technologies enter everyday life, i.e. whether they are primarily implemented via institutions such as schools or public libraries, or whether they occur as a result of private initiative. Accordingly, online media have different significance in different countries – they may be associated with learning functions rather than with recreational activities (Krotz and Hasebrink 2001).

Fragmentation is visible too with respect to TV consumption patterns. Transnational channels like Eurosport or ARTE have very small audiences. Audiences concentrate their viewing mainly on national channels. This is different in small states which border larger states with the same language, as is the case for Austria, Switzerland, Flanders, Wallonia and Ireland. Here, a reasonable share of the audience watches programmes on the neighbouring states' TV stations. Most of the interest in foreign content is given to fiction and entertainment programming, whereas attention towards news is only granted to national news programmes. Entertainment is more internationalized – and less fragmented – than information, although information is regarded as an important element of the European public sphere (Olderaan and Jankowski 1989: 47).

The integrative force of media has long been questioned (Jarren 2000). Regarding media use patterns and access within Europe, it is no longer possible to start from the assumption that audiences gather around commonly shared media content.

Supra-Nationalization and Regionalization of the Public Sphere = A Counterpart to Multi-Layer Governance in Europe?

Europe is marked by two countervailing tendencies. On the one hand, the process of European political integration is advancing; on the other hand, there is an ongoing renaissance of small-scale entities and regional movements. This is reflected within the development of multi-layer governance in Europe. Political, economic and cultural thinking increasingly crosses national borders and orientates towards sub-national entities. These developments are reflected within public spheres. On the other hand, regionalization is a countervailing tendency to European integration with regard to enlargement, as well as to the intensification of cooperation. The renaissance of small regional (in the sense of sub-national) entities and of regional movements has taken place, and this is reflected in some institutions. In 1985, the Assembly of European Regions (AER) was founded as a political organization for these regions, representing their interests at the European, as well as at the international level. Today, more than 270 regions from 33 European countries and 13 international organizations are members of this assembly.[7]

The EU Treaty of 1992 (Article 198a) lays down the constitution of a Committee of the Regions (CoR). In it, 344 representatives have the role of providing advice to the Council and the Commission whenever new proposals are made in areas that have repercussions at regional or local level.[8] The 1997 Treaty of Lisbon even gives the Committee of the Regions the right of appeal before the European Court.

Political, economic and cultural thinking thus transgresses national borders on the one hand, and it is increasingly orientated towards sub-national entities on the other (Faulstich and Hickethier 2000; Schmitt-Egner 2005). Dependent on their strength and acceptance within their respective national settings, we can state that the regions in Europe tend to refer to the European level, in the sense that they aspire to be heard and represented within the European Union.

Several studies have found an increasing role for multi-layer governance within Europe representing the notion of a 'Europe of the Regions' (see Riescher 1991; Knemeyer 1994; Hrbek and Weyand 1994; Walkenhorst 1997; Kohler-Koch 1998). Connected to this development is the belief that the handing over of political decision-making from the national to the European level strengthens the sub-national level (see Knodt 1998; Kohler-Koch 1996; König et al. 1996; Nitschke 1999).

This double process of transnationalization and regionalization in the European Union is reflected within political communication and the public sphere. Because of the development of communication technologies and the globalization of media companies and markets, the European media are also characterized by contradictory tendencies. This can be found with the transnational concentration of media and the homogenization of media content on the one hand, and with the regionalization of media via the production of content for regional audiences and the tendency to give regional communication more weight on the other (Garitaonandía and Moragas 1995). Thus the European public sphere is made of multiple regional public spheres.

The regions have not only acquired increased significance within the institutions of the European Union, but also within the process of mediated policies. Due to citizens' general lack of identification with the European Union and its actions, a regional emphasis was elaborated within the EU communication and PR policies. The Commissioner for Institutional Relations and Communication Strategy, Margot Wallström (Kommission der Europäischen Gemeinschaften 2007), saw the necessity of strengthening European communication policies at the local and regional level, and announcements by the General Directorate of Press and Communication are now addressed immediately to the regional media (Europäische Kommission 2005).

Beyond those territorial regional public spheres, linguistic minorities – which exist within, and across, national and regional borders – create their own public spheres, which adds to the overall complex picture (Husband and Moring 2009).

Commercialization = Depolitization of Public Sphere?

The Euromedia Research Group has long detected and described the processes of media commercialization, initiated by the abolition of a predominantly public service orientated media system (see Meier and Trappel 2007; McQuail and Siune 1999). This has affected the quality of public spheres in the sense that it contributed to a de-politization of public spheres. On the other hand, concepts of the public sphere which mainly refer to a political public sphere do not adequately recognize the contributions to public communication which accrue from culturally-defined communication spaces. So, the quality of public spheres beyond the background of the existing media system has to be considered.

Commercialization is the process by which the logic of commercial enterprise enters the sphere of public communication and culture. It is mainly the longstanding development of privately-owned media which changed the representation of politics in the European media. Commercial broadcasting is known for lower amounts of information content in their programming than public service media. This is relevant for the European public sphere, as it needs to have informed citizens. If the media are expected to have an interest in European affairs, we must ask, under which conditions can this interest develop?

In general, we can say that the news value of EU-news on the national agenda is rather low (AIM 2007; Möra 2009). Typically, the media show interest in European themes only once a certain degree of attention for European issues is already evident. This is particularly the case when it comes to the commercial broadcast media, because attention (that is viewership) results in more commercial income and profits. While coverage of national matters guarantees high ratings, the market for European affairs is more difficult to develop, and this is especially evident in smaller linguistic areas (Meier and Trappel 1992).

To strengthen European reporting, appropriate resources need to be available (competent correspondents and editors, who are able to address news topics for both national and local audiences, enough time slots and so on) – even if this is not translated directly into attention and audience shares (which means revenues). European reporting does require investment in advance. Referring to the market logic of supply and demand, European reporting involves supply without relevant demand for the time being, while the commercialized media market responds mainly to demand. It works as a buyer's market. The resources for a new product – in this case, a new field of reporting – are usually only made available if this is worthwhile in itself, meaning if there is a market for those news topics. This lack of interest in catering for issues which are not demanded by the audience, but which are relevant for the political public sphere can be considered as a structural deficit. It is built into the structure and philosophy of the commercial media, which adopt the logic of the market and ignore the social benefits of the creation of a political public sphere. So more European reporting – even if this does not result in high ratings and therefore revenues – cannot be realized within the framework of commercial media.

A further precondition – taking into account the above-mentioned deliberative model – would be that the media follow the criteria of equality and reciprocity, of openness and discursiveness. The performance of Public Service Broadcasters (PSB) – which is more likely to be able to follow these prerequisites – is dependent both on the existing regulatory framework, which represents the legal-political dimension, and on market competition, which represents the economic dimension. It is true that public institutions do perform within a competitive media ecology and also need to pay attention to ratings, but due to their societal contract which obligates them to fulfil fundamental cultural and social goals, PSBs can more easily be associated with the process of Europeanization of the public sphere than commercial media. This is because PSB is a form of broadcasting regulation based on broadcasting that has to satisfy certain social and cultural needs which exist beyond the interests of the consumer. The PSB system is to a certain degree protected against market forces (for example by its unique method of funding through the licence fee), and specific obligations are imposed upon it (e.g. the condition to provide universal service, or to cater for certain programme genres such as news, children's programmes, regional content, and so on). These privileges and obligations are secured by special statutes or charters (Syvertsen 2003).

Therefore, we can assume that a broadcaster who does not act according to commercial logic, can actually contribute better to the creation of a public sphere (in the sense of an informed participating public) than a broadcaster who responds to commercial interests.

However, empirical findings as to whether PSBs contribute to the realization of a public sphere are contradictory. On the one hand, Lauf and Peter (2004) found little evidence that increasing commercialization of the media system – and a declining significance of the public sector – would lead to less attention being paid to European matters. They analyzed the 1999 European elections with regard to the frequency that European Union representatives were on TV news bulletins in various European countries just before the elections. The research found high coverage of the European elections and of members of the European Commission and European Parliamentarians in the TV news of Scandinavia, Spain, Italy and Austria, but there were no significant differences between reporting by PSBs and commercial broadcasters. On the other hand, Kevin (2001) reported that more news about the European Union appeared in the programming schedules of PSBs than in those of their commercial counterparts. In this study, media coverage of European news was monitored during two one-week periods in 1999 and 2000, in eight European countries (France, Germany, Ireland, Italy, the Netherlands, Spain, Sweden and the United Kingdom). It focused on four newspapers and the primetime news broadcasts of the main public service and commercial channels. The different findings of these two pieces of research might be explained by the fact that electoral coverage, with its tendency for personalization, might not be a very suitable criterion for analyzing the European news agenda, since electoral coverage by commercial channels is typically (but not necessarily) rather good and the range of European subjects in the broadcast media is best analyzed outside of election coverage.

Conclusion: Communication Deficits and Potentials in Europe

As we have seen there are several factors influencing the formation of public spheres in Europe, even if you discount the Euroscepticism revealed in the results of the Eurobarometer survey, which regularly asks Europeans about their attitudes towards the European Union.[9]

We can state that the reason for the prevailing sense of Euroscepticism, which is a common factor in the European public sphere, is not because of the performance of the media but because of the perception of the European Union as a bureaucratic entity, which takes unworldly decisions and has too much regulation. There is also widespread fear and insecurity because of the continued enlargement of the European Union.

Referring to the above-mentioned triad of political actors, media and audiences, the following developments are possible: the actions of political actors in Europe will change with changing structures and processes, in the sense that there will be a greater weight of decisive action compared to that of administrative action. Connected to this there may be more conflicts about European decisions with the trend towards personalization, which will increase media interest in European issues. Media – which have lacked staff until now – will increase their resources: the number of correspondents in Brussels is steadily growing. Correspondents are starting to build teams of experts (especially for economy and editorials). As audience interest grows for European-related issues, Euroscepticism might decrease.

One key element in the promotion of the European public sphere is the question of whether the democratic deficit will be overcome. Supra-nationalization and regionalization will contribute to a growing interest in European affairs. Digital online media will provide more platforms for dialogue and debate. The fragmentation of audiences will persist, so that public spheres at the European level will be focused on different media and different issues. These are trends which the media – especially the commercial ones, which are lagging behind in European coverage – cannot ignore.

The debate about the empirical verification of public spheres in Europe will go on, while its necessity should no longer be an issue.

Acknowledgement

The author would like to thank Inka Salovaara-Moring for her valuable contributions to this chapter.

Notes

1. http://www.europa-digital.de (Accessed 31 July 2009).
2. http://www.europatermine.de (Accessed 31 July 2009).
3. http://www.cafebabel.com/eng (Accessed 31 July 2009).
4. http://ec.europa.eu/citizenship (Accessed 22 September 2009).
5. http://www.eukn.org/eukn (Accessed 22 September 2009).
6. http://pep-net.eu (Accessed 22 September 2009).
7. http://www.aer.eu/en/about-aer/vocation.html (Accessed 1 November 2008).
8. http://www.cor.europa.eu/pages/PresentationTemplate.aspx?view=folder&id=be53bd69-0089-465e-a173-fc34a8562341&sm=be53bd69-0089-465e-a173-fc34a8562341 (Accessed 1 November 2008).
9. On average, only 53 per cent of Europeans support their countries' membership in the European Union. Latest results from December 2008: http://ec.europa.eu/public_opinion/archives/eb/eb70/eb70_first_en.pdf. (Accessed 3 August 2009).

References

AIM Research Consortium (2007), *Comparing the Logic of EU Reporting in Mass Media across Europe: Transnational Analysis of EU Media Coverage and of Interviews in Editorial Offices in Europe*, Working Papers 2007/2, Bochum and Freiburg: Adequate Information Management in Europe (AIM).

Bach, M. (ed.) (2000), *Die Europäisierung nationaler Gesellschaften: Sonderheft 40 der Kölner Zeitschrift für Soziologie und Sozialpsychologie*. Köln: VS Verlag.

Baerns, B. and Raupp, J. (2001), *Information und Kommunikation in Europa: Forschung und Praxis*, Berlin: Vistas.

Bauer, J. (1992), *Europa der Regionen: Aktuelle Dokumente zur Rolle und Zukunft der deutschen Länder im europäischen Einigungsprozess*, 2nd edn, Berlin: Duncker&Humblot.

Berkel, B. (2006), *Konflikt als Motor europäischer Öffentlichkeit. Eine Inhaltsanalyse von Tageszeitungen in Deutschland, Frankreich, Großbritannien und Österreich*, Wiesbaden: VS Verlag.

Boesler, K. A.(ed.) (1998), *Europa zwischen Integration und Regionalismus*, Stuttgart: Steiner.

Conzelmann, T. and Knodt, M. (ed.) (2002), *Regionales Europa – Europäisierte Regionen*, Frankfurt: Campus.

Europäische Kommission (2005): *Mitteilung der Kommission an den Rat, das Europäische Parlament, den Europäischen Wirtschafts- und Sozialausschuss und den Ausschuss der Regionen. Der Beitrag der Kommission in der Zeit der Reflexion und danach. Plan-D für Demokratie, Dialog und Diskussion.* KOM(2005) 494, Brüssel: Europäische Kommission.

DG REGIO (2006), *The Media and European Regional Policy: Key Findings. Summary Report Prepared for the DG REGIO's within the Framework of the Evaluation of its Communication Policy.* Available at: http: //ec.europa.eu/regional_policy/country/commu/document/keyfindings_en.pdf. Accessed 12 January 2010.

Eder, K. (2000), 'Zur Transformation nationalstaatlicher Öffentlichkeit in Europa: Von der Sprachgemeinschaft zur issuespezifischen Kommunikationsgemeinschaft', *Berliner Journal für Soziologie*, 10, pp. 167–84.

Eder, K., Hellmann, K. and Trenz, H. J., 'Regieren in Europa jenseits öffentlicher Legitimation? Eine Untersuchung zur Rolle von politischer Öffentlichkeit in Europa', in Kohler-Koch, B. (ed.) (1998), , PVS-Sonderheft, 29, Opladen: Westdeutscher Verlag, pp. 321–44.

Erbe, J. and Koopmans, R. (2004), 'Towards a European Public Sphere? Vertical and Horizontal Dimensions of Europeanised Political Communication', *Innovation*, 17, pp. 97–118.

European Parliament (1994), *The Role of Regional Television*, Working documents 1–4, EP 208.155, Brussels: European Parliament.

Faulstich, W. and Hickethier, K. (2000), *Öffentlichkeit im Wandel: Neue Beiträge zur Begriffsklärung*, Bardowick: Wissenschaftler Verlag.

Garitaonandía, C. and Moragas, M. (eds) (1995), *Decentralisation in the Global Era: Television in the Regions, Nationalities and Small Countries of the European Union*, London: University of Luton Press.

Gerhards, J., 'Das Öffentlichkeitsdefizit der EU im Horizont normativer Öffentlichkeitstheorien', in Kaebel, H., Kirsch, M. and Schmidt-Gernig, X. (eds) (2002), *Transnationale Öffentlichkeiten und Identitäten im 20. Jahrhundert*, Frankfurt a M.: Gerhards, pp. 135–58.

—— (1997), 'Diskursive versus liberale Öffentlichkeit: Eine empirische Auseinandersetzung mit Jürgen Habermas', *Kölner Zeitschrift für Soziologie und Sozialpsychologie*, 49,Köln: VS Verlag, pp. 1–39.

—— 'Europäisierung von Ökonomie und Politik und die Trägheit der Entstehung einer europäischen Öffentlichkeit', in Bach, M. (ed.) (2000), *Transnationale Integrationsprozesse in Europa: Sonderheft der Kölner Zeitschrift für Soziologie und Sozialpsychologie*, Wiesbaden: Westdeutscher Verlag, pp. 277–305.

—— (1993), 'Westeuropäische Integration und die Schwierigkeiten der Entstehung einer europäischen Öffentlichkeit, *Zeitschrift für Soziologie*, 22, Stuttgart: Lucius&Lucius, pp. 96–100.

Hagen, L. (ed.) (2004), *Europäische Union und mediale Öffentlichkeit: Theoretische Perspektiven und empirische Befunde zur Rolle der Medien im europäischen Einigungsprozess*, Cologne: Halem.

Hasebrink, U., 'Europäische Öffentlichkeit: Zur Konstruktion von Kommunikations-räumen in Europa durch Medienpublika', in Faulstich, W. (ed.) (2000), *Öffentlich-keit im Wandel: neue Beiträge zur Begriffsklärung*, Bardowick: Wissenschaftler Verlag, pp. 97–109.

—— 'Medienrezeption', in Thomaß, B. (ed.) (2007), *Mediensysteme im internationalen Vergleich*, Konstanz: UTB, pp. 145–63.

Herzog, A. (2007), *Media Use and Euroscepticism in the Group of Lower Educated People*, Presentation on the IAMCR Conference 23 July 2007, Paris (not published).

Hickethier, K. (2000), *Veränderungen von Öffentlichkeit. Antrag auf Einrichtung eines Sonderforschungsbereiches*, Hamburg (not published).

Hrbek, R. and Weyand, S. (1994), *Betrifft: Das Europa der Regionen*. München: Beck.

Husband, C. and Moring, T., 'Public Spheres and Multiculturalism in Contemporary Europe', in Salovaara-Moring, I. (ed.) (2009), *Manufacturing Europe: Spaces of Democracy, Diversity and Communication*, Gothenburg: Nordicom, pp. 131–52.

Jarren, O. (2000), 'Gesellschaftliche Integration durch Medien?', *Medien & Kommunikationswissenschaft*, 48: 1, pp. 22–41.

Kaelble, H. (2004), 'Die Genese einer europäischen Öffentlichkeit: Anzeichen und Defizite der politischen Willensbildung auf europäischer Ebene', *Neue Züricher Zeitung*. Available at: http://www.nzz.ch/2004/04/24/zf/article9guq0_1.245039.html. Accessed 31 July 2009.

Kevin, D. (2001), *Europe in the Media: A Comparison of Reporting, Representation, and Rhetoric in National Media Systems in Europe*, London and Mahwah: Erlbaum.

Klein, A., Koopmans, R., Trenz, H., Klein, L., Lahusen, C. and Rucht, D. (2003), *Bürgerschaft, Öffentlichkeit und Demokratie in Europa*, Opladen: Leske&Budrich.

Knemeyer, Franz-Ludwig (1994), *Europa der Regionen, Europa der Kommunen: Wissenschaftliche und politische Bestandsaufnahme*. Baden-Baden: Nomos.

Knodt, M. (1998), *Tiefenwirkung europäischer Politik: Eigensinn oder Anpassung regionalen Regierens?*, Baden-Baden: Nomos.

Kohler-Koch, Beate (1996), 'Regionen als Handlungseinheiten in der europäischen Politik', *WeltTrends* No. 11, pp. 7–35.

KOM, (Kommission der Europäischen Gemeinschaften) (2007), *Mitteilung der Kommission an das europäische Parlament, den Rat, den europäischen Wirtschafts- und Sozialausschuss und den Ausschuss der Regionen. Partnerschaft für die Kommunikation über Europa*, Brüssel: KOM 568. Available at: http://eur-lex.europa.eu/LexUriServ/site/de/com/ 2007/com2007_0568de01.pdf. Accessed 27 May 2010.

König, T. et al. (eds) (1996), *Das europäische Mehrebenensystem. Mannheimer Jahrbuch für eruopäische Sozialforschung*, vol. 1, Frankfurt and New York: Campus, pp. 3–28.

Koopmans, R. (2007), 'Who Inhabits the European Public Sphere? Winners and Losers, Supporters and Opponents in Europeanised Political Debates', *European Journal of Political Research*, 46: 2, pp. 183–210.

Kremer, M. (2004), *Europäische Öffentlichkeit: Missing Link europäischer Politik*. Available at: http://www.auswaertiges-amt.de/www/de/infoservice/download/pdf/eu/missing_link.pdf. Accessed 20 October 2004.

Krotz, F. and Hasebrink, U., 'Who Are the New Media Users?', in Livingstone, S. and Bovill, M. (eds) (2001), *Children and Their Changing Media Environment: A European Comparative Study*, Mahwah, N.J.: Erlbaum, pp. 245–62.

Langenbucher, W. and Latzer, M. (eds) (2006), *Europäische Öffentlichkeit und medialer Wandel: Eine transdisziplinäre Perspektive*, Wiesbaden: VS Verlag.

Lauf, E. and Peter, J.(2004), 'EU-Repräsentanten in Fernsehnachrichten. Eine Analyse ihrer Präsenz in 13 EU-Mitgliedstaaten vor der Europa-Wahl 1999' in Hagen, L. M. (ed.): *Europäische Union und mediale Öffentlichkeit. Theoretische Perspektiven und empirische Befunde zur Rolle der Medien im europäischen Einigungsprozess*. Köln: Halem, pp. 162–177.

McQuail, D. and Siune, K. (eds) (1999), *Media Policy: Convergence, Concentration & Commerce*, London: Euromedia Research Group.

Meier, W. A. and Trappel, J. (eds) (2007), *Power, Performance and Politics: Media Policy in Europe*, Baden-Baden: Nomos.

—— 'Small States in the Shade of Giants', in Siune, K. and Truetzschler, W. (eds) (1992), *Dynamics of Media Politics: Broadcasts and Electronic Media in Western Europe*, London: Sage pp. 129–42.

Meyer, C. O. (2002), *Europäische Öffentlichkeit als Kontrollsphäre: Die Europäische Kommission, die Medien und politische Verantwortung*, Berlin: Vistas.

—— 'Ansätze einer europäischen Öffentlichkeit: Länderübergreifender investigativer Journalismus und der Rücktritt der EU-Kommission', in Baerns, B. and Raupp, J. (eds) (2000), *Information und Kommunikation in Europa: Transnational Communication in Europe*, Berlin: Vistas, pp. 107–32.

Mörä, T., 'The European Union and Ideals of the Public Sphere', in Salovaara-Moring, I. (ed.) (2009), *Manufacturing Europe: Spaces of Democracy, Diversity and Communication*, Gothenburg: Nordicom, pp. 81–96.

Nieminen, H., 'The European Public Sphere as a Network? Four Plus One Approaches', in Salovaara-Moring, I. (ed.) (2009), *Manufacturing Europe: Spaces of Democracy, Diversity and Communication*, Gothenburg: Nordicom, pp. 19–34.

Nitschke, P. (1999), *Die Europäische Union der Regionen. Subpolity und Politiken der Dritten Ebene. Opladen*: Leske + Budrich.

Olderaan, F. and Jankowski, N., 'The Netherlands: The Cable Replaces the Antenna', in Becker, L. and Schoenbach, K. (eds) (1989), *Audience Reponses to Media Diversification – Coping with Plenty*, Hillsdale, N.J.: Erlbaum, pp. 29–55.

Polat, R. K., (2005), 'The Internet and Political Participation: Exploring the Explanatory Links', *European Journal of Communication*, 20: 4, pp. 435–59.

Riescher, G. (1991) (ed.), *Regionalismus ´90 – Zur Dialektik des westeuropäischen Einigungsprozesses*. München: Beck.

Salovaara-Moring, I. (ed.) (2009), *Manufacturing Europe: Spaces of Democracy, Diversity and Communication*, Gothenburg: Nordicom.

Schlesinger, P. and Kevin, D., 'Can the European Union Become a Sphere of Publics?', in Eriksen, E. O. and Fossum, J. E (eds) (2000), *Democracy in the European Union: Integration through Deliberation?*, New York and London: Routledge, pp. 206–29.

Schmitt-Egner, P. (2005), *Handbuch zur europäischen Regionalismusforschung: Theoretisch-methodische Grundlagen, empirische Erscheinungsformen und strategische Optionen des transnationalen Regionalismus im 21. Jahrhundert*, Wiesbaden: VS Verlag.

Semetko, H. A., de Vreese, C. H., and Peter, J. (2000), 'Europeanised Politics – Europeanised Media? European Integration and Political Communication', *West European Politics*, 23, pp. 121–41.

Slaton, C. D., 'Mündige Bürger durch Televoten: Ein fortlaufendes Experiment zur Transformation der Demokratie', in Leggewie, C. and Maar, C. (eds) (1998), *Internet & Politik: Von der Zuschauer- zur Beteiligungsdemokratie*, Köln: Bollmann, pp. 321–41.

Sparks, C. and Kunelius, R. (2001), 'The Emergence of the European Public Sphere?', *Javnost – The Public*. Available at: http: //www.javnost-thepublic.org/issue/2001/1/. Accessed 31 July 2009.

Statham, P., (2007), 'Journalists as Commentators on European Politics: Educators, Partisans or Ideologues?', *European Journal of Communication*, 22: 4, pp. 461–77.

Syvertsen, T. (2003), 'Challenges to public television in the era of convergence and commercialization', *Television & New Media* 4(2), pp. 155–75

Tenscher, J. and Schmidt, S., '„So nah und doch so fern". Empirische Befunde zur massenmedialen Beobachtung und Bewertung des europäischen Integrationsprozesses in einer Grenzregion', in Hagen, L. (ed.) (2004), *Europäische Union und mediale Öffentlichkeit – Theoretische Perspektiven und Befunde zur Rolle der Medien im europäischen Einigungsprozess*, Cologne: Halem, pp. 212–37.

Trenz, H. J. (2005), *Europa in den Medien: Die europäische Integration im Spiegel nationaler Öffentlichkeit*, Frankfurt and New York: Campus.

—— 'Uniting and Dividing: The European Public Sphere as an Unfinished Project', in Salovaara-Moring, I. (ed.) (2009), *Manufacturing Europe: Spaces of Democracy, Diversity and Communication*, Gothenburg: Nordicom, pp. 35–52.

Walkenhorst, H. (1997), *Die Föderalisierung der Europäischen Union: Möglichkeiten und Grenzen im Spannungsfeld der drei politischen Gestaltungsebenen EG/EU, Nationalstaaten, Regionen*. Oldenburg: bis.

van de Steeg, M., 'An Analysis of the Dutch and Spanish Newspaper Debates on EU Enlargement with Central and Eastern European Countries: Suggestions for a Transnational European Public Sphere', in Baerns, B. and Raupp, J. (eds) (2000), *Information und Kommunikation in Europa: Forschung und Praxis*, Berlin: Vistas, pp. 61–87.

Chapter 8

Media Serving Democracy

Hannu Nieminen and Josef Trappel

Media and democracy can hardly be separated. There are intrinsic links to one another. Media require sufficient freedom to unfold which is guaranteed by democratic rules. Democracy, in turn, requires certain active and accountable media for its well functioning. In contemporary democracies, the media conciliate and mediate between those who govern, and those who are governed. Therefore, the media are essential for the political, economic and cultural life in modern societies.

But the relation between media and democracy is not necessarily relaxed. A whole series of trends and media development issues impact on this relation: media concentration and the increase of media ownership power, the 'tabloidization' of the press with less emphasis on the coverage of political issues, and the hyper-commercialization of the media system are just a few endurance tests for the relation between media and democracy. Moreover, the scholarly discourse is controversial: while some argue that democracy works well enough when citizens pay attention to politics once things have evidently gone wrong (Zallers' infamous model of the 'burglar alarm' standard for journalism; 2003), others emphasize the importance of the Habermasian ideals of participation and public deliberation. In any case, it must be remembered that the relationship between media and democracy is always a two-way street. General social, political, economic and cultural developments have always created the basic conditions, as well as restrictions, for the functioning of the media.

Although there are a number of different definitions of democracy, the role of the media has not traditionally been highlighted from the viewpoint of democratic theory (see Habermas 1998; Cunningham 2002; Held 2006). There are considerable differences when attempting to distinguish different models of democracy. In an attempt to define the media tasks addressing different types of democracies, C. Edwin Baker characterizes 'elite democracy' as a model where 'responsibilities of the press are minimal but crucial' (2006: 113ff). The media are essentially society's watchdogs of 'accuracy, honesty, and investigative zeal' (Baker 2006: 114). 'Republican', 'pluralist' and 'complex' types of democracy require the media and journalism to be more active in public life. Journalism should contribute to the public's search for the common good, portray different realms of public life, encourage those with different values and interests to express themselves, and essentially support 'varying types of discourses – bargaining discourses of the liberal pluralist, discourses aimed at the common good emphasized by republicans, and smaller self-definitional as well as minority cultural discourses especially important to the fairness of the democratic participation of smaller or otherwise marginal groups' (Baker 2006: 119).

Other scholars provide similar ways of describing different models of democracy. Christians et al. (2009: 97) list pluralist and administrative democracies under the heading of 'liberalism', and civic and direct democracies under the heading of 'republicanism'. What these attempts of systematizing models of democracy have in common is the notion of 'deliberative democracy' as the most sophisticated – perhaps illusive – form of contemporary democracy (see, for example, Nordenstreng 2006; Curran 2000; Baker 2006). In general terms, in deliberative democracy 'media should encourage and empower different groups in society to express themselves and advocate for their causes' (Trappel and Maniglio 2009: 174). The discussion in this chapter will also be guided by deliberative democracy.

In this chapter, we will first give a short historical review of the relationship between the media and democracy in Europe. This is followed by an introduction to the media's three dimensions in democracy: political, economic and cultural. Thirdly, certain complicating factors will be discussed, followed by a brief elaboration of the democratic potential of the Internet. Before concluding, some research perspectives will be examined.

Media and Democracy: European History

Liberal democracy cannot be thought of without the media. Historically there is an inseparable connection between democracy and the media, as what we understand today as a democratic political system can only emerge on the condition of freedom of speech implemented through the media. Although modern parliamentary democracy was adopted in most European countries from the late nineteenth and early twentieth centuries onwards, the basic elements for the emergence of public culture, which are elemental for liberal democracy, started to develop much earlier (see Habermas 1992: 14–26; Keane 1991.)

We can separate several stages in the slow development towards modern day democratic society. One of the first signs of the birth of modern Europe was the development of the newspaper press in the seventeenth century. With it, the power of public opinion started to emerge (Habermas 1992: 89–102). Newspaper press became the central instrument of the rising European middle classes in their political mobilization for overthrowing the old feudal rule: 'Until the middle of the nineteenth century, in both America and Britain, "liberty of the press" functioned as a bold and infectious utopian notion. It helped to put the wind up the governing classes. It dramatized the state's restrictions upon freedom of expression. It fuelled the struggle for civil rights and political democracy, and familiarized reading publics with such vital subjects as constitutional reform, the need for representative institutions, and the subordination of women, slaves and others' (Keane 1991: 28).

Bourgeois revolutions did not, however, result to the immediate establishment of democratic order in its present form, which is based on universal suffrage and a parliamentary form of government. In many countries it took another hundred years of political struggle to establish a pluralist democracy. The early press, however, was institutionalized as a commercial enterprise with profit goals. (On the British experience, see Curran and Seaton 2003: 5–108).

In the next period, from the late nineteenth to the mid twentieth centuries, the media – first the newspaper press, later broadcasting – served the European nation building process. This was also the main period of political press: different political and ideological factions mobilized their supporters into public contestation for public opinion and popular support. The national public sphere started to form, uniting warring social and political factions for the common aim, the creation and solidification of the nation state (see Eley 1992; Scannell and Cardiff 1991: 3–19). In several European countries, this development took another direction in the early decades of the twentieth century and resulted in authoritarianism and dictatorship. In these countries the media (like other public institutions) were subjected to instruments of dominant ideology and governmental propaganda.

After World War II, another phase opened. In many countries, the slow decline of the political press had already started in the early decades of the twentieth century (first in the United Kingdom). The political press' decline finally gained momentum and led to a slow disappearance of party-related newspapers in most European countries. By the 1980s, papers affiliated to political parties had lost most of their earlier significance. Independent, non-partisan newspapers, the so-called forum press, expanded. In contrast to the political press which had depended heavily on the financial support of political parties, the new independent papers were partly financed by advertisements, subscriptions and single copy sales. The media turned into an industry; a condition for the success of the media was their talent to sell audiences to advertisers. The media served two causes: on one hand, they had their basic social and democratic function, informing citizens of matters of common concern; on the other, they entered the marketplace expecting to make profitable business (see Curran and Seaton 2003: 72–108).

Parallel to the growth of the print media industry, another development took place in the realm of the emerging electronic media. Because of its strategic importance in the after-World War I Europe – from military, as well as from ideological-political viewpoints – radio broadcasting was appropriated by the state and established as a public service. As the United Kingdom was the earliest to do so (1927), many countries followed the BBC example. The European broadcasting ethos, transferred from radio to television after the World War II, adopted the famous definition of its tasks by John Reith, the then Director-General of the BBC: to inform, educate and entertain national audiences. In their more developed forms, the public service principles have been applied into national broadcasting legislation in most European countries (Open Society Institute 2005; Harrison and Woods 2007). In the 1990s, in the seminal Amsterdam Protocol (1997), public service broadcasting philosophy was adopted as an essential part of European cultural policy. It states that the provision for the funding of public service broadcasting is within the competence of European Union member states 'insofar as such funding is granted to broadcasting organizations for the fulfilment of the public service remit as conferred, defined and organized by each Member State, and insofar as such funding does not affect trading conditions and competition in the Community to an extent which would be contrary to the common interest, while the realization of the remit of that public service shall be taken into account' (Amsterdam Protocol 1997).

Media and Democracy in Central and Eastern Europe

In central and eastern Europe, the history of the media and democracy unfolded in a fundamentally different manner than in western Europe. After 1989, when the old regimes collapsed, enthusiasm for the exercise of long missed media freedom spread out over large parts of central and eastern Europe. What followed was a period of vivid activism with numerous newspapers published in the spirit of celebrating the newly gained civic right of freedom of speech. But enthusiasm rapidly vanished, followed by backlash and frustration. Karol Jakubowicz and Miklós Sükösd enumerate what they call 'multiple shocks or traumas that post-communist societies suffered' (2008: 34) during the years of transformation. From the detection that the removal of the Communist regimes does not solve all problems but creates new ones, to the discovery of the true nature of the capitalist system and the tedious process of European unification (instead of a warm welcome by the European Union) – all resulted in tension and exhaustion (Jakubowicz and Sükösd 2008: 34).

Apart from the short period of enthusiasm, the democratization of the media in the post-Communist countries was characterized by imitation. Such mimetic processes were either a deliberate copying of western European arrangements, or the repetition of processes western countries experienced in comparable circumstances (e.g. Portugal and Spain in the 1970s) (cf. Jakubowicz 2007: 305). There is no single model for the institutionalization of democratic media cultures in the countries of central and eastern Europe, despite the enduring efforts from international organizations such as the Council of Europe, the European Union (EU) and US-based organizations like the United States Agency for International Development (USAID) or International Research & Exchanges Board (IREX). The print industry enjoys formal press freedom, but in many countries it was sold to foreign media corporations, mainly from western Europe. Final decisions on the editorial line and on the allotment of resources it taken outside the country. With regard to broadcasting, most countries established public service broadcasters, but political parallelism is still widespread. 'In general, public service broadcasting is so far generally seen as failing to deliver on its promise of independence and political impartiality, as well as of serving as a mainstay of the public sphere and of delivering diverse and pluralistic content of high quality' (cf. Jakubowicz 2007: 309). The processes of democratizing the media in central and eastern Europe is – as indeed also in western Europe – not yet completed. Political interference and strong economic pressure for media company efficiency makes further development towards democratic satisfactory media a long and tedious undertaking.

The two different European media policy regimes – the one emphasizing the democratic function of the media, and the other underlining more the industrial and commercial aims – can today perhaps be seen clearest in the realm of European television policy. Powerful industrial forces have long attempted to narrow down the role of the public service broadcasting, and to reduce it to cover only such contents which are not commercially viable or interesting for mass audiences, such as educational, religious and minority programmes, as well as educational children programmes (see, for example, ACT 2009). Despite this long-standing campaign, the supporters of the public service broadcasting have at least until today been successful in defending the basic ideals of the public service broadcasting, with political reference to the Amsterdam Protocol.

Historically, we can discern three different dimensions in the relationship between the media and democracy: political, economic and cultural. Most research has concentrated on the political dimension; however, today the dimensions are ever more difficult to separate from each other. In what follows, we will first discuss these dimensions one by one, and then we will create a general overview of the field.

Media and Political System

Media's role in – and for – democracy has traditionally been defined from the point of view of news media and journalism. There has been much less discussion of the potential effects of other media forms to democracy, such as diversion, advertisement and different cultural contents. The newspaper press was already elemental in the eighteenth and nineteenth centuries in the building processes of European democracies. Catchphrases such as 'the press as the fourth estate' and 'the watchdog of democracy' have their origins from these times. In modern democracies the media play no less central role, although the division of labour between other social and cultural institutions is much more complex today.

According to the democratic ideal, media's function is, first of all, to *inform the citizens* on the whereabouts of public life. The function is that of servicing citizens with relevant and objective information on common matters, which is a prerequisite for critical and reasoned public debate, leading to public opinion and common will formation (the 'freedom principle'; see Trappel and Maniglio 2009). This first function is closely related to the freedom rights, in particular the right to expression and the right to get informed. The media therefore act as trustees for this fundamental civic right. With it, however, comes an increased level of public accountability. Media cannot interpret their freedom of expression as absolute freedom to act in their own interest.

Recent research findings support the argument that media are essential for information and thus knowledge for the population. In a comparative media study carried out in the United States, Britain, Finland and Denmark, the coverage of the core media on various issues and the level of knowledge of the population in each country were put into relation (Curran, Iyengar, Lund and Salovaara-Moring 2009). Two of the countries had a strong public service broadcaster (Denmark and Finland), one country had a dual system (Britain) and one country followed the market model in broadcasting (United States). It turned out that public service television makes news more accessible for the population, fosters higher news consumption and results in better knowledge of public affairs in the population. The survey data revealed that Scandinavians were best informed both on soft news and on hard (political) news, while Americans were the least informed (Curran et al. 2009: 14). The authors of the study conclude that 'perhaps the most significant result to emerge from this study is the low level of attention that the market-driven television system of the US gives to the world outside America, and to a lesser extent, to hard news generally. This lack of attention contributes to the relatively high level of public ignorance in America about the wider world and about public life in general' (Curran et al. 2009: 22). Thus, media structures and media coverage have strong implications on public knowledge and thereby on the exercise of democratic rights.

Secondly, the media are expected to *monitor and control the power holders* on behalf of citizens – that is, they are supposed to act as the 'watchdog' of the government and other power holders (the 'control principle'; see Trappel and Maniglio 2009). For this reason, it is necessary that the media should be independent from the government and other political forces who might want to use the media to spread their influence (in the form of propaganda). Given the long tradition of the notion of the media exercising watchdog functions, it comes as no surprise that some consider this notion as 'fossilized'. Curran (2007) rightly claims that the traditional watchdog argument requires journalists to expose the abuse of the authority of public officials. 'While there is some merit in this argument, it can lead to an undue concentration on institutionalized political power, and the neglect of other forms of power – economic, social and cultural – that can also injure or restrict' (Curran 2007: 35). Indeed, modern democracy has brought forth new centres of power, in addition to the state. The watchdog role of journalism, therefore, is extended in scope to all other realms of public life where powerful actors determine the life of others. In fact, the watchdog role on non-state power holders is even more important as in many cases no other democratic control is built into the system. The global recession following from the crash of the US sub-prime markets in 2008 and 2009 provided ample evidence, not only for insufficient internal control within commercial banks, but also for insufficient monitoring and surveillance of powerful private companies by the state – and eventually by the media. Single journalists might be overcharged with such complex watchdog duties. 'The watchdog role of the press is perhaps best viewed as mediating the investigative resources of a free society – its whistleblowers, dissenting elite members, civil society watchdogs, independent think tanks, and critical researchers – rather than acting as a substitute for them' (Curran 2007: 37).

The third major function of the media is to *give voice to the citizens*, that is, to act as the creator of public opinion which should then guide decision-makers and power holders to their actions (the 'equality principle'; see Trappel and Maniglio 2009). This way, the role of the media in democracy is understood as being that of a mediator between the government (understood in a wide sense) and its citizens (informing citizens of the actions of the government, and informing the government of the public opinion emanating from citizenry). This notion includes the heroic role of the media as mediators in society, giving voice to the voiceless and managing to conciliate through balanced journalism. Notwithstanding the importance of this mediating function, (commercial) media are probably more interested in conflict than in the search for compromise. Therefore, this function creates contradicting requirements. The contradiction can be overcome through the differentiation of the media, which are indeed not a single entity. Core media – such as television, national press and national radio – should report on divergent viewpoints and produce balanced journalism by supporting the rituals and procedures of the democratic system, while media outside the core sector could – and should – nourish the public debate through controversial positions and partisan coverage (Curran 2007: 39f).

Media and Economy

As mentioned above, most accounts on media and democracy have concentrated on the political dimension of the media, that is, the relation to the state and the government. The other main source and form of power, economic power, has not had an equal emphasis. There are historical reasons for this, as the European concept of democracy was shaped and established in opposition to the absolutist and authoritarian state in the nineteenth century. The media – and with it the demand for freedom of the press – represented at that time a radical political challenge to the old power and the social forces behind it. The main challengers to the old power were the liberal middle classes who were not only advancing their political but also their economic interests, exemplified by their demands for minimal state and free trade (*laissez faire*).

Only later, along with the advance of modern capitalism, did the dangers that corporate power posed to democracy start to be critically discussed. However, the basic concepts with which the debate is conducted are derived from the past (such as press freedom and freedom of speech), often used by oligopolistic media corporations against the attempts to curb their powers (see Curran 2000). The problem is that the media as an industry are – and have always been – a necessary part of the corporate world. Thus, questions concerning corporate influence and financial pressure to the media (e.g. in the form of ownership concentration) are more difficult to discuss than those concerning political influence and governmental pressure. Anthony Giddens points to the fact that 'the growth of giant multinational media corporations means that unelected business tycoons can hold enormous power' (2003: 97). In a similar line of argument, Werner A. Meier identifies a problem for pluralism caused by media ownership concentration and argues that there is 'a fundamental tension between, on the one hand, uncontrolled market forces and, on the other, the requirements of the kind of journalism which is compatible with democracy' (2007: 77).

Since the 1990s there has been an increase in the number of voices criticizing the media's growing commercialization as it is seen as a threat to democracy. It is feared that the ongoing trivialization of media contents is superseding 'serious' and quality journalism, and in its worst, leading to the 'dumbing down' of audiences (Blumler and Gurevitch 1995). This may lead to the public's weakening trust to democratic institutions, the symptoms of which can be seen in the declining participation in elections, and general distrust in politics and politicians. Other scholars consider the change in the news agenda of political journalism that squeezes out hard news as an 'appropriate reflection of a popular democracy in which human interest issues have a role to play [...] The blurring of traditional lines dividing the public from the private spheres is itself [...] a measure of the democratization of political culture' (McNair 2009: 243). In our view, such reasoning, underestimates the long-term adverse effects of citizens exposed to highly commercial and trivial news. The above quoted empirical research by Curran et al. (2009) demonstrates the importance of high quality news for the knowledge level of citizens.

The need to counter-balance the corporate power in the media is as such nothing new. Historically, warnings against the excessive power of media monopolies were already raised in the nineteenth century (see Curran and Seaton 2003). Measures aiming at balancing the situation are first of all represented by the public service broadcasting (discussed in Chapter 11 of this book), which is by definition supposedly free from commercial and financial dependencies. Another form of defending public interest is demonstrated by the system of public subsidies to non-commercial media, such as political press and community media (radio and television).

Media and Culture

In most European countries, the media has had a major influence in defining the national culture: in the nineteenth and twentieth centuries, the newspaper press was elemental in nation building and in creating the public sphere necessary to integrate different social forces to the democratic process. At least as important has been the role of the public service broadcasting in 'creating the nation' (see Scannell and Cardiff 199: 13–17). Public service broadcasting is still being defined mostly in national terms, as even the names of the companies indicate: the BBC, ARD, RAI, etc. (see Chapter 11).

From the viewpoint of cultural democracy, the media principally fulfil two functions: in their role as public disseminators of information, they create a common symbolic sphere uniting their audiences for public debate; and in their role as the facilitators of public opinion, they offer ways to different social and cultural groups to define and identify themselves as members of the national public. In this way, media mobilize different communities for negotiation processes where different interests and values can be commonly weighed (see Young 1996). There is a close correlation between political and cultural dimensions: for an inclusive political democracy to be realized, an inclusive common culture (or 'civic culture', see Dahlgren 2009) is required; on the other hand, the development of common or civic culture needs well-developed political democracy. Media's role here is central: as European history shows, they can be used either to promote socially and politically divisive cultural function (nationalist and xenophobic purposes) or to facilitate pluralist, socially and politically integrative aims (multiculturalism and social pacification). An infamous recent example of the former is Prime Minister Silvio Berlusconi's use of his immense media power in Italy (see, for example, Mazzoleni 2008).

However, it is not only the political dimension that has an effect on the media's cultural function. In the last years, critical debate has (again) been launched on the harmful consequences of the media, especially on the non-controlled adolescent use of the Internet. In the first hand, the criticism is targeted against the commercial media and its recourse to ever more violent and explicit content which is claimed to feed anti-social culture. The consequence, though, has been an increase in the demands for more social and cultural control, leading to new forms of policing of the Internet and to more supervision on the uses of social media.

Political, Economic and Cultural Framework

In order to connect the three dimensions discussed above, we attempt to clarify the concepts presented above and their mutual relations:

- Society is composed of three driving forces: the state, the economy and the civil society.
- In the European model of democracy the state exemplifies the entire political system, with the separation of powers into the legislative, executive and judicial departments.
- The economic dimension is symbolized and structures by the market are imperative. In its essence, the market is about the system of the exchange of goods, services and information, governed by supply and demand, within the boundaries of the legal setting; where the basic functioning principle of the state is 'public interest', and in the economic dimension it is 'private interest' and the 'market'.
- Citizens are the prime actors in democracy, both as citizens in their relations to the state, and as consumers in their relations to the economy. In their everyday life citizens are organized in different formations of civil society, in the form of networks, associations, cultural and social groups, etc.
- The cultural dimension covers all other dimensions as it forms the overall historical environment and basic conditions for the functioning of both the state and the market.
- The media occupy the position in the centre of all these mutual relations, mediating communication between these institutions and attempting to safeguard their own independence, despite manifold (and increasing) pressures from each side.

These relations and the media's role are illustrated in the figure below (modified from Hamelink and Nordenstreng 2007: 226). The cultural dimension should be seen as forming the background for all the activities.

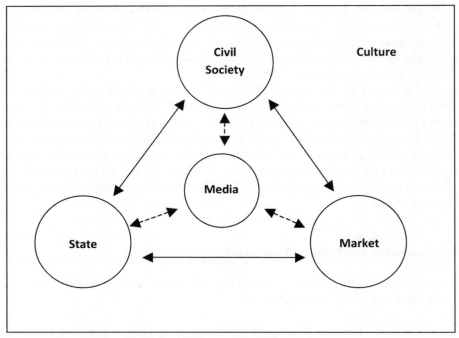

Figure 1: Relations between State, Market, Culture and Civil Society.

The position of the media, however, is unlikely to be exactly in between these forces in society. It is more realistic to consider commercial media closer to the economy/market corner, given the growing commercialization and growth of the media conglomerate. Media closer to the state might be found in autocratic regimes, with the media close to the government and at a distance from economy and civil society. Finally, media close to the civil society are mostly found in the alternative, not-for-profit or 'third sector'.

Complicating Factors

In recent years the role of the media has, if anything, become even more definitive from the viewpoint of democracy than in any time in earlier history. It has become ever more difficult to mark the line between the media and other major social and cultural institutions, as the media have such a central role politically and culturally. This can be seen in children's life, as they are exposed to different modalities of the media from their earliest stages of socialization; first through television, then through different computerized and mobilized media (mobile phones, social media, online contents) (Livingstone 2009). Our leisure time is more and more penetrated by the media (television, Internet, DVDs, etc.) and the media also increasingly define our work life (Internet, intranet, extranet, etc.). The question can be posed, whether this increasing mediatization has also led to an increase in democracy in any of its dimensions – political, economic, cultural? Or, does it have any correlation to democracy?

One major complicating factor is the fact that while democratic institutions are still mostly restricted by national frameworks and they support the political structures of the nation state, many other political institutions play on a transnational or global scale. One such major institution is the European Union, others are the World Trade Organization (WTO), the Organisation for Economic Co-operation and Development (OECD) or the North Atlantic Treaty Organization (NATO), neither of which are democratic organizations in the same sense as national institutions. The media is caught in between: on the one hand, most media infrastructures, as well as media contents, are nationally defined and restricted (national markets, national languages, national politics), but on the other, transnational infrastructures and contents are increasing with accelerating speed, especially promoted by the Internet and different modes of social media. A confusing factor is that national media policies today are being increasingly affected by the European Union's media and communication policies. Although in many respects national legislation still has sovereignty over the European Union, there are more and more examples of the European Union overruling national legislation (see Harcourt 2005).

As a conclusion: although the media systems are still predominantly national in their character and follow national political and cultural logics, the processes of transnationalization and globalization are something that we increasingly need to consider when analyzing media's role in democracy.

The Internet – A Democratizing Force?

Since the Internet became available to mass audiences from the late 1990s onwards, the debate on its democratizing potential was launched. Indeed, there are convincing arguments that the Internet provides for more democracy. Firstly, the Internet gives voice to people who were deprived from any possibility of expressing themselves in public. Internet technologies enable citizens to express themselves on the Internet fora, or somewhere in the endless sphere of Web 2.0 applications. Secondly, the Internet provides citizens with additional sources of information. Apparently, the monopoly of journalism in interpreting events for the public is broken. Some scholars suggest the end of the gatekeeping function of the media. Bruce A. Williams and Michael X. Delli Carpini) argue that 'if there are no gates, there can be no gatekeepers' (2000: 61).

Thirdly, the Internet is highly useful for mobilizing people for any sort of cause. The last two presidential election campaigns in the United States provide ample evidence that indeed the Internet enables new forms of political mobilization, as can be particularly seen in the election campaigns of Howard Dean and Barack Obama. The campaign manager of the former is convinced that the Internet is 'the most democratizing innovation we've ever seen [...] There has never been a technology this fast, this expansive, with the ability to connect this many people from around the world' (Trippi 2004: 235f).

In 2009, the protest movement in Iran following the presidential elections was supposedly organized by using the most basic Internet application: Twitter. There is no doubt that large, loose organizations are able to organize themselves in a highly efficient manner. These arguments suggest that the Internet has essentially forwarded democracy in various ways. In particular, public deliberation is encouraged. 'The Internet's political impacts have often been viewed through the lens that deliberative democrats have provided. The hope has been that the Internet would expand the public sphere, broadening both the range of ideas discussed and the number of citizens allowed to participate' (Hindman 2009: 7).

So, is the Internet empowering citizens to participate in the public discourse? Does the Internet provide different information? And can the Internet foster control of those in power? It might be premature to answer these questions. But there are good reasons to question the democratizing power of the Internet. While the mobilizing power of the Internet can be acknowledged, the case is less clear for the deliberative/participatory and the informative argument. The former argument is compromised by the fact that differences in Internet use remain, not only at the level of Internet access (exclusion of about one quarter of society, along stratification criteria), but also at the level of what people use the Internet for. Jan van Dijk has collected evidence that the Internet is rarely used as an instrument of enlightenment (van Dijk 2005; van Dijk and Hacker 2000). The latter argument is based on the assumption that more voices are available and thus diversity of information is enhanced. Matthew Hindman points out that there is a fundamental difference between speaking and being heard. His conclusion is pessimistic: 'From the perspective of mass politics, we care most not about who posts but about who gets read – and there are plenty of formal and informal barriers that hinder ordinary citizens' ability to reach an audience. Most online content receives no links, attracts no eyeballs, and has minimal political relevance. Again and again, this study finds powerful hierarchies shaping a medium that continues to be celebrated for its openness. This hierarchy is structural, woven into the hyperlinks that make up the Web; it is economic, in the dominance of companies like Google, Yahoo! and Microsoft; and it is social, in the small group of white, highly educated, male professionals who are vastly overrepresented in online opinion' (Hindman 2009: 18f).

Most likely, the full potential of the Internet to further democracy has not yet been explored. But the seemingly vast democratic gains of the Internet require critical analysis. Digital divide, constraints from powerful infrastructure providers (such as search engines and software designs) and new inequalities created by the Internet deserve close observation by social scientists.

Research Perspectives

Academic research of the relationship between media and democracy has generally been based on normative assumptions of the role that the media should play in democracy. One important source for the normative framework is given in the form of international agreements and protocols concerning human rights and the freedom of information. Such documents include, among others: the Council of Europe's 'Convention for the Protection of Human Rights and Fundamental Freedoms' (1950); the 'Universal Declarations of Human Rights' (1948) and the 'International Covenant on Economic, Social and Cultural Rights' (1966) both by the United Nations; the 'Charter of Fundamental Rights' (2000) of the European Union; and UNESCO's 'Universal Declaration on Cultural Diversity' (2001).

In the tradition of normative theories of communication, basic democratic principles are selected and operationalized in order to measure how the performance of the media fits with the normative ideals. Although such criteria may vary, they usually include such issues as the freedom of the press, media pluralism, concentration of ownership, public access, etc. The selected criteria are then deployed in order to measure how the media reality fulfils the normative criteria. As stated above, only in recent years has the approach based on deliberative democracy gained ground among media scholars (see Christians et al. 2009).

Conclusion

Theories on the relation between democracy and the media always sail in the deep waters of the normative. Depending on the democratic tradition, the role of the media is defined as restrictive to the function of information, or as inclusive when embracing the notion of deliberation. Irrespective of which model of democracy is chosen for reflection, the media cannot maintain an equilibrium between the state, the economy and the civil society. Therefore, the overarching democratic request concerns the media's accountability to the public at large. This requires a high degree of political and economic independence, respect and sufficient resources for journalistic practice, clear and predictable media regulation, a well-balanced composition of commercial and not-for-profit media, including media with a public service remit and sufficient financial resources available to media companies. Not each and every television channel, radio operator or daily newspaper needs to live up to all these requirements, but the media landscape as a whole should adhere to these principles.

References

ACT (Association of Commercial Television in Europe) (2009), *ACT Comments on the Second Draft Communication on State Aid and Public Broadcasting*. Available at: http: //www.acte.be/EPUB/ easnet.dll/execreq/page?eas: dat_im=025B1D&eas: template_im=025AE9.

Amsterdam Protocol (1997), 'Protocol on the System of Public Broadcasting in the Member States', *Official Journal of the European Communities*, C 340/109. Available at: http: //www.ebu.ch/ CMSimages/en/leg_ref_ec_treaty_amsterdam_protocol_pb_021097_tcm6-4267.pdf. Accessed 22 February 2010.

Baker, C. E., 'Journalist Performance, Media Policy, and Democracy', in Marcinkowski, F., Meier, W. A. and Trappel, J. (eds) (2006), *Media and Democracy: Experiences from Europe*, Bern: Haupt, pp. 113–26.

Blumler, J. G. and Gurevitch, M. (1955), *The Crisis of Public Communication*, London: Routledge.

Christians, C. G., Glasser, T. L., McQuail, D., Nordenstreng, K. and White, R. A. (2009), *Normative Theories of the Media: Journalism in Democratic Societies*, Urbana (Chicago): University of Illinois Press.

Cunningham, F. (2002), *Theories of Democracy: A Critical Introduction*, London: Routledge.

Curran , J., 'Rethinking Media and Democracy', in Curran, J., and Gurevitch, M. (eds.) (2000), *Mass Media and Society*, London: Arnold, pp.120–154.

Curran, J. (2007), 'Reinterpreting the Democratic Role of the Media', *Brazilian Journalism Research*, 3: 1, pp. 31–54.

Curran, J., Iyengar, S., Lund, A. B. and Salovaara-Moring, I. (2009), 'Media System, Public Knowledge and Democracy', *European Journal of Communication*, 24: 1, pp. 5–26.

Curran, J. and Seaton, J. (2003), *Power without Responsibility: The Press and Broadcasting in Britain*, London: Routledge.

Dahlgren, P. (2009), *Media and Political Engagement: Citizens, Communication, and Democracy*, Cambridge: Cambridge University Press.

Eley, G., 'Nations, Publics, and Political Cultures: Placing Habermas in the Nineteenth Century', in Calhoun, C. (ed.) (1992), *Habermas and the Public Sphere*, Cambridge (Massachusetts): MIT Press, pp. 289–339.

Giddens, A. (2003), *Runaway World: How Globalization is Reshaping our Lives*, New York: Routledge.

Habermas, J. (1992), *The Structural Transformation of the Public Sphere: An Inquiry into a Category of Bourgeois Society*, (trans. Thomas Burger with the assistance of Frederick Lawrence), Cambridge: Polity.

Habermas, J., ‚Three Normative Models of Democracy‘ in Habermas, J. (1998) *The Inlcusion of the Other: Studies in Political Theory* (edited by Cíaran Cronin and Pablo De Greiff), Cambridge: Polity, pp. 239–252.

Hamelink, C. and Nordenstreng, K., 'Towards Democratic Media Governance', in de Bens, E. (ed.) (2007), *Media Between Culture and Commerce*, Changing Media, Changing Europe Series, vol. 4, Bristol: Intellect, pp. 225–40.

Harcourt, A. (2005), *The European Union and the Regulation of Media Markets*, Manchester: University of Manchester Press.

Harrison, J. and Woods, L. (2007), *European Broadcasting Law and Policy*, Cambridge: Cambridge University Press.

Held, D. (2006), *Models of Democracy*, 3rd edn, Cambridge: Polity.

Hindman, M. (2009), *The Myth of the Digital Democracy*, Princeton and Oxford: Princeton University Press.

Jakubowicz, K., 'The Eastern European/Post-Communist Media Model Countries', in Terzis, G. (ed.) (2007), *European Media Governance: National and Regional Dimensions*, Bristol and Chicago: Intellect, pp. 303–13.

Jakubowicz, K. and Sükösd, M., 'Twelve Concepts Regarding Media System Evolution and Democratization in Post-Communist Societies', in Jakubowicz, K. and Sükösd, M. (eds) (2008),

Finding the Right Place on the Map: Central and Eastern European Media Change in a Global Perspective, Bristol and Chicago: Intellect, pp. 9–40.

Keane, J. (1991), *The Media and Democracy*, Cambridge: Polity.

Livingstone, S. (2009), *Children and the Internet: Great Expectations and Challenging Realities*, Cambridge: Polity.

Mazzoleni, G., 'Italy: Media System', in Donsbach, W. (ed.) (2008), *The International Encyclopedia of Communication*, Malden: Blackwell Publishing, Blackwell Reference Online. Available at:http://www.communicationencyclopedia.com/subscriber/tocnode?id=g9781405131995_chunk_g978140 513199514_ss97-1. Accessed 16 February 2010.

McNair, B., 'Journalism and Democracy', in Wahl-Jorgensen, K. and Hanitzsch T. (eds) (2009), *Handbook of Journalism Studies*, New York, London: Routledge, pp. 237–49.

McQuail, D., 'Introduction: Reflections on Media Policy in Europe', in Meier, W. A. and Trappel, J. (eds) (2007), *Power, Performance and Politics: Media Policy in Europe*, Baden-Baden: Nomos, pp. 9–19.

Meier, W. A., 'National and Transnational Media Ownership Concentration in Europe: A Burden for Democracy?', in Meier, W. A. and Trappel, J. (eds) (2007), *Power, Performance and Politics: Media Policy in Europe*, Baden-Baden: Nomos, pp. 75–103.

Open Society Institute (2005), *Television Across Europe: Regulation, Policy and Independence*, Budapest: Open Society Institute.

Nordenstreng, K., '"Four Theories of the Press" Reconsidered', in Carpentier, N., Pruulmann-Vengerfeldt, P., Nordenstreng, K., Hartmann, M., Vihalemm, P. and Cammaerts, B. (eds) (2006), *Researching Media, Democracy and Participation*, The Intellectual Work of the 2006 European Media and Communication Doctoral Summer School, Tartu: Tartu University Press, pp. 35–45.

Scannell, P. and Cardiff, D. (1991), *A Social History of British Broadcasting, Vol. 1, 1922–1939: Serving the Nation*, Oxford: Basil Blackwell.

Trappel, J. and Maniglio, T. (2009), 'On Media Monitoring – The Media for Democracy Monitor (MDM)', *Communications*, 34, pp. 169–201.

Trippi, J. (2004), *The Revolution Will Not Be Televised: Democracy, the Internet, and the Overthrow of Everything*, New York: HarperCollins.

van Dijk, J. (2005), *Deepening Divide: Inequalities in the Information Society*, Thousand Oaks: Sage.

van Dijk, J. and Hacker, K. L. (eds) (2000), *Digital Democracy: Issues of Theory and Practice*, London, Thousand Oaks and New Delhi: Sage.

Williams, B. A. and Delli Carpini, M. X. (2000), 'Unchained Reaction: The Collapse of Media Gatekeeping and the Clinton-Lewinsky Scandal', *Journalism*, 1: 1, pp. 61–85.

Young, I. M., 'Communication and the Other: Beyond Deliberative Democracy', in Benhabib, S. (ed.) (1996), *Democracy and Difference: Contesting the Boundaries of the Political*, Princeton: Princeton University Press, pp. 120–35.

Zaller, J. (2003), 'A New Standard of News Quality: Burglar Alarms for the Monitorial Citizen', *Political Communication*, 20: 2, pp. 109–30.

Chapter 9

From Media Regulation to Democratic Media Governance

Werner A. Meier

From a public interest point of view, the last ten to fifteen years of media policy and media regulation have not been a success story. Five points can be identified, which are suspected to be responsible for the failure of media regulation. Firstly, integration and ownership-concentration has strengthened the leading media corporations in relation to the state. These corporations successfully reject every attempt to limit their growth both in economic and political terms. Secondly, looking at media deregulation measures, one can argue that the state promotes media concentration. The state and its subordinate authorities tend to promote mergers and acquisitions rather than attempt to limit them. Since the 1990s, both across Europe and the United States, politicians and policy-makers have favoured media ownership deregulation without looking closer at the social consequences of such moves. Politicians – always with a keen eye on power, careers, reputation and prestige – try to prevent dissent in relation to corporate interests and ambitious media owners. Thirdly, the application of general competition legislation is insufficient in the case of the media industry. Competition law emphasizes the dangers of market dominance and is not concerned with media pluralism. A fourth reason is that the European Union (EU) Commission usually welcomes economically powerful media companies. Traditionally, the European Union's competition policies distinguish between media power and the abuse of media power. But it is highly unclear in which circumstances media power is acceptable and where the abuse of media power begins. And last but not least, it is becoming more and more evident, again at the European level, that the EU Commission is not willing to protect ownership pluralism. Rather, the Commission promotes strong European media players in the global game. The European Union has no explicit competence for regulating the plurality of opinions in the press, radio and television. The European Commission has left the issue to the European Union member states.

In analyzing the paradigm shifts in media policy, van Cuilenburg and McQuail (2003) identify a shift away from social welfare to economic welfare principles. Following their analysis, the emerging paradigm shifts the core values of media policy away from a (desirable) balance between political, social-cultural and economic values towards a predominance of the latter. Issues like competition, employment and innovation are central to media policy, whereas societal or political concerns are subject to regulation only in the case of consumers' protection or 'where issues of morality, taste, human rights and potential harm to young people and society are concerned' (van Cuilenburg and McQuail 2003: 200).

This perceived decline of public control over the mass media, of media accountability towards society and the lack of public control over new technological developments within

155

media systems, determine the continuity between the 'old' and the 'new' order concerning a 'set of perennial problems arising from the nature of communication and the important (and probably increased) role it plays in organized social life, from global to local' (McQuail 2008: 25). Denis McQuail lists a set of issues with both international and national dimensions, which should be addressed by media policy in general. These are:

- Achieving due accountability for ethical, moral and professional standards of media performance, as decided by the larger community
- Protecting individuals and society from potential harm of many kinds that can occur by way of communication systems
- Setting positive expectations and goals for public social and cultural communication, and steering the development of systems accordingly
- Maintaining essential freedoms of communication under conditions of total surveillance and registration
- Managing relations between state and political power, on the one hand, and communicative power on the other, according to democratic principles

At this point, the concept of governance comes into play. For McQuail the transition from the old order of media policy – characterized by strong public control of broadcasting, and a clear separation between print and electronic media – to the new order of media governance, can be explained through the greater degree of commercialization and marketization of all forms of public communication, by the higher 'centrality and pervasiveness' (2008: 18) of electronic media, and by the decline of national sovereignty over the flow of media content.

Governance

Governance in general is often described as a process where a power shift in policy-making is taking place. The power shift goes from government, states, state agencies and administrations to a network of different stakeholders. The power shift goes from government-driven modes of steering and influencing – mostly in a command and control style – to a more co- and self-regulated mode of decision-making. Governance refers to a network of control that is grounded less on legal rules but more on informal mechanisms, executed by a variety of stakeholders. Private companies and organizations are steered in a decentralized manner, and the power game should be transparent, although complex with multiple objectives, processes, arenas and mechanisms.

The growing interest about all forms of governance is both a normative discourse (about democratic values meaning co-regulation and participation) and an analytical discourse (able to handle the growing societal complexity). Since the beginning of the 1990s, a growing body of academic literature is dealing with the various forms of governance as a new way

Table 1: Old vs. New Control, Regulation and/or Steering Modes.

Old, 'Hard' Government Rules	New, 'Soft' Governance Rules
Statutory regulation by strong state	Co-regulation, regulated self-regulation or self-regulation
State and administrative actors as	All stakeholders participate within open
dominant players within institutionalized processes by law	proceedings and ongoing decision-making processes
Centralized structure and steering mechanism	Decentralized structure and steering mechanism
Vertical-hierarchical processes: ruling by command and control (coercive)	Open and horizontal-heterarchical processes: agreement by deliberations (discursive)
Irreversible, final decisions	Provisional decisions
Intransparent power games behind closed doors	Transparent power games in different arenas with different stakeholders

of steering complex societies and gives the readers the impression of a changing paradigm about taking political decisions. Kooiman (2002: 75), for example, explains through several factors of why the governance approach denoted such a rapid growth during the 1990s. These are:

- A growing awareness that governments are not the only crucial actor in addressing major societal issues
- Traditional and new modes of government-society interactions are needed to tackle these issues
- Governing arrangements and mechanisms will differ for levels of society and will vary by sector
- Concomitantly, many governance issues are interdependent and/or become linked

The use of governance as a scientific construct is relatively new. Although governance as in governing groups or societies may be as old as humanity, the way the concept of governance came to the centre of social and economic sciences is more complex. Governance is ultimately concerned with creating the conditions for ordered rule and collective action. The outputs of governance are therefore not different from those of government. It is rather a matter of different processes (see Stoker 1998: 17), hence a matter of governing. From a political perspective, governance is seen as an answer to the increasing societal complexity that governments all over the world are facing, when addressing political, economic, societal or technical issues. From a corporate angle, governance is also seen as a way of improving the management of firms and companies, so that their accountability and responsibility towards the shareholders increases. Finally, from a societal point of view, governance is seen as a possibility for civil society to gain or to consolidate some (new) forms of participation in political processes and decisions.

Remarkable within the discussion and presentation of governance as a new method for governing and organizing modern societies, is its overwhelmingly positive evaluation. Concepts like participation and co-determination of the political inputs and outputs are dominating the discourse about governance. Governance is presented as something that should enhance, improve and modernize the way politics works. Hence, in this line of thought, the accountability and responsibility of the political system towards civil society, businesses and citizens in general should be improved.

It must, however, be made clear that governance by no means represents a revolutionary approach to politics. It is an attempt to reform the way governments and parliaments dominate the political scene by applying alternative forms of political control, regulation and steering. As an alternative to top-down hierarchical political decision making, governance is about bottom-up approaches and horizontal co-determination of political issues, with political solutions put forward. It must be stated that even if governance is presented as a democratization of politics, the rationale underpinning the emergence of governance relies on other arguments, i.e. the growing complexity of modern societies. Jessop (2003: 103) sees such complexity reflected 'in worries about the governability of economic, political, and social life in the face of globalization and conflicting identities. It implies that important new problems have emerged that cannot be managed or resolved readily, if at all, through top down State planning or market-mediated anarchy'.

In this sense, Tony Bovaird (2005: 222) describes the growing interest in alternative governing processes as the result of a radical reinterpretation of the role of policy-making and service delivery. He defines the policy-making process as 'the negotiated outcome of many interacting policy systems, participation in which is not simply the preserve of "policy planners" and "top decision-makers". Through governance, it is argued, the different aspects and problems of an increasingly global and interdependent political system could be better handled, because of the participation and involvement of more interests groups in the political process with more information and better knowledge than government officials, both politicians and bureaucrats. The co-determination of specific policies and the consultation of involved stakeholders should allow in this sense a better tailoring of political solutions to complex problems modern societies face due to the globalization of the world economy. Kenneth (2008: 4) argues that 'with the change from government to governance, the administration is now only one player amongst many others in the policy arena'. In this sense the government's command over the policy process is said to have transformed. In general, there is a broad perception of governance as an antonym to hierarchical steering, where the state as the exclusive authority from which regulation is implemented steps aside in favour of a more horizontal way of governing. It implies every mode of political steering involving public and private actors, including the traditional modes of government and different types of steering from hierarchical imposition to sheer information measures (Héritier 2002: 185). In a more restricted sense, governance describes different types of political steering, which are employed in order to engage public and private actors in policy formulation.

Media Governance

In recent years, analyses on governance have been high on the national as well as on the global agenda. Studies on governance, and in particular on media governance, seem to be attractive to many political and communication scientists. The basic assumption underlying governance research is that we are moving from 'government' to 'governance'. From this perspective, media governance looks beyond government, market and corporate media management. Especially, media governance focuses on non-governmental modes of institutionalization and organization, on civil society organizations, as well as on the public. Media governance emphasizes the self- and co-regulation modes of media policy. It must be clear that speaking about non-governmental modes of institutionalization does not mean that the government or the state are completely absent from media governance. The state is, and remains, a central actor in the institutionalization of even non-governmental approaches (see Pierre and Peters 2000).

When it comes to the question of how society shapes its media system, the distinction between the three concepts of policy, regulation and governance seems to be helpful. Should the focus be on the actors involved, on the instruments developed or the goals pursued? In a review of the media policy field Des Freedman (2008: 14–15) defined the concepts as follows:

- *Media policy* refers to the development of goals and norms leading to the creation of instruments that are designed to shape the structure and behaviour of media systems.
- *Media regulation* focuses on the operation of specific (often legally binding) tools that are deployed on the media to achieve established policy goals.
- *Media governance* refers to the sum total of mechanisms, centralized and dispersed, that aim to organize media systems according to the resolution of media policy debates.

One can argue that these three concepts are separate phenomena, although they are interconnected and overlap to a certain degree. A similar definition of media governance is given by Denis McQuail (2003: 91), who defines media governance as covering 'all means by which the mass media are limited, directed, encouraged, managed, or called into account, ranging from the most binding law to the most resistible of pressures and self-chosen disciplines'.

In yet other words media governance refers to the total of centralized and dispersed mechanisms with the aim to organize mass media from the inside, as well as the outside. In particular, media governance has to focus on the more institutionalized, as well as the less institutionalized, power relations within media organizations, and between the media – as political, economic and cultural institutions – and society. According to McQuail (2008: 18), the transition from the old order of media policy (which is characterized by strong public control of broadcasting and a clear separation between print and electronic media), to the new order of public governance can be explained through the greater degree of commercialization of all forms of public communication, through the higher 'centrality and pervasiveness' of electronic media, and as the result of the decline of national sovereignty over the flow of media content. The emergence of governance as a concept describing the transition from classical top-down media policy to more horizontal steering represents the assumption that the lawmakers are losing ground in the implementation process of media policies. For Patrick Donges (2007: 326), 'governance refers to the dynamic structure of rules between actors that are linked in different networks and permanently forced to negotiate, without a centre that has the power to command and control'. Thorsten Held (2007) goes one step further and traces back the growing interest in governance as a new regulatory alternative to the failure of traditional regulation of command-and-control. Failure is due to the fact that 'traditional regulation ignores the interests of the regulated objects and that initiative, innovation, and commitment cannot be imposed by law, the increasing knowledge gap of the regulating state, globalization as well as difficulties in intervening in autonomous social systems' (Held 2007: 356).

Co- and Self-Regulation

Governance is also seen as an answer to the growing complexity of social systems, which are traditionally regulated by the state. Due to society's increasing complexity, the state sees itself confronted with a situation whereby it lacks detailed knowledge to implement informed and effective regulation. This lack of knowledge should be compensated through the involvement of a variety of stakeholders in the policy-making process. For Michael Latzer (2007: 345), 'the plurality of public and private norm-setting actors and a plurality of norms, ranging from classical command-and-control-regulations (laws) to various forms of "soft law" and voluntary agreements, are preconditions for regulatory choice'.

Media governance thus entails both co-regulation and self-regulation. Co-regulation refers to private actors, both business and civil society, and the state to co-ordinate the formulation of a specific policy, while self-regulation refers to a situation whereby the media actors and industry associations are left to themselves to decide and propose their own internal regulations. The rationale for such a shift in regulation lies in the dilemma of reconciling media regulation with media freedom. 'While there are legitimate societal, economic, and technical justifications for media regulation, in democratic societies the media should be devoid of governmental influence. Accordingly, media freedom restricts the scope of media regulation. Non-statutory media regulation may be a solution for this dilemma of media regulation: media freedom is respected because the media regulate themselves' (Puppis 2007: 332).

In our view, however, media governance has to focus on power structures in the power vacuum of international relations. Moreover, it has to focus on the power struggle between national and international organizations, businesses and civil society organizations. We suggest looking at media governance as a contested power order or as an ongoing power struggle. Thus, media governance is not only an analytical concept to describe power shifts in media policy-making from a multi-level perspective, but also a normative concept that aims to reformulate the role of government, private actors and civil society in the political process leading to media policies and media regulations. The growing complexity of media systems is often used as a rationale for the emergence of governance, for the shift from top-down hierarchical political decisions to more flexible and horizontal decision-making. Such changes within decision-making structures eventually reflect the need for a more suitable approach to political issues in addition to mandatory regulation. Or put differently, governance is still regulation, although shifting from mandatory to co- and self-regulation.

Julia Black (2002: 20), in her reflections on the nature of regulation and consequently on the role of the state, defines the former as 'the sustained and focused attempt to alter the behaviour of others according to defined standards or purposes with the intention of producing a broadly identified outcome or outcomes, which may involve mechanisms of standard-setting, information-gathering and behaviour-modification'. Eventually this is also the goal of media governance, i.e. producing political and social outcomes that follow the standards of national media policy. It is therefore argued that media governance should be the answer to the shortcomings of traditional media regulation. McQuail (1997: 511) argued that 'the principal dilemma faced is how to reconcile the increasing significance of media with the declining capacity to control them, on behalf of the general good'. According to McQuail (1997: 511), one factor determining this loss of control is 'the greatly increased economic imperative to harness market forces to communication development, on the way toward the widely shared goal of the information society'. Eventually 'the triumph of liberal ideology and the spirit of deregulation and privatization makes it harder than ever for societies to intervene and exert control'.

In this sense, media governance should be a way to tackle this lack of control. However, the question remains: who should exercise this control, if the state is going to step aside? Governance studies put emphasis on co-regulation and self-regulation between media companies and other groups, mainly civil society organizations. In the case of self-regulation, media companies are motivated to regulate themselves in order to avoid state mandatory regulation. Within co-regulation, the actors should reach an agreement on a set of standards regulating the entire system. Control should be exerted either directly by media companies or through coordination between civil society and media companies. In other words, within media governance, the object of regulation – the media organization – either regulates itself or discusses the regulation with relevant civil society organizations. Needless to point out that the first solution denotes considerable, if not total, lack of democratic legitimacy, because of the conflict of interests created by a regulator regulating itself. The control issues pointed out by McQuail are clearly not resolved and it remains to be seen whether the problems can be solved through co-regulation.

Not Easy to Grasp

In the academic discourse on media governance there are some additional aspects that need to be discussed. The first aspect is that hierarchy and power are frequently neglected within networks and when it comes to single actors. Although scholars writing about media governance outline the importance of participation of all involved stakeholders and the coordination required between them in order to produce efficient output, the power relations between the actors and the power stemming from their individual resources are not discussed in the literature. This is, however, important because it would be naïve to assume that by simply gathering representatives of media organizations and civil society organizations around the table all participants would have the same power to co-determine the outcome of the deliberations. In such thinking, command and control by the state and the economy are severely underestimated.

A second aspect is the overestimation of the social actors' willingness to participate in governance agreements. Civil society organizations do not – and cannot – dispose of the same resources like media organizations do. However, in order to participate in such intensive decision-making processes, an organization needs remarkable resources to make its interests not only heard and represented, but also – and more importantly – implemented. Without resources or with resource asymmetry between the bargaining parties there is a power asymmetry, which is neglected in most of the literature. Without access to power or the possibility to hold media power accountable for deficits in the provision of public goods, interactions, coordination and participation, the governance regimes merely offer civil society freedom of speech within consultation forums. Considering the mere participation in consultative bodies as synonymous with a new form of democratic bargaining, results in a trivialization of the democratic bargaining mechanism altogether. Without the possibility to expose, criticize or sanction media power for its unsatisfactory provision of public goods, mere consultation structures represent no more than a protest channel. In fact, mainstream media governance allows more self-regulation at the level of the industry, without providing civil society with a proper institutional setting for criticizing the outcomes of self-regulation.

To sum up, most media governance studies assume that networks of command and control are losing ground, while on the contrary multi-stakeholder networks of deliberation are gaining ground. These studies assume that the autonomy of the involved actors grows when it comes to the decision-making process. Media governance studies do not seem to be concerned with the problems of unchallenged societal power structures and media power itself. They tend to overestimate the problem-solving capacities of co- and self-regulation and to underestimate the legitimacy problems, which come along with new governance solutions. Finally, media governance studies seem to overlook social actors, who are not ready – or not willing – to participate in organized governance networks.

Democratic and Participatory Media Governance

The rationale behind the involvement of actors, other than those actually having the decision-making power, lies in the need for legitimate input and output processes through the participation of all involved actors. In addition, the growing complexity of societal and political matters forces decision-makers to open their consultation and decision-making process to other actors, who may contribute to the decision process with their specific knowledge.

According to Meier and Perrin (2007: 338), the fact that media governance is based on a systematic, comprehensive and institutionalized multi-stakeholder approach allows to integrate (neglected) stakeholder interests at various levels, i.e. civil society organizations should participate in media governance processes alongside established stakeholders, such as media organizations, economic interests and state authorities.

Why is such a participatory framework important for media policy? The involvement of civil society in policy decisions remains a central issue in participatory media governance. Yet, the aim should not simply be the consultation of civil society groups, but their full participation in the decision-making process. This can only be achieved through some form of decision rights provided to the participants. Gbikpi and Grote (2002: 25) point out that 'participatory governance also and still requires some kind of democratic institutional settings. As a matter of fact, if participatory governance is a matter of ensuring that relevant actors participate in all the various governance arrangements, their quality must depend on their representativeness, as well as upon the decision-making procedures chosen by them to perform the arrangement.' The authors stress the fact that with a view to the quality of the governance arrangement, it is important 'that every holder community has a real opportunity to be involved in the decision and that every holder in his or her collectivity feels properly represented'.

Participatory media governance should also contain elements of direct democracy that allow civil society groups to co-determine particular policy outcomes. This would allow a more transparent political process and the political legitimacy of policies would be enhanced through co-determination. Summing up, participatory media governance can enhance the legitimacy of the political process, the accountability of media companies and finally provide a better interaction between citizens, civil society, economic interest and the state with benefits for the whole democratic process.

In this context, the participatory approach of Fung and Wright (2003) who developed an understanding of a participatory *modus* of governance is of particular interest. They propose a model of empowered participatory governance by analyzing institutional reforms aimed at improving citizens' participation in local political matters. On the basis of these participatory experiments, they identified three general principles that are fundamental to sketching the participatory approach: (1) a focus on specific, tangible problems; (2) the involvement of ordinary people affected by these problems, and officials close to them; and (3) the deliberative development of solutions to these problems (see Fung and Wright 2003). Participatory media governance can therefore be distinguished from other forms of participatory governance by keeping the state outside the governance agreements. This does not mean that the state has no longer a role to play. On the contrary, the state remains an important player, but only in establishing the institutional setting in which private actors and civil society can meet to discuss and regulate media matters.

From Media Regulation to Participatory Media Governance?

The growing complexity of media systems is often used as a rationale for the emergence of media governance, for the shift from top-down hierarchical political decisions to more flexible and horizontal decision-making. Eventually a change within the decision-making structures reflects the need for a better approach to some political issues through some kind of regulation, because as we have seen, media governance is still regulation, regardless of whether it is mandatory regulation, or co- or self-regulation.

However, it must be noted that in the academic discourse about media governance, there are only a few examples which can show that up until now neglected interests are articulated in the media policy process. From a democratic point of view, this is regrettable. If we are moving from top-down media policy to more horizontal and self-regulation processes, one could wonder: what about the democratic legitimacy of such processes? If the democratic state is going to step aside, who is going to replace the democratically elected politicians who participate in media politics as representatives of different constituencies? Freedom of the media should not mean freedom from regulation or freedom from democratic control. More concretely, if the benefit of the governance approach is the shift away from over-politicized media regulations towards multi-stakeholder approaches, then there should be more reflection about neglected stakeholders. Denis McQuail (1997: 511) argued that 'the principal dilemma faced is how to reconcile the increasing significance of media with the declining capacity to control them, on behalf of the general good'. We argue that it would be counterproductive to let the media regulate themselves in response to this growing media complexity and the loss of control over media systems.

Conclusion

We conclude with three recommendations aimed at fostering democratic and participatory media governance in media sectors that are vital for the diffusion of political and social information:

- In order to achieve more democratic regulation of media matters, media organizations should be encouraged to adopt self-regulating codes, which must be open to public scrutiny and discussion in every field, from media ownership issues to editorial policies.
- Following the deliberative experience of advertising regulation, various councils should be set up, in which civil society representatives and media professionals can interact in a constructive way. This would allow an open exchange of information that may help both parties.
- Within this 'mediation' process the state still has a role to play, especially by requesting the media industry adopts self-regulating codes and fosters governance agreements in which civil society organizations can participate as stakeholders. Moreover, the state could institutionalize some form of professional training for civil society organizations affected by mass media.

Participatory media governance could reinvigorate the democratic legitimacy of mass media towards civil society, firstly by giving organized interests within civil society some decision power – at least over the implementation of professional codes – and secondly, by assuring media companies that they are on the right track to satisfy the needs of their most important stakeholders, namely the public who consumes their products.

References

Black, J. (2002), *Critical Reflections on Regulation, Centre for Analysis of Risk and Regulation at the London School of Economics and Political Science*. Available at: http: //www.lse.edu/collections/CARR/pdf/Disspaper4.pdf. Accessed 23 February 2010.

Bovaird, T. (2005), 'Public Governance: Balancing Stakeholder Power in a Network Society', *International Review of Administrative Sciences*, 71: 2, pp. 217–28.

Donges, P. (2007), 'The New Institutionalism as a Theoretical Foundation of Media Governance', *Communications*, 32: 3, pp. 325–30.

Freedman, D. (2008), *The Politics of Media Policy*, Cambridge: Polity Press.

Fung, A. and Wright, E. O., 'Thinking about Empowered Participatory Governance', in Fung, A. and Wright E. O. (eds) (2003), *Deepening Democracy: Institutional Innovations in Empowered Participatory Governance*, London: Verso, pp. 3–42.

Gbikpi, B. and Grote, J. R., 'From Democratic Government to Participatory Governance', in Grote J. R. and Gbikpi, B. (eds) (2002), *Participatory Governance: Political and Societal Implications*, Opladen: Leske+Budrich, pp. 17–34.

Held, T. (2007), 'Co-Regulation in European Union Member States', *Communications*, 32: 3, pp. 355–62.

Héritier, A., 'New Modes of Governance in Europe: Policy Making without Legislating?', in Héritier, A. (ed.) (2002), *Common Goods: Reinventing European and International Governance*, Boston: Rowman & Littlefield Publishers, pp. 185–206.

Jessop, B., 'Governance and Metagovernance: On Reflexivity, Requisite Variety, and Requisite Irony', in Bang, H. P. (ed.) (2003), *Governance as Social and Political Communication*, Manchester: University Press, pp. 101–116.

Kenneth, P., 'Introduction: Governance, the State and Public Policy in a Global Age', in Kenneth, P. (eds) (2008), *Governance, Globalization and Public Policy*, Cheltenham: Edward Elgar Publishing, pp. 3–18.

Kooiman, J., 'Governance: A Social-Political Perspective', in Grote, J. R. and Gbikpi, B. (eds) (2002), *Participatory Governance: Political and Societal Implications*, Opladen: Leske+Budrich, pp. 71–96.

Latzer, M. (2007), 'Regulatory Choices in Communication Governance', *Communications*, 32: 3, pp. 343–49.

McQuail, D. (1997), 'Accountability of Media to Society: Principles and Means', *European Journal of Communication*, 12: 4, pp. 511–92.

—— (2003), *Media Accountability and Freedom of Publication*, Oxford and New York: Oxford University Press.

—— 'The Current State of Media Governance in Europe', in Terzis, G. (ed.) (2008), *European Media Governance: National and Regional Dimensions*, Bristol and Chicago: Intellect, pp. 17–26.

Meier, W. A. and Perrin, I. (2007), 'Media Concentration and Media Governance', *Communications*, 32: 3, pp. 336–43.

Pierre, J. and Peters, G. B. (2000), *Governance, Politics, and the State*, London: Macmillan.

Puppis, M. (2007), 'Media Governance as a Horizontal Extension of Media Regulation: The Importance of Self- and Co-Regulation', *Communications*, 32: 3, pp. 330–36.

Sarikakis, K. (ed.) (2007), *Media and Cultural Policy in the European Union*, Amsterdam: Editions Rodopi.

Stoker, G. (1998), 'Governance as Theory: Five Propositions', *International Social Science Journal*, 50: 155, pp. 17–28.

van Cuilenburg, J., 'Media Diversity, Competition and Concentration: Concepts and Theories', in de Bens, E. (ed.) (2007), *Media between Culture and Commerce*, Bristol and Chicago: Intellect, pp. 25–54.

van Cuilenburg, J. and McQuail, D. (2003), 'Media Policy Paradigm Shifts: Towards a New Communications Policy Paradigm', *European Journal of Communication*, 18: 2, pp. 181–207.

Chapter 10

Media Industries: Ownership, Copyright and Regulation

Elena Vartanova, Laura Bergés Saura, Jeanette Steemers and
Stylianos Papathanassopoulos

Although conventional European media, the press and broadcasting in particular, continue to operate largely according to traditional business models, convergence and digitization are transforming the sector, offering consumers a proliferation of choices across many media platforms (Deloitte 2006; Küng, Picard and Towse 2008: 19–23). Bearing in mind these ongoing economic and technological developments, and drawing on the concepts of political economy, commodification, and marketization, this chapter focuses on the changing status and development of European media industries in the light of technological convergence, the multiplication of media outlets, changing distribution models, the fragmentation of audiences and funding, and globalizing markets. This chapter considers the impact of these factors on European media industries. We will start by outlining the historical context, basic features and media ownership dynamics of European media industries before considering a further issue of growing relevance: intellectual property (IP) rights, their impact on business models, and the implications of IP for who owns and controls the production and distribution of content.

Historical and Theoretical Contexts

While European media represent an important component of the European economy, their economic impact has been far more modest than the larger consolidated US media industry for a number of reasons. The most obvious explanation for this is the existence of unconsolidated economies. In spite of the intensification of European unification since the mid-1990s, which has been promoted by the European Union, European media still mainly comprise of a large number of unconsolidated national media markets, representing very diverse national contexts, business models and professional cultures.

However, there is another reason for the weaker position of the European media economy. For many years, particularly after World War II, most states regarded the mass media more as national institutions in need of strict regulation for a variety of social, cultural or political reasons, which were not subject to global- or market-based logic. So in the first half of the twentieth century, there may have been powerful privately-owned press and publishing entities in many countries, but these were usually counter-balanced by a strictly regulated and often monopolistic public service or state broadcasting.

History has also played its part in other ways. For many years several European countries were characterized by totalitarian (e.g. Germany and Italy before World War II) and authoritarian regimes (e.g. the Soviet Union, Spain, Portugal, Greece, eastern Europe), and this placed a number of national media systems outside market-based media economics. The end of the World War II in 1945 was particularly important for the sharp economic and political distinctions it brought to the European media landscape. Eastern and central European media (state-owned media under the ideological control of Communist parties) on the one hand, and North western European media (mixed-market media within a liberal democratic system) on the other, developed within dissimilar economic frameworks rooted in different political systems which prioritized different degrees of state control and economic intervention. In southern Europe dictatorships in Spain, Portugal and Greece did allow private media, but these were subject to strict censorship and state control until the demise of these regimes from the 1970s onwards. The significance of these ideological divides is that they reinforced economic unevenness and inhibited global competitiveness. However, differences within Europe became less marked after 1989 following the end of the Communist/Socialist system when private ownership and market economics came to dominate eastern and central European media in much the same way as they did in western Europe (Williams 2005).

Another key aspect of European media after 1945 has been the continued existence of a strong public service tradition, particularly in western European broadcasting, which challenges the principle of profit-oriented media giving 'primacy to the needs of society or collective needs of citizens rather than to individual rights, consumer freedom or market forces' (McQuail 2005: 179). In practice, the application of public service models has been variable across Europe in terms of quality, independence and funding, but the public service tradition has inspired a European tradition of political economy research, which focuses on the pursuit of social justice (Holt and Perren 2009: 7), drawing sharp distinctions 'between capitalist enterprise and public intervention' (Wasko 2004: 311).

The liberalization of regulation from the 1980s, combined with the growth of satellite and cable distribution, propelled the commercialization of European broadcasting (in breach of the public service and state broadcasting monopolies) (Weymouth and Lamizet 1996: 21) as free-market thinking and the pursuit of profit replaced the collectivist and socialistic approaches of the 1960s and 1970s (Küng-Shankleman 2000: 24). This has impacted the practice of public service media as well, blurring the distinctions between public and market models (de Bens 2007: 11), and encouraging the growth of European *infotainment* giants such as Bertelsmann (Germany), Vivendi (France) and Mediaset (Italy).

Media Industries in Europe: Basic Features Today

The European media landscape today comprises of many media systems including the 27 member states of the European Union (EU), as well as Norway, Switzerland, Russia and a number of post-Socialist countries outside the European Union. This constitutes a potential market of almost 700 million people, three times the size of the US market (Hardy 2008: 174), making Europe one of the most attractive and largest markets for print, audio-visual services and advertising (Williams 2005: 15). Even in 2008, under conditions of economic crisis, entertainment and media spending rose in the region by 2.8 per cent, with media spending on Internet access, video games, TV subscriptions and licence fees, each of which grew more than 5 per cent on a compound annual basis (PricewaterhouseCoopers 2009–10: 64).

However, in their totality the European media industries also demonstrate uneven economic development. According to the World Bank, Russia is the largest country in terms of population (142 million) and audience size, but the media industries in Germany (82 million), France (62 million), the United Kingdom (61 million), Italy (59 million) and Spain (45 million) are substantially larger in terms of value (see Table 1).

According to Denis McQuail (cit. in Kelly, Mazzoleni and McQuail 2004: 2–3), the key issues dominating the development of European media industries since the 1980s have been:

- The deregulation and 'commercialization' of electronic media, particularly in television, which have increased the scope for commercial enterprise and private ownership.
- The development of new technologies that ignited 'a smouldering conflict between public and private forces'.
- Commercial pressures that altered the structure of media ownership in favour of larger, transnational, cross-media enterprises
- Pressures to integrate the media at a European level in respect to economic activity and policy.

These key issues still characterize European media industries today. Firstly, public service broadcasting is still significant, accounting for 35 per cent of all broadcasting income for the broadcasters of the 27 states of the European Union (European Audiovisual Observatory 2008). Yet competition with commercial operators has become more intense because of the ongoing deregulation and 'commercialization'. Advertising was key in this transformation, fuelling the growth of both commercial broadcasting and the advertising industry from the 1980s. However, declining advertising revenues have raised questions about the sustainability of the advertising model for television, and in some countries, such as Britain, subscription revenues now exceed television advertising revenues (Ofcom 2009).

Table 1: Media Industries in Selected European Countries (2008) – US $ million.

Country	Volume of Advertising Market	Entertainment and Media Market	Consumer/end-User Spending for Entertainment and Media
United Kingdom	23 652	92 173	60 453
Germany	21 078	95 505	59 920
France	12 604	67 224	47 433
Russia	4 569	23 533	11 023

Source: PricewaterhouseCoopers (2009–10: 66–74).

Secondly, the progress of digital technologies and the emergence of online media have placed new pressures on traditional media business models. With the rise of online news, the press has experienced a decline in both circulation and advertising revenues, but online revenues have not yet compensated for the losses experienced from falling subscriptions and advertising revenues. As 'old' and 'new' media compete for the consumer's time and attention, some are even questioning the practice of providing newspaper content for free online. For example, in 2009 News Corporation signalled that it would be introducing payment for its online news services. No one knows what this content will cost and whether consumers will pay, but the availability of large swathes of free content (particularly news and entertainment) on the Internet raises serious questions about the sustainability of traditional content production (Open Society Institute 2008: 23).

Thirdly, it is worth noting that the political and economic unification of Europe after the demise of the Socialist system, stimulated expansion into central and eastern Europe by western European media companies. Even those media companies which were not particularly active outside their own national markets, such as the Swiss publisher Ringier, have been attracted by liberalized eastern European media markets. Central and eastern European media companies have not been quite so successful at expanding their businesses beyond national frontiers; instead, they have seen their own markets targeted by transnational corporations such as Central European Media Enterprises (CME), a Bermuda-based company with interests in approximately twenty commercial TV stations across the region.

Fourthly, the European media industry must operate in accordance with EU rules. The Audiovisual Media Services Directive (AVMSD) came into force in 2007, adapting and

---

Box 1: Economic Challenges of the Digital Age
The number of economic challenges facing European media industries has increased considerably as digital technologies undermine traditional business models. Among them are audience fragmentation and the migration of audiences to online media. European content producers are looking to the online domain to increase revenues. Research commissioned by the European Commission in 2006 noted that revenues in Europe from online content would reach 8.3 billion Euros by 2010, representing a growth of over 400 percent within a five-year period. The study assessed the potential growth of digital content across new distribution platforms and technologies, such as interactive TV, broadband and mobile, and also attempted to identify economic, technical and legal obstacles that might hinder the exploitation of digital content in Europe. The research found that the spread of broadband, the roll-out of advanced mobile networks and the mass adoption of digital devices means that online content has become mass market, especially in music and games where the proportion of revenues made online already represents a significant percentage of the overall income (Screen Digest et al. 2006).

replacing the previous Television Without Frontiers Directive (TVWF) for a new digital environment involving light-touch regulation of some audio-visual media services. The AVMSD creates a single market for all audio-visual media services, including video-on-demand services in addition to traditional linear television services. It is too early to assess the impact of the AVMSD upon European media businesses, but the aim is to create a legal basis for increasing European competitiveness.

Media Ownership Dynamics in Europe

The question of media ownership and the impact of ownership concentration on pluralism and diversity has been a core issue for European media industries (European Audiovisual Observatory 2001). Another important industry focus has been the impact of US-based transnational conglomerates on European media industries (Iosifidis, Steemers, Wheeler 2005: 83), including the impact of foreign investment – both European and non-European – on national media structures (Gulyás 2005).

In terms of media ownership, it is important to note that in recent years there has been an emergence of a small number of larger western European media companies within the first tier of global players (Herman and McChesney 1997; NORDICOM 2009), alongside US-based global giants Disney, Time Warner and News Corporation. German-based Bertelsmann AG is present in about 50 countries, and Vivendi, which has its origins in France, is present in more than 70. These companies like their US counterparts conduct diversified activities, are engaged in all types of media production and are present in regional/national media markets across the globe. Similarly, a number of European advertising agencies are global players including WPP (United Kingdom), Publicis (France), Aegis (United Kingdom) and Havas (France). Although focused on a small number of players, the ownership dynamics of European-based transnationals follows the tendencies of media ownership and control identified by Flew as 'part of a wider tendency of globalization to shift the balance of political and economic power from nationally based institutions, such as governments and trade unions, towards geographically mobile multinational corporations' (2007: 73).

A second tier of European players is represented by large media companies that mainly serve regional markets (Herman and McChesney 1997). Gulyás (2005: 13–15) classifies this second tier of European media companies according to their interests at the global and regional level. These include:

- Companies with some degree of global focus: Lagardère (France), Pearson (United Kingdom), Reed Elsevier (Netherlands), VNU (Netherlands)
- Companies with an EU regional focus:
  - All Europe: ProSiebenSat.1 Media AG (Germany)
  - Northern and East central Europe: Sanoma (Finland), Bonnier (Sweden)

- Central Europe: Axel Springer (Germany)
- Southern Europe: Mediaset (Italy)
- Companies with non-EU regional interests
  - Focusing on Spanish-speaking countries: Prisa, Planeta (both Spain)
  - Focusing on English-speaking countries: Daily Mail and General Trust (United Kingdom), Independent News & Media (Ireland), Pearson (United Kingdom)
  - Focusing on eastern Europe: Hubert Burda Media, WAZ-Mediengruppe (both Germany)
  - Focusing on French-speaking countries: Socpresse (France)
  - Focusing on a variety of different geographical markets: EMAP (United Kingdom), Heinrich Bauer (Germany), Holtzbrinck (Germany)

A third tier is represented by many smaller companies targeting largely national and local markets. One notable characteristic of European companies across all three tiers is their focus on infotainment production, thus contradicting the perception of European mass media as a non-commercialized public sphere (Thussu 2007: 50; Habermas 2005: 27). At the same time, public service broadcasters in Germany (ARD) and the United Kingdom (the BBC) are also among the world's largest audio-visual companies. Secondly, any list of the top European companies is always dominated by those from the largest West European countries (Germany, Britain, France and Italy) which have long-standing commercial media industries. However, European players have yet to establish a global player in the online domain, with Google, Yahoo! and Facebook all originating in the United States.

In contrast to the consolidated nature of the European audio-visual sector, European print media industries (press, magazines, books) exhibit a wider range of players and more national differences, although internationalization is becoming increasingly evident. The reason for this greater diversity in the print sector can be found in the existence of diverse and uneven linguistic markets. German, French and Russian-speaking countries/communities create large audiences within Europe. Spain and Portugal benefit from non-European markets in Latin America, while smaller linguistic communities in Nordic or central/eastern European countries are concerned with the protection of their languages and cultural traditions through the support of print media. Audio-visual and new media markets, by contrast, tend to be more open to domination by global (US) players, either through direct investment or through the European subsidiaries of global conglomerates.

Within Europe a number of media ownership trends are identifiable. Firstly, the largest European media companies have been, or are being, transformed into multinational corporations with ownership and professional management structures, which can no longer be attributed to either national or family affiliations. The most significant European merger of recent times, the creation of Thomson Reuters, from the merger of Reuters and Thomson in 2008, created an Anglo-Canadian company with extensive interests in financial, legal, scientific and healthcare markets, as well as media. It is also worth noting that some European companies have come under non-European ownership. For instance, the 'French' group Vivendi is classified as French but it is 90 per cent owned by US registered stakeholders.

The 'British' BSkyB, the 'Italian' Sky Italia, Premiere Germany and Premiere Austria come under the control of the US-based News Corporation (Harcourt 2008: 14). Secondly, the western European tradition of 'family' ownership associated with the names of first owners (e.g. Reuters, Havas, Burda, Lagardère, Bonnier, Holtzbrinck, Springer, etc.), particularly in publishing, has become less common as media companies become more internationally active and publicly listed; the only exception is in the Nordic countries. Bertelsmann AG provides one example of company that is not publicly listed. It is majority-owned by the Bertelsmann foundation (76.9 per cent) and the founding Mohn family still own a 23.1 per cent share.

The issue of foreign media ownership within Europe is in fact multi-faceted, increasingly transnational, multi-sectoral and complex (International Federation of Journalists 2006: 6; Aris and Bughin 2005: 254). However, most of the largest media companies operating in Europe are in fact subsidiaries of multinational conglomerates who are well placed to take advantage of the digital revolution, industry convergence and Europe's move to an information society. For instance, during the 1980s and 1990s in Greece, Ireland, Italy, Sweden, Norway and Spain, investments in the cable and satellite sectors came from both national players and US media conglomerates such as Time Warner, Liberty Media, News Corporation and Viacom (Harcourt 2008: 14; Koulouvari 2004). As well as investing in areas such as audio-visual content production, cable and satellite TV, these companies are also investing in online content and services, reflecting the shift to 'virtual' consumption of non-material and digital goods.

Thirdly, the dynamics of European media ownership have been affected by the technological and ownership convergence of telecommunications, cable, satellite and mobile communications on the one hand, and traditional media (print, broadcasting) on the other. This has implications for the way in which media content is funded, as audiences and funding become fragmented across numerous outlets on different media platforms.

Fourthly, the dynamics of media ownership in Europe have been affected by social change in central/eastern Europe and the former USSR. Media ownership here has become a lucrative area for national politicians, as well as foreign media investors. For politicians, media ownership brings a combination of political influence and business advantages. According to Voltmer, 'the experience from Latin American and post-communist countries shows that ownership is frequently highly politicized in that influential actors – politicians or oligarchs – purchase media outlets in order to bring them under their control for the purpose of the instrumentalizing them for their own political ambitions' (2008: 37). Seeing a market for advertising and content, European and US media and entertainment companies have entered central and eastern European media markets, setting up new business alliances and establishing subsidiaries. For instance, German and Swiss companies own about 80 per cent of Czech print media outlets. German, Austrian, Swiss, French and Scandinavian media interests also dominate the print media markets in Bulgaria, Hungary, Poland and the Baltic states.

It has been argued that the concept of a single global market is an illusion, particularly in relation to Europe (see Flew 2007: 82–83). What exists instead are a series of regionalized production and market blocks, dominated by the 'triad' markets of North America, the European Union and Japan. In this case, international expansion strategies generally require a large degree of 'local knowledge'. By contrast, extension within a region is often more straightforward and less risky. In other words, the issues facing a French company seeking to expand into eastern Europe are probably less complex than those raised by similar plans to expand into South East Asia.

Content Ownership and Media Business Models

Alongside shifts in media ownership, transformations in the economic, political and technological dynamics of the media have resulted in new business models. Where media companies, such as publishers and broadcasters, once integrated all their production operations internally, many media and communication firms have now moved to decentralized production models, using either group affiliates or external producers and suppliers. At the same time, there has been a transformation of traditional media revenue structures, involving the redistribution and fragmentation of advertising and consumer expenditure among traditional and new media. There has been a growth in free newspapers and free online content, but there has also been growth in subscription services (television, online).

In this more complex value chain, new alliances and conflicts have arisen among different actors (creatives, producers, distributors) because the economic rights associated with intellectual property have become a key asset not only for traditional media industries, but also for the telecommunications and ICT (information and communication technologies) industries which now occupy an important position in business models designed to make content available to consumers across many different platforms (mobile, online).

Growing competition for content has increased the value of certain content rights, including popular US serials, some reality formats and above all sports. For these reasons, large European media companies try to exert stronger control over the provision of TV programming, through long-term agreements with producers, through the creation of production and rights management affiliates, as well as through the acquisition of the most successful independent producers. For example, Mediaset acquired format producer Endemol in 2007, and others have sealed alliances with US companies. Strong competition has also led to a number of conflicts between media companies related to copyright and broadcasting rights. The centrality of intellectual property for the media, ICT and telecommunications industries, the intangible nature of rights, their complex valuation, and the continuous revision of business models due to technological innovation and social change, help to explain why some companies are moving away from competition with rivals to alliances and long-term agreements in order to reduce risk.

One good example of this trend is reflected in the relations between Google and traditional media companies, involving lawsuits about rights as well as commercial agreements to exploit them.

Authors and content producers are therefore trying to reinforce their copyright position in a number of ways by:

Box 2: European Media vs. Google

Most European broadcasters, besides operating their own websites, have also reached agreements with Google to distribute content on the video/file sharing website YouTube (owned by Google). Others, such as Mediaset in Italy and its affiliate Telecinco in Spain, have sued YouTube for copyright infringement, demanding the removal of their content from the site.

While the vast majority of newspapers tolerate Google News as a new distribution channel that brings consumers to their own websites, some news organizations (France-Presse in 2005; Belgian editors in 2007) have also taken Google to court for copyright infringement. In 2009, some media giants (notably News Corporation) discussed the possibility of removing all their content from Google, and making agreements with rival ICT companies, such as Microsoft or Yahoo.

Google has infuriated some book publishers, who have denounced the Google Books service for copyright infringement. In 2009, Google negotiated an agreement with US publishers to pay for copyright; an agreement later extended to Canadian, British and Australian publishers. However, Google has faced legal actions in France and Germany against its digital books service, and by the end of 2009 there was still no resolution to the conflict between Google, libraries and publishers.

This case exemplifies the conflict between the fair use of content and the right to culture and education on the one hand, and the economic rights of publishers and rights owners on the other. It also highlights the conflict between the 'old' oligopolistic media industries and the 'new' digital industry, where Google now occupies a quasi-monopolistic position. One could argue that the digitization and internationalization of content has unsettled and undermined traditional media industry structures, but strengthened the position of the largest media conglomerates and ICT companies, who have the resources and expertise to manage large amounts of content and its distribution via traditional publication and broadcast networks, as well as online.

- Taking advantage of technologies to control and protect the use of their creations through digital rights management (DRM) applications which restrict access and copying
- Improving the coordination of the different national copyright collecting agencies/societies across different territories and networks
- Adopting a more active role in negotiations with content distributors
- Demanding stronger protection of primary authors' rights versus the secondary rights of producers and distributors (in contrast to the US model and some European countries – Spain, the United Kingdom, Portugal, Norway and Finland – which attribute these rights to employers rather than the individual)
- Searching for new income sources such as levies on private copying

On the other hand, technological innovation – particularly online with the rise of social networking sites – has allowed authors, content creators and independent producers to seek out a more direct relationship with consumers. This can be seen in the music field, where peer-to-peer (p2p) technologies have had a major impact with many authors making their music available online. This is also the case with personal sites and blogs created by journalists. However, it is not clear how these sites generate revenues. Online distribution of content and p2p file sharing has also raised the problem of piracy and the protection of owners' rights.

State Interventions in the European Media Economy

Media ownership, the promotion of production and the regulation of copyright are three of the main areas for state intervention in the media economy. Ownership represents one area where individual countries within Europe have sought to regulate in order to encourage content diversity and multiple voices (Hamelink and Nordenstreng 2007: 227). However, the impact of state interventions to enhance pluralism and democracy varies between countries and for different media sectors (including the press and audio-visual production).

In respect of the press, some European states apply direct press subsidies (Finland, Sweden) targeted 'to arrest the decline in the number of newspapers, to promote more competition in newspaper markets, to combat Europe-wide trend towards press concentration, and – importantly – to help sustain a diversity of opinion in the press' (Humphreys 2006: 39). As a form of state intervention, these subsidies can take different forms including fiscal advantages and indirect subsidies (France, Austria, Netherlands, Belgium). In the Nordic countries, they take the form of direct aid linked to the cultural and political goals of media organizations (Picard 2006: 214).

At both the national and EU level, there are policies to support television and film production (Lange and Westcott 2004: 19). For audio-visual markets as a whole, the European Union has elaborated a clear protectionist policy to safeguard economic stability and to facilitate the expansion and competitiveness of European audio-visual media. Policy responses, especially in relation to television, have been undertaken to overcome national barriers on the free flow of content. For example, the European Union's Television Without Frontiers Directive (TVWF) of 1989 (later revised in 1997) established liberal rules about the reception of television within the European Union, in the hope of creating a pan-European market for television and stimulating audio-visual production (Iosifidis, Steemers and Wheeler 2005), which would allow European companies to compete with America in global markets (Flew 2007: 125). The recent AVMS Directive (European Commission 2007), which replaced the TVWF Directive, has reaffirmed these principles and extended them to audio-visual services in the digital environment. Yet the TVWF and AVMS Directives (European Commission 2007) are not simply an economic intervention, but also a cultural intervention designed to protect national cultures, in that they demand 'where practicable' a majority of European content by broadcasters. In recent years the European Commission has also been trying to boost Europe's online content sector, although problems associated with rights management, piracy and copyright have yet to be effectively resolved at an EU level.

In this more competitive situation, the regulation of intellectual property (IP) and the derived economic rights – the right to copy, to perform, to reproduce, the right to public communication and free speech (e.g. to make content available) – becomes a crucial matter for the media industries, because copyright is the mechanism which guarantees financial rewards not only to authors, but also to producers and distributors who receive a return on their investment.

IP also has social and cultural implications, since it affects access to cultural creations, including access to information and knowledge (Lessig 2004; Haynes, 2005). So the regulation of copyright and the market regulation of relations in the value chain, stretching from creators to audiences, does not only affect the economic rights of authors. It also affects authors' moral rights (the individual right to attribution and to protect their work from alteration – Droit Moral) and human rights (the right to information, education, culture, and to just and favourable remuneration) (art. 19, 26, 27, 23 Universal Declaration of Human Rights).

Faced with these challenges and conflicting interests around intellectual property, the European Union has adopted the perspective represented by the General Agreement on Tariffs and Trade (GATT) agreement on the Trade-Related Aspects of Intellectual Property Rights (TRIPS), and the World Intellectual Property Organization (WIPO) on the extent of copyright and derived rights (the right to distribution and rental, the right to public communication). At the national level, different regulatory traditions and different industrial structures are still recognizable in the different systems of the copyright collecting societies and author remuneration, in the sanctions for infringement and in the definition of limits and exceptions to these rights. Nevertheless, throughout the 2000s the European Union has been promoting greater harmonization in the approach to copyright.

The main issues EU policy-makers have to deal with are the exceptions to exclusive economic rights and the establishment of mechanisms to guarantee fair remuneration in the value chain, particularly in view of imbalances between authors, producers and distributors, and also in relation to the problem with piracy.

EU regulations[1] recognize: the possibility of a limitation on exclusive rights on content motivated by the general interest and related to the rights to education and information; the need for public security and legal procedures, or the principle of universal access to knowledge. The perspective adopted on this issue can be compared to the regulations on public aid to public radio and television media, inasmuch as there are attempts to guarantee that the considerations of general interest and public service do not jeopardize the functioning of the market and do not lower the 'normal profit' of the private sector. Thus, EU member states must specifically define the exceptions, may not 'enter into conflict with the normal exploitation of the work' (EC 2001: article 4.5, Directive 2001/29/EC), and should there be any harm to the interests of the holders of the rights, equitable compensation must be valued and set up.

European regulation also recognizes the core role of copyright collection societies. However, despite greater coordination, the effectiveness of these agencies in different EU countries still varies considerably in terms of legally binding enforcement. For instance, in Greece or Belgium, there are no specific laws regulating the operations of copyright collecting agencies. In Italy and, to a lesser extent, Germany there is stronger regulation, which seems to result in more effective royalty collection. The control and effectiveness of copyright protection in France, Spain and Britain is somewhat lower (Rochelandet 2002).

The EU directives extend authors' rights for equitable remuneration to new modes of commercial exploitation, but there are no mechanisms to guarantee fair remuneration, and no harmonization in the attribution of the rights in work-for-hire, leaving authors in a weak position. Instead EU norms emphasize the harm that private copying and p2p technologies can cause to authors and distributors. As such, they authorize taxes on electronic devices to compensate for the damages caused by private copying and the termination of individual Internet connections to counteract illegal downloading, subject to adequate procedural safeguards.

To counter the extension of proprietary rights and market relations to all new technological possibilities, and all social uses of culture and social communication, other initiatives are also being proposed. General Public Licenses, Copy-Left proposals and Creative Commons Licenses are designed as alternative instruments for the protection of public domains, for the creation and exchange of content. These licensing systems authorize the free use of content in the public domain, without excluding commercial exchanges, but limiting the exclusive rights of the authors and especially those of content distributors. These represent attempts to counterbalance the market power of commercial organizations that use copyright and associated exclusive rights, to consolidate their dominant position in the market.

Conclusion

Modern European media industries today represent a diverse field characterized by uneven features in respect to ownership and regulation. It is obvious that there is no unified media industry, neither in geographical, nor in media sectoral terms, but the following conclusions can be drawn:

- History has played a key part in shaping the different development of European media industries. However, with the demise of totalitarian and authoritarian systems and the rise of liberalized commercially-led media economies, media industries across Europe now exhibit some similarities with commercial media existing alongside public – or state-owned – audio-visual media.

- However, across different media sectors there are different levels of international engagement: in print media and radio, national and regional dimensions are still dominant, in contrast to television and the Internet which are more globalized in both their ownership and the scope of their activities.
- Public service broadcasting is still a significant force in European media but faces strong competition from commercial players.
- The dynamics of ownership in European media are clearly moving away from family-owned enterprises to multi-sectoral conglomerates operating in pan-European and global markets. This trend is supported by the European Union whose initiatives for a single market clearly aim to support the economic power and competitiveness of the European media.
- Traditional European media players within press and broadcasting face considerable challenges from digital and online media, both in terms of competition for consumers and revenues, and also in respect of copyright issues. Advertising-based funding models for the press and broadcasting, no longer look sustainable in the long term, forcing players to think about alternative revenue sources.
- Copyright has become a key issue as authors and rights owners seek to protect their creations in the face of growing piracy. Efforts to resolve copyright issues at a pan-European level, by the European Union for example, are complex with no uniform solutions, because there are conflicting interests between authors' rights and the rights of employers and corporations.

Note

1. Council Directive 91/250/EEC, Directive 96/9/EC, Council Directive 92/100/EEC, Council Directive 93/98/EEC, Council Directive 93/83/EEC, Directive 98/84/EC, Directive 2001/29/EC, Directive 2004/48/EC, Directive 2006/116/EC; Telecoms Reform adopted in November 2009. Annex 1: The new Internet Freedom Provision: Article 1(3)a of the new Framework Directive.

References

Aris, A. and Bughin J. (2005), *Managing Media Companies: Harnessing Creative Value*, Chichester: John Wiley & Sons.

Deloitte (2006), *Turn on to Digital: Getting Prepared for Digital Content Creation and Distribution to 2012*, London: Deloitte.

de Bens, E. (ed.) (2007), *Media Between Culture and Commerce*, Bristol: Intellect.

European Audiovisual Observatory (2001), *Television and Media Concentration: Regulatory Models on the National and the European Level*, Strasbourg: European Audiovisual Observatory.

European Audiovisual Observatory (2008), *Yearbook Online Premium Service 2008*. Available at: http://www.obs.coe.int/yb2008/members/CNumPage.html. Accessed 14 February 2010.

European Commission (2007), Directive 2007/65/EC, European Parliament and Council, 11 December 2007 (L 332). Available at: http: //ec.europa.eu/avpolicy/reg/tvwf/index_en.htm. Accessed 14 February 2010.

Flew, T. (2007), *Understanding Global Media*, Basingstoke: Palgrave Macmillan.

Gulyás, Á. (2005), 'Multinational Media Companies in a European Context', Paper Presented at the MECCSA and AMPE Joint Annual Conference, Lincoln: University of Lincoln.

Habermas, J. (2005), *The Structural Transformation of the Public Sphere*, Cambridge: Polity.

Hamelink, C. and Nordenstreng, K., 'Towards Democratic Media Governance', in de Bens. E. (ed.) (2007), *Media Between Culture and Commerce*, Bristol: Intellect, pp. 225–40.

Harcourt, A., 'Introduction', in Terzis, G. (ed.) (2008), *European Media Governance: The Brussels Dimension*, Bristol and Chicago: Intellect, pp. 13–23.

Hardy J. (2008), *Western Media Systems*, London and New York: Routledge.

Haynes, R. (2005), *Media Rights and Intellectual Property*, Edinburgh: Edinburgh University Press.

Herman, E., and McChesney, R. (1997), *The Global Media: The New Missionaries of Corporate Capitalism*, London and Washington: Cassell.

Holt, J. and Perren, A. (eds) (2009), *Media Industries: History, Theory, and Method*, Oxford: Wiley-Blackwell.

Humphreys, P., 'Press Subsidies in the Context of the Information Society: Historical Perspective, Modalities, Concept and Justification', in Alonso I., de Moragas, M., Gil, J. and Almiron, N. (eds) (2006), *Press Subsidies in Europe*, Barcelona: Col-lecció Lexikon, pp. 38–55.

International Federation of Journalists (2006), *Media Power in Europe: The Big Picture of Ownership*. Available at: http: //www.ifj.org/en/articles/media-power-in-europe-the-big-picture-of-ownership. Accessed 14 February 2010.

Iosifidis, P., Steemers, J., and Wheeler, M. (eds) (2005), *European Television Industries*, London: BFI Publishing.

Kelly, M., Mazzoleni, G., and McQuail, D. (eds) (2004), *The Media in Europe: The Euromedia Handbook*, London: Sage.

Koulouvari, P. (2004), 'Family-Owned Media Companies in the Nordic Countries: A Portrait of Structures and Characteristics of 25 Firms', Working Papers No. 2004–4, Jönköping: Jönköping International Business School.

Küng, L., Picard, R., and Towse, R. (2008), *The Internet and Mass Media*, London: Sage.

Küng-Shankleman, L. (2000), *Inside the BBC and CNN: Managing Media Organizations*, London and New York: Routledge.

Lange, A., and Westcott, T. (2004), *Public Funding for Film and Audiovisual Works in Europe: A Comparative Approach*, Strasbourg: European Audiovisual Observatory.

Lessig, L. (2004), *Free Culture: How Big Media Uses Technology and the Law to Lock Down Culture and Control Creativity*, New York: Penguin Press.

McQuail D. (2005), *McQuail's Mass Communication Theory*, London: Sage.

NORDICOM (2009), *Media Trends*, Gothenburg: Nordicom, 2009.

Ofcom (2009), *Communications Report 2009*, London: Ofcom.

Open Society Institute (2008), *Television Across Europe: More Channels, Less Independence. Follow-up Reports*, Budapest: Open Society Institute.

Picard, R. (1989), *Media Economics: Concepts and Issues*, London: Sage.

—— 'Issues and Challenges in Provision of Press Subsidies', in Alonso., I., de Moragas, M., Gil, J. and Almiron, N. (eds) (2006), *Press Subsidies in Europe*, Barcelona: Collecció Lexikon.

PricewaterhouseCoopers (PwC) (2009–10), *Global Entertainment and Media Outlook*, London: PricewaterhouseCoopers.

Rochelandet, F. (2002), 'Are Copyright Collecting Societies Efficient? An Evaluation of Collective Administration of Copyright in Europe', The Society for Economic Research on Copyright Issues, Inaugural Annual Congress 2002, Madrid: Universidad Autónoma de Madrid. Available at: http: // www.serci.org/2002/rochelandet.pdf. Accessed 17 February 2010.

Screen Digest, CMS Hasche Sigle, Goldmedia Gmbh, Rightscom (2006), *Implications for the Information Society: A Study for the European Commission (DG Information Society and Media)*, London: Screen Digest Limited.

Thussu, D. K. (2007), *News as Entertainment: The Rise of Global Infotainment*, London: Sage.

Universal Declaration of Human Rights, adopted by the General Assembly of the United Nations in 1948. Available at: http: //www.un.org/en/documents/udhr. Accessed 31 March 2010.

Voltmer, K. (2008), 'Comparing Media Systems in New Democracies: East Meets South Meets West', *Central European Journal of Communication*, 1: 1, pp. 23–40.

Wasko, J., 'The Political Economy of Communications', in Downing, J. (ed.) (2004), *The SAGE Handbook of Media Studies*, London: Sage, pp. 309–30.

Weymouth, T. and Lamizet, B. (1996), *Markets and Myths: Forces for Change in the European Media*, London and New York: Longman.

Williams, K. (2005), *European Media Studies*, London: Bloomsbury Academic.

Chapter 11

From Public Service Broadcasting to Public Service Media

Leen d'Haenens, Helena Sousa and Olof Hultén

The Amsterdam Protocol (1997) has made it clear that the duality of the European broadcasting landscape is explicitly recognized by the European Union institutions. One consequence is that the European Union (EU) goes along with government subsidization of public broadcasters, on condition that there should be a sufficient degree of transparency and proportionality between the funding provided and the services rendered. What output is being delivered by Public Service Broadcasters (PSB) and in what circumstances, given their budget, the degree of market competition, and the taste cultures of the audiences targeted, will be the topic of this chapter.

Statement of the Problem: Main Challenges

New information technologies, liberalizing the European Union and national policies, together with rapidly changing societies – from mono- to multicultural – undoubtedly entail serious consequences for the prospects of public service broadcasters in Europe. Consequently, they will need to solve their current identity crisis, reformulate their remit and reorganize their institutions in order to stay in tune with the societies they want to serve. Offering a one-size-fits-all model, which would allow public service media to 'reinvent' itself while responding to all social, ideological and cultural changes since the 1920s when public service broadcasters were born, is an impossible task since the concept of public service broadcasting has developed along partly converging and partly distinct lines in each European country (d'Haenens and Saeys 2007). This chapter will touch upon a number of ingredients which we believe are necessary to strike a healthy and durable balance between the mission attributed to the European public service broadcasting – universal service, quality, diversity, public value, etc. – and institutional security.

This balance cannot be achieved without taking the technical innovations, as well as the political, economic, legal and cultural conditions, to determine how broadcasting systems can and should be operated into account. Obviously, these contextual conditions are paramount to the structure, production, distribution and consumption of media content. In the wake of digitization, internationalization and convergence, the broadcasting sector throughout the western world has gone through some sweeping changes in the last few decades (Broeders, Huysmans and Verhoeven 2006). However, this evolution has not led to greater uniformity per se, as critics feared when the deregulation and advent of commercial broadcasting began to be felt in Europe as of the second half of the 1980s (Dahlgren 1995).

Even though commercial channels spread like wildfire, and regulation and interventions at the level of the European Commission led to policy convergence, this did not result in identical structures and strategies being set up by public broadcasters throughout Europe, nor did it end in extreme superficiality of output. Major differences continue to exist in the European context, which is characterized by more than just one single national public broadcasting model (e.g. PSB obligations are shared by the BBC, ITV, Channel 4 and Five in the United Kingdom; the 'pillarized' model in the Netherlands; the PSB function outsourced to a private broadcaster, the RTL group in Luxembourg; Portugal's test with public channel RTP2 as a 'civil society' channel for content from various public and private organizations).

The differences observed among the various European Union member states are not only – and not even primarily – linked to the members' time of accession. The long-standing cultural, economic and social diversities found in Europe have always been apparent in the broadcasting systems of the members.

Resulting from their comparison of media and political systems in several western countries, Hallin and Mancini (2004) developed three 'ideal types': (1) the 'liberal model', mainly to be found in Great Britain and its former British colonies (United States, Ireland and Canada); (2) the 'polarized pluralist model' with considerable levels of politicization, state intervention and clientelism in Mediterranean countries like France, Italy, Spain, Portugal and Greece; and (3) the 'democratic corporatist model' which is present in the Scandinavian countries, the Netherlands, Austria, Switzerland, Belgium, as well as Germany, and which strongly relies on the role of organized social groups in society, as opposed to a more individualistic concept of representation in the liberal model. In Great Britain, for instance, the monopoly of the public broadcaster was broken as early as the 1950s, while the evolution towards a dual system was much slower in the Nordic countries. In between these two extremes, one can find countries such as Germany, France, the Netherlands and Belgium, while the radically commercial broadcasting system of Luxembourg can be regarded as an exception. The newcomers from eastern Europe obviously have their own history and traditional broadcasting contexts, and can find it hard to adapt to the standards laid down by the European Union straightaway, since these EU standards are fashioned on a fairly western pattern.

The multiplication of the number of broadcasting stations in Europe is to be considered the direct cause of the fragmentation of the audience (see, among others, Picard 2000). In so doing, the nature of the media as a force that binds people together is weakened and the shared media experience risks disappearing. Also, the following question can be raised: will this overwhelming presence of the media be effectively utilized? Research into time-spending patterns reveals that we do not spend more time on media, but that shifts have occurred from the 'old' to the 'new' media and that functions of the media are also shifting. A final argument is that a further increase in the number of content providers is bound to result in the fragmentation of financial resources, inevitably leading to a loss of quality (Picard 2000).

This chapter will be looking into public service broadcasting in the multimedia environment or, put differently, into the transition from public service broadcasting to public service media. The one thing, among others, that this chapter proves is that the demise of public service broadcasting is far from being as serious as forecast. In recent years, public broadcasters in some European countries managed to be at the heart of public attention, as the problems are obviously numerous: commercialization, the individualization of society, and political climates not being too keen on finding adequate and future-proof financing mechanisms. Digitization – the most recent battlefield for public broadcasters – entails new media platforms offering user interactivity and a more targeted, thematic supply of content. This is aimed at audiences (especially the younger segments of under 40 years of age) who although still continue to view in a linear fashion, they gradually devote more time to non-linear viewing (viewing-on-demand), irrespective of the content carrier.

Within this context of blurring borders between media, it is becoming increasingly hard to continue referring to separate media carriers. Hence, more and more voices are raised advocating a functional approach to the media: in outlining a media policy, policy-makers should no longer focus on the separate media platforms, but rather on the needs of society at large, i.e. on the social functions which the media landscape as a whole must definitely meet (van de Donk et al. 2005). The role of the public service concept behind this background will be centrally dealt with in this chapter, as well as the specificity and distinctiveness of the European full-fledged, 'all-in-one' PSB model versus the US 'niche' model which has more modest pretensions in relation to popular reach and social impact.

The European concept of public service broadcasting as a comprehensive and universal service is challenged by both European authorities and national governments at three levels: (1) mission and programme task (comprehensive or complementary programming?); (2) organization (central organization, publishing model or 'distributed public service'?); and (3) financing (license fee, advertising or 'state aid'?) (see also Bardoel and d'Haenens 2008b; Donkers and Pauwels 2008). At the European level and in many western countries there have been pressures towards a more 'pure' model of public service broadcasting and/or towards the de-institutionalization of PSB and 'distributed public service'. More in general, the traditionally close relationship between public broadcasters and national politics has become more distant and problematic; at the same time, the viewing and listening public has abandoned public broadcasting stations in favour of their commercial competitors. Moreover, recent European competition policies and jurisdiction make it imperative to formulate the public remit in a much more explicit manner, and to make public funding much more transparent and proportional in order to ensure an equal level playing field for both public and commercial broadcasters.[1]

In other words, looking at the current map of the EU media space – a complex regulatory framework, structural-financial constraints, technological changes due to the information society's uncertainties and opportunities, as well as more individualized consumer behaviour – we ask ourselves: where can the public service media go from here? Or, to put it differently: what content strategies are there for public broadcasters in terms of remedying market failure and offering public value, in a world of rampant commercialism, fragmentation, time and place shifting?

Therefore, this chapter deals with the concept, performance and transformation of public service broadcasting in Europe, in light of dramatic technological and political changes. The Euromedia Research Group has for a long time followed the different phases of this evolution, from the fall of the old national public service monopolies and the rapid growth of the commercial sector in most countries, to today's paradigmatic shifts in the media field thanks to the Internet.

Early in their competition with commercial rivals, many public service broadcasters were struggling with how to position their channels, programme output and schedules in relation to private channels with their heavily entertainment-oriented schedules. Soaring prices for attractive sports, major movies and TV series as well as media personalities, required more money and demanded more efficient operations. Until digital distribution was introduced, analogue public broadcasters retained strong – albeit declining – market shares of viewing and listening. They were, however, often criticized for lowering their traditional quality and becoming too commercial (Hultén and Brants 1992).

Competition grew tremendously when digital TV distribution was introduced, first via satellite and cable, later via terrestrial networks. In northern Europe, most TV households today receive a great number of channels; in southern Europe, this diffusion process is significantly slower. Fragmentation of audiences is a reality for all channels, but commercial broadcasters are able to offer bigger bundles of services. This is especially the case in the bigger EU markets. The opposite trend can be identified in the smaller European Union countries, where the public broadcasters prove to be the initiators of digital initiatives, and the commercial broadcasters are following. Overall, the challenge facing public service broadcasters is how to keep a broad output, to remain distinct and different, offer public value, and be attractive to their audiences (Hultén 2007).

Structure: Regulation and Policy Actors

The governments of the European Union member states have to engage in a good deal of give-and-take between their own media policies on the one hand, implemented at the local, regional and national levels, and the rules established by the European Union on the other hand. In the initial stages, European regulation mainly focused on the creation of competitive, creative and diverse content industries (see Biltereyst and Pauwels 2007). In the 1980s and 1990s, increasing competition between public and commercial broadcasters led to the convergence of content, which caused the former to suffer a fundamental identity crisis. Europe-wide, a cautious trend towards the re-regulation – instead of deregulation – of broadcast policies can be observed, in which the focus is on policies that are more flexible and more effective (e.g. contributing to the Lisbon agenda and acting as a crucial component to the 2010 policy strategy adopted by the European Commission in June 2005), but which are also more selective in regulating the media. Recent regulatory changes at both the national and EU levels also show a tendency to favour a market-orientated approach (Steemers 2003; Michalis 2007). Also, traditional regulation is felt to be too static to cope with the rapidly changing context. New concepts such as 'self'- or 'co-regulation' and 'process regulation' are thus introduced.

Against this liberal(izing) policy climate illustrated in the 1989 Television without Frontiers Directive (TVWF), the last public service broadcasting monopolies in the European continent came to an end around 1990, and 'dual' broadcasting structures comprising of public and commercial actors were put in place. At the same time in eastern Europe, state-controlled media complexes were dismantled and often a shift was made towards highly commercial media landscapes. The Amsterdam Protocol of 1997 has made it clear that the duality of the European broadcasting landscape is now explicitly recognized by the EU institutions. One important consequence is that the European Union now goes along with government subsidization of public broadcasters, admittedly on condition that there should be a sufficient degree of transparency and proportionality between the funding provided and the services rendered (Pauwels 2006; Hirsch and Petersen 2007; Broeders, Huysmans and Verhoeven 2006; Coppens 2005). The funding of PSB is subject for debate, both because of the questionable willingness of the public to continue paying the licence fee, and the uncertain future of mixed-funded PSBs which have resulted in numerous 'unfair competition' complaints by commercial competitors. Most public broadcasters are mixed income-based (see Table 1). As the counterbalance of commercial income (advertising) tends to decrease, public funding only becomes more important.

Given its public mission and the notions of independence attached to it, one could expect public funding to be the major source of income for public broadcasters. However, when analyzing Table 1, this seems far from obvious, and in some countries (e.g. Spain and Poland) it is rather the exception than the rule. In general, the clearest financial fracture can be identified between the more solid public broadcasting systems of the United Kingdom, Germany and the Nordic countries (with a public income ratio between 80–95%) on the one hand, and on the other hand one finds the more privately funded public broadcasters of the Mediterranean basin (Spanish TVE running with less than 10% of public funding; the Italian and French public broadcasters operating on 49–57% public funding; and EU newcomer Poland with 30% of public funding). In France, for instance, the financing issue is hot, as it is the intention to considerably increase the licence fee. Less advertising income should be compensated by taxes stemming from private broadcasters, mobile telephone operators and Internet providers. Small countries like Switzerland, Slovenia, Belgium and the Baltic states tend to rely on public funding for two-thirds of their total budget. In addition to these differences in the income sources, large discrepancies remain in terms of total income. Whereas the total public broadcasters' income of large countries such as the United Kingdom and Germany fluctuates around five billion Euros, their smaller Belgian, Slovenian, Baltic and Scandinavian counterparts have to make do with a budget ranging between 17 million and 480 million Euros. The question how these budgets are spent and on which programme genres will be dealt with later in the chapter (see also Table 2).

Table 1: Sources of Income of Public Broadcasters According to Size and Region.

Countries		Total In Euros thousand	Public In %	Private In %	Other In %
SIZE					
Large Countries					
United Kingdom					
BBC	2004	5 561 637	73.7	26.2	0.2
	2005	5 578 730	77.0	22.9	0.1
	2006	5 745 438	81.4	18.5	0.1
	2007	6 141 739	80.3	19.7	–
	2008	5 552 000	81.0	19.0	–
Germany					
ARD	2003	5 703 253	85.9	12.6	1.4
	2004	5 818 075	85.1	13.3	1.6
	2005	5 948 998	86.1	13.6	0.4
	2006	6 056 268	86.3	12.7	0.1
	2007	6 075 270	86.3	13.0	0.8
ZDF	2003	1 763 366	85.8	11.7	2.6
	2004	1 795 797	84.8	12.4	2.8
	2005	2 061 601	78.6	12.0	9.4
	2006	1 965 622	84.9	13.4	1.7
	2007	1 927 218	86.6	12.9	0.5
France					
FR2	2004	1 133 400	54.4	41.1	4.5
	2005	1 096 800	56.9	42.9	0.3
France Televisions	2006	2 961 000	61.9	34.4	3.6
Poland					
TVP	2003	353 100	32.7	56.1	11.2
	2004	394 100	32.4	61.2	6.4
	2005	486 800	28.2	60.1	11.7
	2006	509 000	27.2	59.7	13.1
Small Countries					
Switzerland					
SRG SSR Idée Suisse	2004	1 136 470	64.4	35.6	–
	2005	1 126 710	64.2	35.8	–
	2006	1 108 270	63.2	36.8	–
	2007	1 105 130	62.3	37.7	–
Slovenia					
RTVSLO	2004	107 974	70.7	28.2	1.1
	2005	109 814	71.4	28.6	1.1
	2006	116 877	66.1	18.5	15.4
	2007	114 524	–	–	–

Countries		Total In Euros thousand	Public In %	Private In %	Other In %
REGIONS					
Mediterranean Countries					
Spain					
RTVE (replaced in 2007	2004	874 377	9.3	86.2	4.5
by the Corp. de Radio y	2005	858 667	9.5	85.8	4.7
Television Española)	2006	1 320 280	43.9	55.2	0.9
	2007	1 183 805	–	–	–
Portugal					
RTP	2005	266 100	75.3	24.7	–
	2006	292 100	76.8	23.2	–
	2007	314 900	76.3	23.7	–
Greece	–	–	–	–	–
Italy					
RAI	2004	3 021 300	51.8	46.2	2.0
	2005	3 152 900	49.6	47.5	2.9
	2006	3 217 400	49.3	49.2	1.5
	2007	3 290 200	50.4	48.2	1.4
Benelux					
Belgium					
Flanders VRT	2004	367 840	62.9	27.1	10.0
	2005	405 670	62.5	27.0	10.1
	2006	456 300	61.4	13.1	25.4
Wallonia RTBF	2003	276 540	63.2	31.8	5.1
	2004	297 960	59.9	27.7	12.3
	2005	257 081	72.7	26.1	1.1
	2006	266 614	72.1	25.9	2.0
Netherlands					
Dutch public broadcasting	2003	771 500	66.2	29.0	4.8
system	2004	805 900	64.1	26.9	9.1
	2005	837 900	66.4	22.4	11.2
	2006	678 900	54.6	29.1	16.3
Luxembourg	–	–	–	–	–
Baltic States					
Estonia					
Eesti Television (ETV)	2003	12 095	–	–	–
	2004	14 182	–	–	–
	2005	13 898	–	–	–
	2006	16 672	–	–	–

Countries		Total In Euros thousand	Public In %	Private In %	Other In %
Eesti Rahvursringhaaling	2006	25 439	–	–	–
(ERR)	2007	27 725	–	–	–
Lithuania					
LNRT	2003	15 100	70.2	29.8	–
	2004	17 300	63.6	36.4	–
	2005	17 400	63.8	36.2	–
	2006	19 900	61.8	38.2	–
Latvia	–	–	–	–	
Scandinavian Countries					
Denmark					
DR	2004	457 977	87.5	12.5	–
	2005	469 850	88.3	11.7	–
	2006	474 908	92.1	7.9	–
	2007	484 384	91.9	8.1	–
Sweden					
SVT	2003	449 100	93.1	0.6	6.2
	2004	478 900	92.7	1.1	6.1
	2005	444 317	93.5	–	6.5
	2006	452 837	90.9	–	9.1
	2007	426 682	93.0	–	7.0

Sources: European Audiovisual Observatory (2005b, 2008a).

Bearing in mind that the present-day media landscape is in transition and there is now a superseded notion of separate platforms for print-media and broadcasting, the Television without Frontiers Directive has been amended in light of the provision of non-linear services (such as video-on-demand) and has been renamed into the Audiovisual Media Services without Frontiers Directive (AVMSD), which is currently in the process of being implemented in the different member states (Nikoltchev 2006). Worthwhile in this context is the attention-grabbing report 'Focus on Functions: Challenges for a Future-Proof Media Policy', produced by the Scientific Council for Government Policy of the Netherlands (WRR 2005), which suggests a number of stimulating scenarios for the future of the media.

The fact is that the Internet, and the headlong internationalization and commercialization of media companies, are rapidly and radically transforming the media landscape (Küng, Picard and Towse 2008). Technological developments connect old media with new ones, making it possible to watch television on the Internet and listen to radio on mobile phones. Infrastructural facilities that used to be strictly separated, such as cable and telephone lines, are now competing with each other for the distribution of digital media, the growth of which is truly explosive. The impact of European regulation in this sector has become so substantial that the national governments' scope for legislation has shrunk: the European Union can now label national support for Internet activities as disproportionate and as a distortion of competition; it can be forbidden and the government concerned can be censured. The logical outcome of technological convergence, therefore, is legal convergence and the move towards a functional media policy. However, the tide seems to be turning in several EU member states, with public broadcasters not only regaining a part of the market but also finding back their *raison d'être* (Coppens and Saeys 2006).

In this respect, radio tells us an interesting story. When comparing radio use with television, Internet, newspaper and magazine exposure, the former continues to show a remarkable strength with its weekly average of 13.2 hours, representing one of the highest absolute media use figures (EIAA 2008a). While analogue audiences, especially young people, are declining (EBU 2007a), digital radio (DAB and DRM) may change the tide thanks to its wider variety of content supply, and its higher availability on multiple platforms and standards. This new situation entails a shift in the production from traditionally-passive-flow radio to active-demand radio where the audience can pick, choose and mix preferred content whenever and wherever it suits them. With a more and more demanding audience, the real challenge is not to make listeners choose between parallel universes of linear programming but to offer all content on one platform which can be controlled and personalized according to audience preferences.

An obviously important partner in this radio development is the Internet. While television and the Internet are often experienced as mutually competing platforms, the radio and the Internet are complementary by their very nature. Among young Internet users (25–34 year olds), 36 per cent listen to the radio while searching the Internet (EIAA 2008b). Nowadays ARD, BBC and SR radio sites already stand out as the most popular radio websites among European Broadcasting Union (EBU) members (EBU 2007b). Nevertheless, in an effort to reach young audiences in particular, specifically targeted channels and initiatives are being launched and tested. By way of example, focus groups conducted by the Danish radio DR (Danmarks Radio) revealed that young people do not always fit in the audience groups as outlined by radio producers since they like to go their own way. As a result, DRDK recently experimented with a personalized Internet radio platform, a mix of radio on-demand and podcasting, on which one can create one's own radio stream by picking and mixing different kinds of contents (Heiden 2009). Furthermore, by attempting to visualize entire radio programmes on multiple platforms, BBC Radio 1 tried a visual version of two radio programmes in January 2009, providing live footage of the radio programme's presenter simultaneously with text messages sent in by listeners on the Internet (Spencer 2009). Another recent example of combining multi-platform and mobile radio is the Swedish SR Pod Radio, which made use of an MP3-browser and player allowing to podcast content from the Swedish public radio through WiFi or 3G (Torberg 2009).

Beyond and above these promising initiatives, a stable and dedicated transmission network will need to remain vital in order to maintain public radio broadcast prominence and avoid public radio being relegated to a merely supplementary function. As the EBU (2007a) formulated, the challenges for public radio broadcasters in the future will be to 'support open standards, secure provision of adequate spectrum, secure PSB's free access to digital platforms, secure digital content rights including music rights, provide distinct and competitive content on all platforms, increase availability of programmes in a convenient form, and create new forms of intriguing, innovative, involving and interactive radio formats'.

Conduct: Mission, Content and Driving Forces

The demand to renew the PSB mission premise first became pressing after the Amsterdam Protocol (1997) and Communication on State Aid (2001). As Jo Bardoel and Gregory Ferrell Lowej (2007: 14) rightly state, 'this period coincides with the rapid development of non-linear media, especially the Internet, and the associated escalation of convergence phenomena. It has become increasingly clear that making the transition from PSB to PSM [Public Service Media] requires effectively renewing the public service ethos because it alone remains the ground for any convincing case.' The main contextual drivers stimulating PSB to become PSM are digitization, globalization, convergence, fragmentation, individualization and a paramount market logic (see also Bardoel and d'Haenens 2008a). In this respect, the match between radio and the Internet dealt with in the former section is an interesting point in case.

In its 2001 Communication on the application of State aid rules to public service broadcasting, the European Commission stipulates that the definition of the public service mandate should be 'as precise as possible. It should leave no doubt as to whether a certain activity performed by the entrusted operator is intended by the Member State to be included in the public service remit or not. [...] Without a clear and precise definition of the obligations imposed on the public service broadcaster, the Commission would not be able to carry out its tasks.' From this, it is clear that on the basis of 'subsidiarity' the European Commission leaves it to the member states to formulate the task – broad if necessary – of public service broadcasting, while at the same time making it quite clear that as far as the Commission is concerned this task cannot be concrete enough.

Obviously a central component of the mission is the programme assignment of public broadcasting. The current debate on this issue can be summarized by the catchwords 'comprehensive or complementary'. In practice, most public broadcasters have chosen, principally or pragmatically, for the middle way of compensation. The discussion about the future of PSB revolves around two competing visions: that of the pure 'monastery model' on the one hand, and the 'full portfolio model' on the other (Jakubowicz 2003). The former vision is shared by the critics of PSB's commercialization, while the latter is likely to be adopted by most of the public service broadcasters themselves and policy-makers that hold PSB dear. Among them are the Digital Strategy Group members of the EBU, unmistakably stating in their *Media with a Purpose* (2002) that the public service broadcasters should meet the diverse needs of all audience members and therefore remain a 'full portfolio' content provider. Thompson (2005) also believes there is still a place for 'building public value' in an era of private value and individual consumer choice, as public goods like broadcasting or national defence cannot be handled well by conventional markets. In his view, the market is not well equipped to deliver the social and cultural value of public broadcasting to the entire population. Therefore public intervention is required. Although there is much debate in most countries on the mission of public service broadcasting, no country has made the choice to really narrow the task and focus of PSB. In response to this critical debate, most public broadcasters look for arguments in favour of the full-scale model and want to stress their distinctiveness more than ever before.

Based upon empirical evidence on the programme supply (see Table 2), the present chapter will take a pragmatic look at the mission of European public service broadcasting. This look is comparative in scope, distinguishing between the two main television players in smaller and bigger markets, 'old' EU member states and 'newcomers' such as the Baltic states, and between different regions such as the Nordic countries and the Mediterranean basin, which have a strong and poor public service tradition respectively. Market failure has become the main rationale for public service media. The market failure argument goes as follows: as commercial broadcasters are mainly supplying popular programmes, an under supply of information, education and cultural programmes may be a consequence should public service media not exist. Therefore, the latter have the mission to correct market failure and to guarantee content as a public merit good. In light of the current state of media markets in many EU competitive markets, one may wonder whether market failure will indeed continue to be a valid policy argument to be supported as an institutional public arrangement.

As can be seen in Table 2, public broadcasting time mainly goes to fiction, information, news, and to a lesser degree to arts, humanities and sciences. This genre division can be noticed in all the countries under study. Irrespective of origin, fiction leads in most cases, although information and news take the lead in the programming schedules of BBC, Das Erste (ARD), La Primera (TVE), NED 1/2/3, SVT and DR. As stated before, public broadcasters tend to reinforce their public mission and legitimization in light of market failure, but how does this reflect in their programme output? After all, most commercial broadcasters also provide viewers with fiction, news, and to a lesser degree, information. When looking back at the grid, only a small portion of public broadcasting time is allocated to art, humanities, sciences and education (except for BBC2, FR2, TVE, RAI and RTBF which dedicate more air time to such content). Notwithstanding the important role public broadcasters can fulfil here, there still seems to exist a vacuum concerning the latter programme genres.

A note of caution is in place when using output analyses with very simple genre structures as in Table 2. In order to make comparisons possible, statistics may have to be categorized in ways that conceal important differences in underlying categories. Many national studies on broadcast output from public and private channels find systematic differences in character also within categories and sub-categories of content. This is not the place for a detailed

Table 2: Programme Genres of Public Broadcasters According to Size and Region.

	SIZE	Large Countries								Small Countries			
		GB		DE		FR	PL		RU	SI		CH	
Genres In % (based on hours)		BBC1	BBC2	Das Erste (ARD)	ZDF	FR2	TVP1	TVP2	Perviy Kanal	RTVSLO	SF ½ (1)	TSR ½ (1)	TSI ½ (1)
Fiction	2003	–	–	28.5	26.7	27.0	–	–	–	23.2	–	–	–
	2004	23.6	16.9	28.8	26.7	25.7	43.2	36.6	42.2	22.7	35.6	33.1	21.4
	2005	–	–	32.2	30.6	–	–	–	41.7	21.2	–	–	–
	2006	23.7	13.4	34.6	28.6	–	35.1	43.5	35.0	22.1	39.4	27.0	20.9
	2007	–	–	36.1	28.0	–	–	–	–	–	–	–	–
Entertainment	2003	–	–	8.3	8.2	15.4	–	–	–	7.3	–	–	–
	2004	10.5	22.0	8.2	6.0	16.5	3.0	9.2	10.3	8.8	5.7	2.7	8.7
	2005	–	–	6.9	5.6	–	–	–	10.5	8.1	–	–	–
	2006	7.3	18.4	4.4	5.8	–	5.4	7.1	11.4	9.4	7.7	2.8	5.3
	2007	–	–	4.2	6.3	–	–	–	–	–	–	–	–
Music	2003	–	–	1.9	1.7	1.1	–	–	–	10.2	–	–	–
	2004	1.0	1.4	1.6	1.7	1.2	3.0	7.4	4.4	8.7	7.8	0.9	1.1
	2005	–	–	1.5	1.0	–	–	–	3.9	7.5	–	–	–
	2006	0.5	2.7	1.3	1.2	–	2.9	4.9	2.5	7.9	5.9	0.6	1.3
	2007	–	–	1.6	1.3	–	–	–	–	–	–	–	–
Sport	2003	–	–	8.6	6.0	6.6	–	–	–	10.6	–	–	–
	2004	9.1	11.3	9.6	7.5	8.0	4.8	6.7	2.6	9.8	12.5	11.4	15.3
	2005	–	–	6.7	5.5	–	–	–	2.0	9.7	–	–	–
	2006	10.0	12.4	8.0	7.5	–	5.1	4.8	3.3	11.7	10.2	10.4	17.2
	2007	–	–	6.0	5.9	–	–	–	–	–	–	–	–

	Year												
News	2003	–	–	10.1	10.1	13.1	–	–	–	7.3	–	–	–
	2004	–	6.3	9.5	9.4	12.5	7.6	6.6	9.7	8.8	8.9	12.1	20.2
	2005	31.2	–	9.7	9.6	–	–	–	9.4	9.5	–	–	–
	2006	–	7.4	9.3	9.2	–	6.6	7.7	9.2	10.0	7.1	21.5	26.7
	2007	30.0	–	9.4	9.4	–	–	–	–	–	–	–	–
Information	2003	22.2	–	33.0	–	6.6	–	–	–	20.5	–	–	–
	2004	–	18.5	32.2	39.0	6.4	8.9	9.0	5.8	18.8	6.9	9.9	9.0
	2005	24.4	–	33.4	39.2	–	–	–	5.7	20.7	–	–	–
	2006	–	22.9	32.5	38.6	–	12.4	9.7	6.7	20.2	6.3	6.9	9.9
	2007	–	–	33.8	40.2	–	–	–	–	–	–	–	–
Arts/Humanities/Sciences	2003	0.8	–	–	–	16.8	–	–	–	4.2	–	–	–
	2004	–	3.5	–	–	16.1	12.5	9.4	4.3	4.4	5.4	4.4	5.5
	2005	2.8	–	–	–	–	–	–	3.8	4.2	–	–	–
	2006	–	4.0	–	–	–	7.6	7.9	3.7	3.8	10.6	9.2	8.0
	2007	–	–	–	–	–	–	–	–	–	–	–	–
Religion	2003	1.0	–	–	–	2.9	–	–	–	0.8	–	–	–
	2004	–	0.5	–	–	2.8	1.8	0.8	0.3	1.0	0.8	0.9	0.5
	2005	1.3	–	–	–	–	–	–	0.3	1.1	–	–	–
	2006	–	0.3	–	–	–	2.5	1.2	0.2	1.0	0.5	1.1	0.4
	2007	–	–	–	–	–	–	–	–	–	–	–	–
Education	2003	0.7	–	–	–	–	–	–	–	5.6	–	–	–
	2004	–	19.7	–	–	–	2.0	0.2	0.0	6.2	1.8	0.0	0.2
	2005	0.0	–	–	–	–	–	–	–	5.6	–	–	–
	2006	–	18.5	–	–	–	1.9	0.5	–	5.9	1.4	0.0	0.2
	2007	–	–	–	–	–	–	–	–	–	–	–	–
Children's programmes	2003	–	–	6.0	5.2	–	–	–	–	–	–	–	–
	2004	–	–	6.2	5.9	–	–	–	–	–	–	–	–
	2005	–	–	5.7	5.0	–	–	–	–	–	–	–	–
	2006	–	–	6.0	5.6	–	–	–	–	–	–	–	–
	2007	–	–	5.1	5.1	–	–	–	–	–	–	–	–

Genres In % (based on hours)		Large Countries								Small Countries			
SIZE		GB	GB	DE	DE	FR	PL	PL	RU	SI	CH	CH	CH
		BBC1	BBC2	Das Erste (ARD)	ZDF	FR2	TVP1	TVP2	Perviy Kanal	RTVSLO	SF ½ (1)	TSR ½ (1)	TSI ½ (1)
Advertising	2003	–	–	1.3	1.3	3.1	–	–	–	3.2	–	–	–
	2004	–	–	1.5	1.5	3.0	6.9	6.0	9.9	4.4	6.0	6.9	3.0
	2005	–	–	1.4	1.3	–	0	–	11.1	5.1	–	–	–
	2006	–	–	1.5	1.4	–	–	9.6	12.6	3.5	4.5	4.6	2.3
	2007	–	–	1.5	1.5	–	–	–	–	–	–	–	–
Others (2)	2003	–	–	2.3	2.1	7.4	–	–	–	6.9	–	–	–
	2004	–	–	2.4	2.5	7.7	6.3	8.0	10.6	6.2	8.5	17.7	15.0
	2005	–	–	2.5	2.3	–	–	–	11.7	7.2	–	–	–
	2006	–	–	2.4	2.2	–	20.7	3.2	15.5	4.5	6.5	15.9	7.7
	2007	–	–	2.4	2.3	–	–	–	–	–	–	–	–
Total	2003	–	–	100	100	100	–	–	–	100	–	–	–
	2004	100	100	100	100	100	100	100	100	100	100	100	100
	2005	–	–	100	100	–	–	–	100	100	–	–	–
	2006	100	100	100	100	–	100	100	100	100	100	100	100
	2007	–	–	100	100	–	–	–	–	–	–	–	–

Genres
In % (based on hours)

Region groupings: **Mediterranean Countries** (ES, PT, GR, IT, NL, LU) · **Benelux** (VL, BE, WA) · **Scand. States** (DK, SE) · **Baltic States** (EE, LT, LV)

Genre	Year	ES La Primera (TVE)	ES La 2 (TVE)	PT	GR ERT1	GR NET (ERT TV)	IT RAI 1/2/3	NL NED 1/2/3	LU	VL Eén (VRT)	VL Canvas/Ketnet (VRT)	BE La Une (RTBF)	WA La Deux (RTBF)	DK DR1	DK DR2	SE SVT	EE ETV	LT LRT	LV LTV1
Fiction	2003	–	–	–	33.0	14.9	25.0	18.8	–	–	–	–	–	–	–	22.0	28.7	15.8	–
	2004	19.0	17.6	–	–	–	24.0	16.8	–	38.2	55.5	40.9	30.2	23.7	27.2	23.8	31.3	–	28.1
	2005	–	–	–	–	–	20.1	14.3	–	–	–	–	–	31.0	26.3	23.7	33.1	24.2	–
	2006	16.1	28.1	–	–	–	19.0	17.1	–	27.0	58.6	29.6	28.1	–	–	23.8	31.5	–	–
Entertainment	2003	–	–	–	26.0	1.8	19.0	7.8	–	–	–	–	–	–	–	8.4	2.8	6.9	–
	2004	5.2	3.1	–	–	–	19.0	6.9	–	8.7	3.1	2.6	0.5	2.3	0.3	9.6	3.1	–	15.0
	2005	–	–	–	–	–	22.3	6.7	–	–	–	–	–	5.2	1.7	10.8	3.2	18.5	–
	2006	6.7	2.2	–	–	–	21.6	5.8	–	8.7	3.1	2.3	1.8	–	–	11.9	2.9	–	–
Music	2003	–	–	–	4.3	2.0	0.0	3.6	–	–	–	–	–	–	–	4.5	6.2	8.4	–
	2004	1.5	2.7	–	–	–	0.0	3.9	–	2.9	3.5	0.1	7.0	9.3	2.7	4.0	6.0	–	1.4
	2005	–	–	–	–	–	0.3	3.2	–	–	–	–	–	5.2	1.6	4.7	4.9	8.4	–
	2006	1.3	3.7	–	–	–	0.4	3.6	–	2.2	1.6	0.1	1.0	–	–	3.9	4.4	–	–
Sport	2003	–	–	–	18.4	2.6	5.0	7.1	–	–	–	–	–	–	–	9.3	5.3	4.3	–
	2004	5.7	16.0	–	–	–	6.0	9.4	–	4.8	10.4	6.3	14.5	8.4	5.5	12.0	9.0	–	9.6
	2005	–	–	–	–	–	5.1	10.7	–	–	–	–	–	5.4	2.3	9.3	5.7	5.9	–
	2006	1.6	13.0	–	–	–	6.4	11.3	–	10.3	14.2	8.2	15.2	–	–	11.6	8.6	–	–
News	2003	–	–	–	11.1	23.5	11.0	24.3	–	–	–	–	–	–	–	22.0	12.3	5.8	–
	2004	29.9	2.3	–	–	–	11.0	27.4	–	15.4	0.0	11.2	6.1	9.9	5.2	17.6	8.8	–	6.1
	2005	–	–	–	–	–	9.5	31.5	–	–	–	–	–	10.8	6.4	16.2	8.2	5.6	–
	2006	29.7	1.1	–	–	–	13.3	27.5	–	13.5	0.4	34.5 (3)	11.6 (3)	–	–	11.2	7.7	–	–
Information	2003	–	–	–	4.1	50.5	14.0	30.4	–	–	–	–	–	–	–	16.3	32.6	20.6	–
	2004	4.0	8.9	–	–	–	15.0	28.2	–	22.8	19.6	3.5	0.9	35.0	38.6	16.2	30.1	–	14.9
	2005	–	–	–	–	–	13.2	27.2	–	–	–	–	–	32.4	40.2	19.3	29.9	14.8	–
	2006	4.9	10.5	–	–	–	13.4	28.6	–	28.5	15.7	–	–	–	–	25.5	32.1	–	–

REGION		Mediterranean Countries								Benelux				Scand. States			Baltic States		
		ES	ES	PT	GR	GR	IT	NL	LU	BE / VL	BE / VL	BE / WA	BE / WA	DK	DK	SE	EE	LT	LV
Genres In % (based on hours)		La Primera (TVE)	La 2 (TVE)		ERT1	NET (ERT TV)	RAI 1/2/3	NED 1/2/3		Eén (VRT)	Canvas/Ketnet (VRT)	La Une (RTBF)	La Deux (RTBF)	DR1	DR2	SVT	ETV	LRT	LTV1
Arts/ Humanities/ Sciences	2003	–	–	–	1.2	–	16.0	–	–	–	–	–	–	–	–	13.5	6.6	5.7	–
	2004	14.8	16.7	–	–	2.6	16.0	–	–	6.1	6.7	2.6	6.7	4.6	11.6	12.5	6.4	–	5.6
	2005	–	–	–	–	–	14.6	–	–	–	–	–	–	–	–	12.6	8.7	3.3	–
	2006	19.2	17.9	–	–	–	15.6	–	–	7.7	5.4	–	–	3.2	13.8	10.3	8.4	–	–
Religion	2003	–	–	–	–	–	1.0	–	–	–	–	–	–	–	–	1.7	–	1.2	–
	2004	0.0	1.9	–	–	–	0.0	–	–	1.0	0.1	0.0	0.6	0.6	1.6	1.7	–	–	1.3
	2005	–	–	–	–	–	0.6	–	–	–	–	–	–	–	–	1.4	–	1.4	–
	2006	0.0	2.0	–	–	–	0.3	–	–	1.0	0.1	–	0.9	0.9	1.4	0.9	–	–	–
Education	2003	–	–	–	0.8	–	0.0	–	–	–	–	–	–	–	–	–	0.9	0.5	–
	2004	0.0	3.9	–	–	2.1	0.0	–	–	–	–	18.1	26.3	2.3	3.0	–	0.8	–	3.6
	2005	–	–	–	–	–	2.0	–	–	–	–	–	–	–	–	–	1.6	0.0	–
	2006	0.0	4.3	–	–	–	1.9	–	–	–	–	12.6 (4)	33.4 (4)	2.5	4.1	–	0.7	–	–
Advertising	2003	–	–	–	–	–	3.0	7.8	–	–	–	–	–	–	–	–	0.0	2.0	–
	2004	14.2	11.5	–	–	–	3.0	7.3	–	–	–	7.8	2.6	–	–	–	0.0	–	–
	2005	–	–	–	–	–	4.0	6.3	–	–	–	–	–	–	–	–	0.0	1.4	–
	2006	14.8	12.7	–	–	–	4.0	6.2	–	–	–	7.0	4.3	–	–	–	0.0	–	–
Others (2)	2003	–	–	–	1.1	–	5.0	0.2	–	–	–	–	–	–	–	2.4	4.7	28.8	–
	2004	5.7	15.4	–	–	0.0	4.0	0.1	–	0.0	1.1	6.9	4.4	3.8	4.2	2.8	4.4	–	5.1
	2005	–	–	–	–	–	8.3	–	–	–	–	–	–	–	–	1.5	4.5	16.4	–
	2006	5.7	4.6	–	–	–	4.1	–	–	1.0	0.9	5.7	3.7	3.5	2.3	0.6	3.7	–	–
Total	2003	–	–	–	100	–	100	100	–	–	–	–	–	–	–	100	100	100	–
	2004	100	100	–	–	100	100	100	–	100	100	100	100	100	100	100	100	–	100
	2005	–	–	–	–	–	100	100	–	–	–	–	–	–	–	100	100	100	–
	2006	100	100	–	–	–	100	100	–	100	100	100	100	100	100	100	100	–	–

1. SSR–SRG and SVT figures refer to TV only; 2. Presentation/Promotion/Home shopping; 3. Including Information in 2006; 4. Including Arts/Humanities/Sciences in 2006.

discussion on content analysis and methodology. Interested readers can find examples from many countries where this topic is debated.

Here, only two examples will illustrate the need for caution when using condensed categories of content. For example, as illustrated above, the origin of production can be an important aspect of programming (is it a foreign production or a domestic one?); scheduling is another important aspect (prime time or not? weekdays or weekends? first time broadcast or re-run?), as are target audience groups. Public service broadcasters have obligations to serve their audiences in different ways.

One example is the yearly output study published by the Swedish Broadcasting Commission (SBC) of the main TV channels in the country. The news category consists of ten different sub-categories, the genre information is divided in 45 sub-categories, fiction has 40, and there is a category used called mixed/infotainment with 12 sub-categories. These yearly studies have established differences between the public and commercial channels in profiles, orientation and variety of schedules.[2] Another longitudinal project is carried out in Germany and it is based on the content profiles and orientations of the biggest TV channels. Over the years, these detailed analyses have reported differences between public service broadcasters and the main private channels in, for example, their news and current affairs, but also in other categories. The public channels concentrate on politics and current affairs, the latter concentrate on human interests and 'softer' news (see, for example, Krüger and Zaph-Schramm 2009, 2008).

Europe's fragmentation in regard to languages and cultures may be considered an asset, but it does have adverse consequences for the marketing potential of European audio-visual products. The smaller linguistic and cultural communities in particular find it difficult to generate enough home-made production, let alone show it outside their own borders. The Italian- (TSI 1) and French-language (TSR 1) channels in Switzerland, for example, broadcast 25.9 per cent and 27.9 per cent European originated fiction respectively, of which only 10.2 per cent and 3.9 per cent is national, as can be seen in Table 3. The imposition of a quota system is not always appreciated and it is, at any rate, no solution to the financial problems. Programmes from other European countries are often felt as 'alien', as non-European products. European countries differ with respect to the broadcasting of foreign television productions (i.e. fiction and films) originating from Europe and outside Europe. Commercial channels clearly broadcast more non-European productions than public service channels do, the differences being highest in Germany, France, the Netherlands and Sweden. An explanation often voiced by private channels broadcasting more foreign (often US) productions is that the latter are much less expensive than producing programmes themselves, and are therefore more cost-effective (Steemers 2004). Remarkably, the United Kingdom shows an opposite picture. With an average of 53.3 per cent for ITV 1 and 2 against 42.3 per cent for BBC 1 and 2, the commercial broadcaster takes the lead in broadcasting European fiction (including national) in the United Kingdom. Despite this unusual situation, the BBC maintains its strong position in transmitting national fiction in Europe (a total of 38 per cent on BBC 1 and 2 in 2005). The German PSB leads with an average of 50 per cent national fiction.

Table 3: Origin of Fiction Broadcast by Main Players According to Size and Region in 2007.

ORIGIN OF FICTION BROADCAST BY TV CHANNELS IN EUROPE 2007 COUNTRIES	Includes TV films, Series & Soaps, TV Animation, Feature films, Short films Total (in hours broadcast)						EUR origin (in % based on hours)			Non-EUR Origin (in % based on hours)		
	% Fiction (2006)	Total	Total EUR	Total non-EUR	% EUR incl. nat.	% non EUR + not id.	National	Other EUR	EUR & mixed co-prod.	US	Other non-EUR + not id.	Non-EUR co-prod
SIZE												
Large Countries												
United Kingdom												
BBC1*	23.7	2213	1206	1007	54.5	45.5	85.8	1.4	12.7	67.8	25.9	6.4
BBC2	13.4	2157	1139	1018	52.8	47.2	75.4	2.3	22.1	81.5	10.1	8.3
ITV1 Carlton Central**	19.4	1892	1424	468	75.3	24.7	80.8	0.5	18.8	91.2	3.8	4.9
ITV2	–	2904	1689	1215	58.1	41.9	82.2	0.0	17.8	91.2	1.2	7.6
Channel 4	32.4	3272	1235	2037	37.8	62.2	55.1	1.1	43.8	89.9	6.5	3.5
Germany												
ARD*	34.6	3522	2784	739	79.0	21.0	74.3	10.9	14.8	91.6	5.8	2.4
ZDF	28.6	2875	2201	675	76.5	23.5	57.9	14.7	27.1	80.4	11.1	8.3
RTL**	24.8	2839	1576	1263	55.5	44.5	84.0	0.2	15.9	72.9	1.9	25.3
RTL2		5135	600	4535	11.7	88.3	6.0	29.0	65.0	68.9	17.6	13.5
Sat.1	27.7	2369	1205	1165	50.8	49.2	72.8	2.4	24.9	90.5	2.9	6.6
Pro 7	32.1	3540	744	2796	21.0	79.0	39.2	9.5	51.2	92.1	2.0	5.8
France												
FR2*	24.1	1857	1251	606	67.4	32.6	31.4	23.3	45.2	96.7	2.0	1.0
FR3	32.9	2028	1515	513	74.7	25.3	53.5	32.4	14.1	95.7	3.5	0.9
TF1**	41.9	3541	1533	2008	43.3	56.7	34.2	46.6	19.2	83.6	3.1	13.3
M6	33.7	3245	1030	2215	31.7	68.3	27.1	53.7	19.3	89.2	2.0	8.8

Small Countries

Switzerland

SF 1*(German-speaking)	39.4	2030	1679	351	82.7	17.3	7.9	75.5	16.7	92.3	5.1	2.8
TSI 1 (Italian-speaking)	20.9	3503	1159	2344	33.1	66.9	6.6	38.7	54.9	77.6	11.9	10.5
TSR 1 (French-speaking)	27.0	4029	1396	2633	34.7	65.3	3.7	66.0	30.3	87.8	4.3	7.9

REGION

Mediterranean Countries

Italy

RAIUno*	24.5	2154	1486	668	69.0	31.0	65.1	14.1	20.8	74.0	20.1	6.0
RAIDue	15.6	2448	835	1613	34.1	65.9	54.3	25.9	19.9	83.0	9.9	7.3
Canale5**	–	3728	1849	1879	49.6	50.4	56.2	26.3	17.4	94.1	1.8	4.2
Italia 1	–	6061	1140	4921	18.8	81.2	40.0	9.5	50.5	71.2	16.5	12.3

Benelux

Belgium (Flanders)

Een*	27.0	1699	1309	389	77.1	22.9	33.9	60.9	5.4	49.4	30.6	20.1
Canvas	58.6	629	522	106	83.1	16.9	3.4	67.6	29.3	76.4	14.2	10.4
Ketnet	–	2455	1650	805	67.2	32.8	23.2	45.3	31.5	60.2	39.5	0.4
VTM**	–	4145	2067	2078	49.9	50.1	34.3	55.4	10.3	86.2	7.2	6.6
Kanaal 2	–	3091	223	2868	7.2	92.8	15.2	25.1	60.5	73.9	14.3	11.8
VT4	–	2689	301	2388	11.2	88.8	0.7	28.6	70.8	83.3	4.0	12.7

Netherlands

NOS1*	6.9	946	827	119	87.4	12.6	36.6	59.3	4.6	99.2	0.8	0.0
NOS2	5.9	926	786	140	84.9	15.1	23.0	57.5	19.7	67.1	27.1	6.4
NOS3	37.8	3900	3341	559	85.7	14.3	23.2	54.4	22.3	61.7	35.6	2.5
RTL 4**	–	2911	1288	1623	44.2	55.8	45.7	49.5	4.8	87.0	1.2	11.9
SBS 6	–	1804	209	1595	11.6	88.4	11.0	24.4	65.1	82.8	11.7	5.5

ORIGIN OF FICTION BROADCAST BY TV CHANNELS IN EUROPE 2007

Includes TV films, Series & Soaps, TV Animation, Feature films, Short films

COUNTRIES	% Fiction (2006)	Total (in hours broadcast)					EUR origin (in % based on hours)			Non-EUR Origin (in % based on hours)		
SIZE		Total	Total EUR	Total non-EUR	% EUR incl. nat.	% non EUR +not id.	National	Other EUR	EUR & mixed co-prod.	US	Other non-EUR + not id.	Non-EUR co-prod
Scandinavian States												
Denmark												
DR1*	31.0	2825	1718	1107	60.8	39.2	20.7	60.8	18.6	75.9	14.3	9.8
DR2	26.3	1256	623	633	49.6	50.4	6.6	75.9	17.5	91.6	6.8	1.7
TV2**	43.2	4413	1372	3041	31.1	68.9	13.6	61.4	25.1	93.4	5.5	1.2
TV3	–	6075	532	5543	8.8	91.2	22.4	36.7	41.4	94.9	1.2	3.9
Sweden												
SVT 1*	28.2	2519	1925	594	76.4	23.6	33.4	54.1	12.6	76.1	22.2	1.7
SVT 2	18.3	989	433	556	43.8	56.2	12.9	67.4	19.9	85.1	12.6	2.3
TV3 Sweden**	–	5574	374	5200	6.7	93.3	2.9	39.0	58.6	90.1	3.9	6.0
TV4 Sweden	–	3693	1291	2402	35.0	65.0	22.0	61.5	16.7	91.7	7.4	0.9

* Main public broadcaster
** Main private broadcaster
Sources: European Audiovisual Observatory (2008a, 2008b).

These findings tend to underline the public service broadcaster's distinctiveness when it comes to its central carrier's role of home-grown and European fiction production. This is illustrated by the fact that the supply of fiction on most public channels is more or less evenly distributed between European fiction (including national) and fiction from outside Europe. In general, however, European fiction outnumbers non-European output. On commercial channels, the opposite is true: here fiction mainly originates from outside Europe, a clear preference going to US productions. Public broadcasters air on average between 1000 and 3000 hours of non-European fiction per year. The Dutch, Flemish, Danish and Swedish public channels air notably less foreign fiction than their commercial counterparts. In Germany, Italy, Denmark and Sweden, one commercial channel airs over 4000 hours of non-European fiction per year. In the United Kingdom, we noted that commercial channels have much less foreign fiction on offer.

Broadcasters find themselves under heavy pressure to gear their programming to market-oriented factors such as price, and viewing and listening figures. Furthermore, the sensitivity to outside cultural influences and to financial pressures is a problem that not only smaller cultural communities, but also the bigger European markets are faced with.

Performance: Implications for Media Use and Public Opinion Making?

A sound relationship with the public and civil society has become of vital importance, since a relation with politics has proven to have its drawbacks. Popular support can also compensate for an all too close relationship with, or dependence on, politics. A key problem is the gradually diminishing reach of public service broadcasters among 'problematic groups' such as younger generations, migrants and the lower educated. Collins et al. (2001: 8) introduce the term 'audience universality' which is achieved 'by serving all, the poor as well as the rich, with a range of programmes, including those which may be unprofitable'.

As illustrated in Table 3, the position of the public service broadcasters on the viewer market greatly differs among countries. In the large countries (except for France) the public broadcasters stand ground against commercial competitors. The same situation holds for small countries like Austria, the Benelux (except for the French community of Belgium) and the Nordic countries. Public broadcasters in these countries continue to be major players on the broadcasting market with market shares ranging from 30 per cent up to 45 per cent. However, public broadcasters from the Mediterranean basin and the Baltic States have to leave the biggest chunk of the market to their private counterparts, ending up with a mere 15 to 35 per cent.

In many European countries which went through a period of intense deregulation, a tendency can be observed to conclude clearly defined performance agreements between the public broadcaster and the government, particularly with regard to mission and programme supply, as well as funding. Several European countries are evolving towards a more integrated approach to media policy, as is shown in successive management contracts

Table 4: Market Share of Main Players According to Size and Region.

COUNTRIES	Daily Share							Prime Time (18:00–24:00)****						
SIZE	2001	2002	2003	2004	2005	2006	2007	2001	2002	2003	2004	2005	2006	2007
Large Countries														
United Kingdom														
BBC1*	26.9	11.42	25.6	24.7	23.3	22.8	22.0	28.1	28.5	27.6	26.8	25.2	24.2	23.9
BBC2	11.1	11.4	11.0	10.0	9.4	8.8	8.5	9.4	10.4	9.8	9.1	8.9	9.0	9.2
ITV1**	26.7	24.1	23.7	22.8	21.5	19.7	19.2	34.8	30.1	30.2	29.3	27.8	26.8	24.5
ITV2	–	–	–	1.1	1.5	1.6	1.7	–	–	–	0.9	1.3	1.3	1.4
C4	10.0	10.0	9.6	9.6	9.6	9.6	8.4	8.0	9.1	9.1	8.8	9.1	8.6	8.4
Germany														
ARD1*	13.9	14.3	14.0	13.9	13.5	14.2	14.6	14.4	15.2	15.5	15.9	15.4	15.5	13.4
ARDIII	13.2	13.4	13.5	13.7	13.6	13.5	15.7	15.2	15.6	15.6	15.8	15.7	15.7	13.5
ZDF	13.2	13.9	13.2	13.6	13.5	13.6	14.3	14.8	15.2	15.1	15.8	15.2	15.2	12.9
RTL1**	14.7	14.6	14.9	13.8	13.2	12.8	12.9	16.2	15.8	15.0	13.5	12.9	12.7	12.4
RTL2	4.0	3.8	4.7	4.9	4.2	3.8	3.5	3.6	3.7	4.3	4.8	4.0	3.5	3.9
SAT1	10.1	9.9	10.2	10.3	10.9	9.8	8.2	10.3	9.7	9.7	8.9	9.8	8.9	9.6
PRO7	8.0	7.0	7.1	7.0	6.7	6.6	6.2	7.3	6.9	6.9	6.7	6.3	6.3	6.5
France														
FR2*	21.1	20.8	20.5	20.5	19.8	19.2	18.1	20.5	21.2	20.7	21.0	20.0	19.6	18.1
FR3	17.1	16.4	16.1	15.2	14.7	14.7	14.1	18.2	16.8	16.7	16.1	16.7	16.8	16.0
TF1**	32.7	32.7	31.5	31.8	32.4	31.6	30.7	34.0	33.7	33.4	33.4	33.3	33.1	32.6
M6	13.5	13.2	12.6	12.5	12.6	3.4	3.4	14.0	13.8	13.1	12.9	12.7	4.4	4.6

*TV Audience Market Share In %, 4 years + ****

Poland														
TVP1*	24.4	25.4	25.6	24.9	24.6	24.0	23.2	24.5	25.5	26.3	24.8	25.0	25.1	23.6
TVP2	19.7	20.0	20.5	20.5	21.7	20.1	18.0	18.1	18.6	20.3	21.4	21.7	19.9	18.3
Polsat**	22.6	18.3	16.5	16.2	16.7	16.1	16.8	24.3	20.8	17.8	18.0	18.0	17.0	18.3
TV Wisla/TVN	13.9	13.9	14.0	14.7	15.0	16.7	16.5	17.4	16.2	17.1	17.3	17.7	20.9	20.6
Russia														
Perviy Kanal (ex-ORT)*	25.7	27.2	24.3	25.7	23.0	20.3	20.2	27.7	29.4	27.6	29.4	23.9	20.7	22.4
Rossiya (ex-RTR) (1)	17.0	18.4	18.7	20.0	22.5	18.6	16.3	16.7	20.5	20.1	21.4	25.2	20.3	17.6
MTV**	17.5	13.3	12.3	11.9	11.2	12.3	13.3	19.9	13.5	12.9	12.1	11.5	12.5	14.9
CTC (STS)	5.9	6.2	8.7	9.8	10.3	9.8	8.5	5.6	6.1	8.7	9.7	10.4	11.3	8.7
Small Countries														
Switzerland (German-speaking)														
SF1*	26.5	26.7	26.0	24.8	23.8	23.7	24.1	35.1	35.4	34.9	33.6	32.9	32.2	32.6
SF2	6.4	8.1	8.0	8.9	8.5	9.7	8.2	6.1	8.4	8.1	9.5	8.6	9.6	7.5
ARD	5.5	5.8	5.7	5.7	5.8	6.0	5.7	5.6	5.9	5.8	6.0	6.1	6.1	6.1
RTL**	7.7	7.9	8.0	7.9	7.4	7.3	7.0	7.0	7.1	7.0	6.7	6.3	6.3	6.4
SAT1	5.1	6.4	5.7	6.2	6.7	6.4	6.0	4.4	4.6	4.3	4.3	4.7	4.6	4.1
Switzerland (Italian-speaking)														
TSI*	26.1	24.5	27.4	27.1	26.2	23.7	24.3	32.4	31.4	34.4	33.8	33.0	31.1	31.6
TSI2	5.4	5.1	5.6	7.0	6.5	7.6	6.2	5.4	5.2	5.5	7.1	6.4	8.2	6.0
RAI1	11.7	12.0	10.1	10.0	10.0	10.1	10.9	11.2	10.6	9.2	9.4	8.8	8.8	9.8
Canale 5**	14.7	13.8	13.1	12.9	11.9	11.6	10.9	14.2	13.8	12.9	12.2	11.5	10.2	10.1
Italia1	7.4	8.2	7.9	7.7	7.9	8.0	8.0	6.9	7.5	7.0	6.4	7.6	8.1	7.6
Switzerland (French-speaking)														
TSR1*	26.0	25.3	25.4	24.6	25.4	24.5	24.3	31.5	30.8	31.2	30.6	31.6	31.1	30.2
TSR2	5.1	5.0	5.2	5.7	6.2	7.9	6.4	4.7	5.3	5.3	6.2	6.5	8.2	6.0
FR2	9.3	9.5	9.5	9.8	9.4	8.9	8.8	7.7	8.1	7.8	8.1	8.0	7.7	7.6
TF1**	15.9	16.8	16.7	16.5	16.9	16.6	15.1	15.6	16.2	16.6	15.9	16.0	15.6	15.2
M6	8.8	9.2	9.0	9.1	8.9	9.2	9.1	9.1	9.4	9.1	9.0	8.6	9.0	9.2

TV Audience Market Share
In %, 4 years + ***

COUNTRIES	Daily Share							Prime Time (18:00–24:00)****						
REGION	2001	2002	2003	2004	2005	2006	2007	2001	2002	2003	2004	2005	2006	2007
Mediterranean Countries														
Spain														
TVE-1*	24.8	24.7	23.4	21.4	19.6	18.3	17.2	24.8	26.5	24.1	21.8	19.9	18.3	16.8
TVE-2/La 2	7.8	7.7	7.2	6.8	5.8	4.8	4.6	7.7	7.4	6.5	5.8	4.9	4.3	4.1
Tele 5**	21.0	20.2	21.4	22.1	22.3	21.2	20.3	20.6	20.2	21.9	22.5	22.9	21.4	20.9
Antenna 3	20.4	20.2	19.5	20.8	21.3	19.4	17.4	20.1	19.0	18.8	21.1	21.9	19.1	16.8
Autonomic TV Channels	17.0	17.8	18.2	17.6	17.5	15.4	14.7	18.0	17.8	18.4	17.7	17.5	15.7	15.3
Portugal														
RTP1*	20.1	21.1	23.8	24.7	23.6	24.5	25.2	18.1	19.7	22.4	23.6	22.3	22.4	24.4
RTP2	5.6	5.3	5.0	4.4	5.0	5.4	5.2	4.3	5.0	5.2	4.2	4.5	4.9	4.8
SIC**	34.0	31.5	30.3	29.3	27.2	26.2	25.1	31.8	29.5	29.8	29.0	27.9	26.7	24.9
TVI	31.9	31.4	28.5	28.9	30.0	30.0	29.0	40.1	37.8	33.4	33.6	34.1	34.7	33.0
Greece														
ET1*	5.5	5.9	5.5	5.2	4.2	4.0	3.8	5.9	5.8	6.5	6.4	4.1	3.8	3.9
NET	4.0	5.0	6.9	8.8	9.1	10.1	9.6	4.3	4.4	5.4	10.2	10.4	10.4	9.7
Antenna 1**	22.9	21.8	22.5	20.8	19.4	18.0	16.5	23.3	20.6	22.5	22.4	20.8	18.4	15.0
Mega Channel	21.3	20.1	17.3	16.9	18.5	18.8	18.5	22.8	25.1	20.5	19.3	20.5	22.8	22.5
Italy														
RAIU no*	23.6	23.1	23.0	23.0	22.9	23.0	22.3	23.6	23.1	23.0	25.7	23.9	24.2	23.3
RAID ue	13.5	12.1	11.7	12.2	11.3	11.3	10.4	13.5	12.1	11.7	11.1	10.6	10.5	10.3
Canale5**	24.1	23.8	23.9	22.5	21.8	21.0	20.7	22.5	24.1	23.8	22.2	22.5	22.0	21.6
Italia 1	10.9	12.2	12.4	11.6	11.5	11.1	11.2	10.9	12.2	12.4	11.2	11.5	10.5	10.7

Benelux

Belgium (Flanders)														
EEN*	25.0	26.4	27.9	28.2	27.0	28.7	30.1	28.0	29.5	31.3	31.8	30.8	32.2	33.5
CANV AS/ KETNET	8.5	9.6	10.0	9.4	9.4	9.6	9.4	8.1	8.2	8.9	8.4	8.1	7.8	7.9
VTM**	27.2	25.4	23.6	22.9	22.0	21.3	20.7	31.8	30.2	28.1	27.7	27.8	27.3	26.6
KANAAL 2	7.3	6.4	6.2	5.2	5.6	6.7	5.9	8.1	7.0	6.7	5.9	6.2	7.3	6.1
VT4	6.4	6.3	6.8	6.7	6.4	7.0	6.4	6.2	6.2	6.8	7.3	7.3	7.6	7.4
Belgium (Wallonia)														
LA1*	17.2	16.3	15.3	15.3	14.0	14.7	15.1	20.8	19.5	18.5	17.5	16.2	16.7	16.8
LA2	3.6	3.4	3.4	3.7	3.0	4.9	4.5	2.4	2.2	2.3	3.6	2.6	4.8	4.7
FR2	9.7	9.7	9.8	8.9	8.5	9.2	9.6	7.3	7.8	7.4	13.0	6.4	6.7	6.7
RTL-TVi**	18.9	18.1	17.9	17.9	17.9	19.1	19.3	26.9	24.9	24.9	24.6	25.6	27.3	27.1
ClubRTL	5.5	5.2	5.4	5.8	5.1	5.1	4.8	6.1	6.5	6.2	6.7	6.1	6.6	6.8
TF1	16.6	16.6	16.3	15.7	16.4	17.5	17.1	13.4	13.5	13.6	13.0	12.4	13.1	12.9
Netherlands														
Ned-1*	11.9	11.1	11.2	11.1	11.9	13.1	17.8	13.4	12.4	12.2	12.1	12.6	14.0	19.0
Ned-2	16.3	17.2	15.7	18.4	15.1	13.5	6.9	16.6	17.0	16.5	19.4	15.9	13.2	6.8
Ned-3	7.8	7.6	7.5	6.6	6.3	6.2	6.6	8.4	8.2	7.9	7.0	6.5	6.7	7.3
RTL 4	15.1	15.8	16.4	15.4	14.7	13.6	12.9	16.2	17.1	17.7	16.6	16.0	14.7	14.1
SBS 6	10.2	9.3	9.6	9.6	9.8	9.6	10.0	10.8	10.5	11.5	11.4	11.8	11.5	11.8
Luxembourg														
RTL Tele Lëtzebuerg**	15.7	(3) 15.5	(3) 12.7	(3) 14.4	14.3	13.1	12.6	52.9	54.2	(3) 50.8	(3) 52.9	(3) 53.5	44.5	42.0
TF1	9.4	9.4	8.8	8.6	9.2	8.7	11.3	5.7	5.7	5.9	6.3	6.6	8.4	9.4
RTL	11.2	11.2	11.3	9.4	8.9	6.7	6.2	6.5	7.0	7.0	4.9	4.8	4.0	6.3

Baltic States

Estonia														
Eesti Televisioon*	17.1	18.0	16.7	18.0	17.1	17.3	16.4	23.8	22.9	22.0	22.3	19.8	18.1	17.1
TV3**	17.5	21.1	24.4	23.6	22.2	20.0	18.9	14.4	15.3	16.4	20.8	24.0	20.3	18.8
Kanal2	14.1	16.5	20.0	19.6	19.7	21.9	22.1	11.2	10.9	13.8	17.2	22.1	26.0	26.9

TV Audience Market Share
In %, 4 years + ***

COUNTRIES	Daily Share							Prime Time (18:00–24:00)****						
	2001	2002	2003	2004	2005	2006	2007	2001	2002	2003	2004	2005	2006	2007
Lithuania														
LTV1*	9.1	12.2	11.8	12.5	13.0	14.8	13.4	12.6	14.8	13.6	13.7	14.0	15.3	13.4
LTV2	–	–	–	0.6	0.6	0.9	0.9	–	–	–	0.6	0.7	1.1	1.0
Tele-3/TV3**	25.6	23.7	25.2	27.5	25.7	24.5	26.6	27.7	25.7	26.7	28.2	26.4	26.1	27.5
LNK	24.1	15.4	28.3	26.2	24.8	23.4	22.0	25.5	27.1	31.2	28.3	28.6	27.6	27.9
Latvia														
LTV1*	14.5	13.3	13.7	13.8	12.5	11.1	11.4	21.2	20.0	20.5	21.5	18.5	16.1	15.5
LTV7	–	–	–	4.9	4.9	5.3	3.9	–	–	–	4.8	4.2	5.0	3.6
LTN**	27.5	25.4	24.0	22.1	21.0	20.4	19.0	24.5	22.4	21.5	18.9	21.0	20.5	19.3
TV3	12.1	14.4	16.1	17.1	18.5	18.4	18.0	11.7	13.7	15.5	16.8	18.7	18.4	19.1
Scandinavian States														
Denmark														
DR1*	27.6	28.4	29.8	29.9	28.0	27.7	26.5	33.5	33.9	35.8	36.3	34.0	34.1	33.2
DR2	3.3	3.7	3.8	4.2	4.7	4.7	4.6	3.7	4.1	4.3	4.6	5.1	5.0	5.1
TV2**	34.7	35.2	35.2	35.0	35.8	34.2	33.4	37.2	37.6	37.2	36.5	37.6	35.5	34.9
TV3	8.6	7.2	6.6	6.0	5.4	5.0	5.3	7.1	6.5	5.9	5.3	4.7	4.5	4.8
Sweden														
SVT-1*	25.0	26.5	25.1	24.8	24.3	21.8	19.0	29.6	32.2	29.4	30.7	28.9	28.5	28.2
SVT-2	16.9	16.4	15.0	14.9	14.4	14.5	12.5	20.4	17.7	17.7	16.4	15.2	14.2	11.2
TV3**	11.3	9.9	10.4	10.1	10.4	9.4	9.3	8.9	8.7	9.2	9.2	10.0	8.8	8.7
TV4	27.5	25.3	25.1	24.4	23.2	22.2	21.2	26.5	24.2	24.8	23.5	22.8	23.3	23.6

*Main public broadcaster
**Main private broadcaster
***Germany, Switzerland, Denmark and Sweden: 3 years +; the Netherlands: 6 years +; Luxembourg: 12 years +; Lithuania: 15 years +
****Prime time varies from country to country
(1) Partially state-owned
(2) Kanal A: figures combined from 2003.
(3) Monday–Friday, September–June

between governments and the public broadcasters. Radio, television, digital applications and interactive services are increasingly looked upon as a coherent package. The next step could be that the cultural sector, education, information services and communication with the citizen – including those at regional and community levels – are included in writing public-service contracts. At any rate, it looks as if the issue of the legitimacy of public service media will increasingly crop up in the fundamental debate about public service. And despite globalization, this debate, which is primarily a social one, is still to a significant degree influenced by values and norms that differ from one region to another.

After all, the media user continues to seek specific contents, doing so consciously and purposefully. This quest can be illustrated with the example of the migrant population who are dissatisfied with the programmes supplied by the mainstream media and require additional culture-specific media input (d'Haenens 2003; Peeters and d'Haenens 2005). In view of these findings, notions such as 'pluriformity' and 'quality', which are both closely linked with the concept of PSB, must be re-examined and be effectively made operational. Whereas in the past the paternalist public broadcaster ('giving the people what they need') and the mercantilist commercial broadcaster ('giving the people what they want') used to be diametrically opposed, a newly defined concept of public service may help the individual media user to find a high-quality answer to a wide diversity of needs (see also Nikoltchev 2007). The notion of PSB could thus be widened to include the whole range of public media services that can – and may – be expected from the media in a converging and globalizing context.

It is a firm grasp of the obvious that the audience will use more platforms and channels next to the currently available open broadcast channels. This kind of viewing habits are currently already fully explored among young people who have apparently lost the routine of viewing the evening news on television as the 'main source' of information, but rather browse through the news items that are of interest to them on the Internet at the time and place of their preference. Specialists tend to converge in the conviction that these viewing patterns are not going to disappear with older age but are here to stay. The main challenges for the content- and policy-makers of public broadcasters is to decide upon what cross-media strategies and platforms need to be adopted and explored in order for them to remain full-service public communicators and not become redundant. They will need to find the tools to leave the old fashioned path of transmission and instead bring about communication in the public interest, with the public as a partner rather than a passive receiver.

Despite profound and rapid changes, the notion of quality, diversity and innovation, remain key concepts for public service. It is difficult to measure quality adequately and it varies according to whom the beholder is. It is the accumulated value of many aspects, all discussed by politicians, public broadcasters and academic researchers over the years: total output, schedules, genres, taste. In the United Kingdom, just like in other European countries, the 'dumbing down' debate concerning the lowering of the quality of the BBC TV services led to the policy of public value testing which promises to be more accountable to its distinctiveness.

Traditional and conventional measures of market shares, viewing and listening behaviour are of less and less value when determining the performance of public broadcasters. There are more and more linear viewing opportunities, blurring the distinction between original broadcasts and re-runs. On the Internet, there is an increasing number of programmes available on-demand, radio and TV, new digital services, as well as old programmes. It is becoming very complicated to put together a clear picture of, for example, the audiences of public service TV news. Formerly influential national evening newscasts lose many of their viewers. This does not necessarily mean that audiences abandon public service TV news. Instead, they adjust their use of a widely diversified output, as well as adapt to new opportunities offered to them through the Internet platform. The same reasoning goes for all broadcasters, of course.

Conclusion

Marc Raboy (2008: 364) reminds us of the primary purpose of a public broadcaster: 'To do what no other mainstream media institution can be expected to do, and that is: put aside the interests of the State and commercial investors and work to promote democratic practices.' As we are moving towards a post-broadcasting environment, 'it must do this by being at the cutting edge; it must make itself *indispensable* to anyone who wants to be informed, educated and entertained. And as we move towards a post-broadcasting environment, it must think of itself as a full-service public communicator' (Raboy 2008: 364).

The next decade will decide whether public service media as a broad, European concept has the power to reinvent itself. Some fear that the current European public broadcasting systems will converge towards a more limited, liberal model; others believe that the European diversity in media systems will continue to persist as strongly and as visibly in the digital age. Most important, however, is that the European concept of public service media – as a universal and comprehensive service, reflecting Europe's cultural diversity, and independent from both the state and the market – will still be able to be put into practice throughout Europe. As it is now becoming possible with consumer-generated content to speak up on all sorts of participatory media platforms (such as Flickr, YouTube or MySpace), the next question is: who is listening? Where can the public service media make a difference in order to create this inter-cultural, diverse public platform? The EU legal framework needs to be made future-proof. Only under those circumstances can European public service media continue to be prominent and successful actors boosting Europe's creative industries and optimally be a model for the rest of the world. Karol Jakubowicz's (2007: 44) inspiring words in this respect read as follows: 'There is no guarantee that PSM will survive in the twenty-first century. It is, however, certain that it will not survive unless it fundamentally transforms itself. Public service media need to mobilize public support for the institution and their programme of transformation [...] If they are successful in winning strong popular support and participation, and this can only be done by remaining relevant to the audience and partners among the general public, policy will take its cue from that. There is a chance of a new beginning. It must be seized.'

Acknowledgements

The authors would like to thank Barbara Thomass, Laura Berges, Tristan Mattelart, Josef Trappel, Jeremy Tunstall, Hans J. Kleinsteuber and, last but not least, Anna Van Cauwenberge for their valuable contributions to this chapter.

Notes

1. The BBC model for determining the public value of its services (Public Value Test) is an example of how to relate the services and activities of public broadcasters to what the private market offers. All significant proposals of BBC management (to alter its domestic public service) are subject to transparent and public scrutiny (including market impact) before the BBC Trust makes its decisions (see, for example, www.bbc.co.uk/bbctrust/our_work/pvt/ Accessed 29 May 2010). For a pure market position on the relation between public service and private sector services, see, for example, Europe's big publishers' call for radical change to public service obligations; this fits the pure 'monastery model' mentioned by Jakubowicz (2003) (www.epceurope.org/presscentre/), released 10 March, 2008. Accessed 31 March 2010.
2. See, for example, the Swedish Broadcasting Commission (Swedish TV output 2008, Report no. 25). Available (in Swedish only) at www.grn.se. Accessed 29 May, 2010.

References

Bardoel, J. and d'Haenens, L. (2008a), 'Public Service Broadcasting in Converging Media Modalities: Practices and Reflections from the Netherlands', *Convergence: The International Journal of Research into New Media Technologies*, 14: 3, pp. 351–60.
—— (2008b), 'Reinventing Public Service Broadcasting in Europe: Prospects, Promises and Problems', *Media, Culture & Society*, 30: 3, pp. 337–55.
Bardoel, J. and Lowe G. F. (2007), 'From Public Service Broadcasting to Public Service Media. The Core Challenge', in Lowe, G. F. and Bardoel, J. (eds) (2007), *From Public Service Broadcasting to Public Service Media*, Gotenburg: Nordicom. pp. 9–27.
Biltereyst, D. and Pauwels, C., 'Our Policies Keep on Reinventing the Past: An Overview of EU Policy-Making in the Audiovisual Domain', in d'Haenens, L. and Saeys, F. (eds) (2007), *Western Broadcasting at the Dawn of the 21st Century*, Berlin: Mouton de Gruyter, pp. 25–59.
Broeders, D., Huysmans, F. and Verhoeven, I. (2006), 'Setting the Scene: Ontwikkelingen in het medialandschap' (Setting the Scene: Developments in the Media Landscape), *Tijdschrift voor Communicatiewetenschap*, 34: 2, pp. 116–32.
CEC, (Commission of the European Communities) (2001), *Application of State Aid Rules to Public Service Broadcasting*, C 320/04, Brussels: CEC (Commission of the European Communities).
—— (2003), *Green Paper on Services of General Interest*, C 270, Brussels: CEC (Commission of the European Communities).
—— (1997), *Protocol on the System of Public Broadcasting in the Member States Attached to the Treaty of Amsterdam*, C 340/109, Brussels: CEC (Commission of the European Communities).

Collins, R., Finn, A., McFadyen, S. and Hoskins, C. (2001), 'Public Service Broadcasting Beyond 2000: Is there a Future for Public Service Broadcasting?', *Canadian Journal of Communication*, 26, pp. 3–15.

Coppens, T. (2005), *Opdracht volbracht? Een studie naar de taken van de VRT* (Mission Accomplished? Assessment of the Tasks of the Flemish Public Broadcaster), Brussels: Ministry of the Flemish Community and Ghent: University of Ghent.

Coppens, T. and Saeys, F. (2006), 'Enforcing Performance: New Approaches to Govern Public Service Broadcasting', *Media, Culture & Society*, 28: 2, pp. 261–84.

Dahlgren, P. (1995), *Television and the Public Sphere: Citizenship, Democracy and the Media*, London: Sage.

d'Haenens, L. (2003), 'ICT in Multicultural Society. The Netherlands: A Context for Sound Multiform Media Policy?', *Gazette: The International Journal for Communication Studies*, 65: 4/5, pp. 401–21.

d'Haenens, L. and Saeys, F. (eds) (2007), *Western Broadcast Models: Structure, Conduct and Performance*, Berlin and New York: Mouton de Gruyter.

Donders, K. and Pauwels, C. (2008), 'Does EU Policy Challenge the Digital Future of Public Service Broadcasting? An Analysis of the Commission's State Aid Approach to Digitization and the Public Service Remit of Public Broadcasting Organizations', *Convergence: The International Journal of Research into New Media Technologies*, 14: 3, pp. 277–94.

EBU Digital Strategy Group (2002), *Media with a Purpose: Public Service Broadcasting in the Digital Age*, Geneva: EBU.

—— (2007a), *Public Radio in Europe 2007*. Available at: http: //www.drace.org/index.php?ID= Pages&counter=7. Accessed 27 April 2009.

—— (2007b), *Radio in Europe: Trends and Audiences*. Available at:http://www.rte.ie/ebu/english/speaches/day1. Accessed 27 April 2009.

EIAA, (EIAA Mediascope Europe) (2008a), *Launch Presentation*. Available at: http: //www.eiaa.net/research/media-consumption.asp?lang=6. Accessed 27 April 2009.

—— (2008b), *Pan-European Executive Summary*. Available at: http: //www.eiaa.net/research/media-consumption.asp?lang=6. Accessed 27 April 2009.

European Audiovisual Observatory (2005a), *Yearbook 2005: Household Audiovisual Equipment – Transmission – Television Audience (volume 2)*, Strasbourg: European Audiovisual Observatory.

—— (2005b), *Yearbook 2005: Television Channels – Programme Production and Distribution (volume 5)*, Strasbourg: European Audiovisual Observatory.

—— (2008a), *Yearbook 2008: Television in 36 European States (volume 1)*, Strasbourg: European Audiovisual Observatory.

—— (2008b), *Yearbook 2008: Trends in European Television (volume 2)*, Strasbourg: European Audiovisual Observatory.

Hallin, D. C. and Mancini, P. (2004), *Comparing Media Systems: Three Models of Media and Politics*, Cambridge: Cambridge University Press.

Heiden H. (2009), Delivering Innovative Services, Presentation on the Multimedia Meets Radio Conference, Prague 5–6 April. Available at: http: //multimediameetsradio.ebu.ch/index.php. Accessed 27 April 2009.

Hirsch, M. and V. G. Petersen (2007) 'Enlargement of the Arena: European Media Policy', in Meier, W. A. and Trappel, J. (eds) (2007), *Power, Performance and Politics*, Baden-Baden: Nomos, pp. 21–39.

Hultén, O., 'Between Vanishing Concept and Future Model: Public Service Broadcasting in Europe on the Move', in Meier, W. A. and Trappel, J. (eds) (2007), *Power, Performance and Politics*, Baden-Baden: Nomos, pp. 197–221.

Hultén, O. and Brants, K., 'Public Service Broadcasting: Reactions to Competition', in Siune, K. and Truetzschler, W. (eds) (1992), *Dynamics of Media Politics: Broadcast and Electronic Media in Western Europe*, London: Sage, pp. 116–28.

Jakubowicz, K. (2007) 'Public Service Broadcasting in the 21st Century. What a Chance for a New Beginning?' in Lowe, G. F. and Bardoel, J. (eds) (2007), *From Public Service Broadcasting to Public Service Media*, Gotenburg: Nordicom. pp. 29–51.

—— (2003) 'Bringing Public Service to Account', in Lowe, G. F and Hujanen, T. (eds) (2003), *Broadcasting & Convergence: New Articulations of the Public Service Remit*, Göteborg: NORDICOM, pp. 147–67.

Krüger, U. and Zapf-Schramm, T. (2009), 'Politikthematisierung und Alltagskultivierung im Infoangebot', *Media Perspektiven*, 4, pp. 201–22.

—— (2008), 'Sparten, Sendungsformen und Inhalte im deutschen Fernsehangebot 2007', *Media Perspektiven*, 4, pp. 166–89.

Küng, L., Picard, R. G. and Towse, R. (eds) (2008), *The Internet and the Mass Media*, London: Sage.

Michalis, M. (2007), *Governing European Communications, From Unification to Coordination*, New York: Lexington Books.

Netherlands Scientific Council for Government Policy (WRR) (2005), *Focus op functies: Uitdagingen voor een toekomstbestendig mediabeleid* (Focus on Functions: Challenges for Future-Proof Media Policy), Amsterdam: Amsterdam University Press.

Nikoltchev, S. (ed.) (2006), *IRIS Special: Audiovisual Media Services without Frontiers. Implementing the Rules*, Strasbourg: European Audiovisual Observatory.

—— (2007), *IRIS Special: The Public Service Broadcasting Culture*, Strasbourg: European Audiovisual Observatory.

Pauwels, C. (2006), 'Europa als testlab voor de toekomstbestendige mediabeleidsverkenning van de WRR' (Europe as Test Lab for Future-Proof Media Policy Explorations by the Netherlands Scientific Council for Government Policy), *Tijdschrift voor Communicatiewetenschap*, 34: 2, pp. 189–99.

Peeters, A. and d'Haenens, L. (2005), 'Bridging or Bonding? Relationships between Integration and Media Use among Ethnic Minorities in the Netherlands', *Communications: The European Journal for Communication Research*, 30: 2, pp. 201–31.

Picard, R. G., 'Audience Fragmentation and Structural Limits on Media Innovation and Diversity', in van Cuilenburg, J. and van der Wurff, R. (eds) (2000), *Media and Open Societies: Cultural, Economic and Policy Foundations for Media Openness and Diversity in East and West*, Amsterdam: Het Spinhuis, pp. 180–91.

Raboy, M. (2008), 'Dreaming in Technicolor: The Future of PSB in a World beyond Broadcasting', *Convergence: The International Journal of Research into New Media Technologies*, 14: 3, pp. 361–65.

Spencer, B. (2009), *Thinking Multiplatform*, Presentation on the Multimedia Meets Radio Conference, Prague 5–6 April. Available at: http: //multimediameetsradio.ebu.ch/index.php. Accessed 27 April 2009.

Steemers, J., 'Public Service is not Dead Yet: Survival Strategies in the 21st Century', in Lowe, G. F and Hujanen, T. (eds) (2003), *Broadcasting & Convergence: New Articulations of the Public Service Remit*, Göteborg: NORDICOM, pp. 123–37.

—— (2004), *Selling Television: British Television in the Global Marketplace*, London: British Film Institute.

Thompson, M., 'Foreword', in Helm, D., Green, D., Oliver, M., Terrington, S., Graham, A., Robinson, B., Davies, G., Mayhew, J. and Bradley-Jones, L. (2005), *Can the Market Deliver? Funding Public Service Television in the Digital Age*, Eastleigh: John Libbey Publishing, pp. vii–x.

Torberg, H. (2009), *Thinking Multiplatform*, Presentation on the Multimedia Meets Radio Conference, Prague 5–6 April. Available at: http: //multimediameetsradio.ebu.ch/index.php. Accessed 27 April 2009.

van de Donk, W.B.H.J., Broeders, D.W.J. and Hoefnagel, F.J.P.M. (eds) (2005), *Trends in het medialandschap* (Trends in the Media Landscape), Amsterdam: Amsterdam University Press – WRR verkenningen (Netherlands Scientific Council for Government Policy Explorations).

Chapter 12

Changing Practices of Journalism

Auksė Balčytienė, Karin Raeymaeckers and Elena Vartanova

Those who consider democracy as a fundamental principle for society have to monitor carefully the status of journalism. As we trust our elected politicians to represent us and our core interests in policy-related issues, we also attribute journalists a core position within that process. Journalism provides the necessary information to citizens to form opinions and to take decisions. Journalism is therefore a key element in democratic societies since journalists have the moral and ethical duty to provide correct and relevant information, and to analyze factual information in context within a critical perspective. In that perspective, the media as representatives of the Fourth Estate, have the obligation to monitor public affairs and to make sure that political or business elites do not cross the borders of their power. In addition to these tasks and functions, as Peter Dahlgren succinctly adds, the democratic role of journalism should even go beyond the information provision and watchdog function: 'It must also touch us, inspire us and nourish our daily democratic horizons' (Dahlgren 2009: 146).

In recent years, the journalistic field was challenged by a number of critical developments, among which the ongoing diffusion of interactive technologies, digitization of messages and convergence of media formats are clearly some of the most crucial ones. According to new media proponents, interactive media applications clearly democratize representation by making it a more direct relationship: as citizens gain access to inexpensive communication technologies the gatekeeping monopoly once enjoyed by editors and broadcasters is waning (Gurevitz et al. 2009; Coleman 2005). The Internet has indeed shifted communication to a much more personalized level, and both media and politicians are forced to address more channels in order to compete for the attention of a more fragmented audience, as well as target their messages to more fragmented groups than ever before. Therefore, the new media applications could be called the Fifth Estate, since they possess several key distinctive and important characteristics such as the ability to support institutions and individuals to enhance their 'communicative power' with opportunities to network within and beyond various institutional arenas, and the provision of capabilities that enable the creation of networks of individuals which have a public, social benefit (e.g. through social networking websites) (Dutton 2008).

At the same time, however, although there are major changes in the consumption of news and information (Meijer 2006; Mindich 2004; Jenkins 2006), a large majority of the public in many European countries still counts on traditional and professional media for information on political, cultural, economic and societal issues. Indeed, the Internet may have admitted an impressive number of alternative information channels, and the public may have been attributed with more access than ever before to participate in the news production cycle, but traditional journalists in traditional news media still keep their role as main gatekeepers (Domingo et al. 2008).

Dynamics of Journalistic Professionalization: Who Are the Professional Journalists Then and Now?

Any observer of recent developments and challenges in the media sphere, who keeps a detached and critical perspective towards this ever faster cycle of future-forecasting on the impact of new technologies on journalistic professionalization, does not believe in simple or one-way answers. Indeed, some media scholars sketch a doom scenario and predict the death of core media, while others expect that new media distribution platforms will become the major players in contemporary societies. There are also opinions that journalism will become dependent on aggregated news sites that gather and recycle content, whereas some other scholars use the term 'user-generated content' (UGC) as a buzz word that might save the future of journalism, especially the future of local news. There is also the prediction that journalism will further enlarge with input from social and professional network sites. And these predictions, statements and suggestions are just a limited selection of arguments in the current debate on the real and fundamental challenges of digitization and their impact on journalism's professionalization.

In the context of ongoing debates about the real and fundamental challenges of digitization for media and journalism, a historical perspective on the development of the journalistic profession seems particularly relevant here.

Indeed, the first steps towards the professionalization of journalism can be noticed at the end of the nineteenth century, when journalists started to form their professional and formal associations. For instance, in 1886 in Belgium we note the foundation of the first union and professional organization for journalists. Similarly, in many countries around Europe, professional associations for journalists and writers were founded around the turn of the twentieth century (Terzis 2009). The International Federation of Journalists (IFJ) was founded in 1926. This organization today has more than 600,000 members from more than 100 different countries. The IFJ authored the first international code on journalism ethics that was formally approved at a special convention in Bordeaux as early as in the year 1954. In 1972, this code was enlarged with another influential international code of journalistic ethics, the statement on duties and obligations for professional journalists. These ethical codes, based on agreed statements of peers, were an impulse for the further professionalization and institutionalization of journalism in many countries around Europe where national institutions for self-regulation were founded to control the compliance with the regulation.

Generally, the academic research on the profile of professional journalists – their roles and functions, relationships with news sources, as well as news management routines adopted in particular news media – is rooted in the media sociological research tradition. The first academic studies were published in the 1950s and the focus of research was on gatekeeping processes (White 1950; Galtung and Ruge 1965). Other research on journalists and journalism zooms in on newsroom organization and news practices (Breed 1955; Rühl 1969; Tunstall 1971). The first profiling research on professional journalists was conducted in the United States: in 1971 three sociologists, John Johnstone, Edward Slawski and William Bowman, conducted the first large-scale survey with a representative sample of 1313 American professional journalists (Johnstone et al. 1976). The results show a rather homogeneous picture of the professional group. The average American journalist was male, young, white and was working in the newspaper industry. It could be noticed that the educational level was rather modest. Less than 30 per cent of journalists who participated in the survey had a formal schooling in journalism. Also, almost six out of ten journalists were younger than 40 years old, and eight out of ten were men. Despite some correcting trends for education and gender-specific characteristics this typology is quite stable. The follow-up research project by David Weaver and G. Cleveland Wilhoit in 1982, 1992 and 2002 (Weaver and Wilhoit 1986, 1996; Weaver et al. 2007) demonstrates this clearly.

Recently, a significant number of comparative studies were conducted with a goal to disclose the differences and similarities of journalists' characteristics from different countries. For example, David Weaver (1998) collected the results of national journalists' surveys in more than twenty countries and on different continents. He concludes that it is rather difficult to detect universal patterns in the opinions and ethical values of journalists. Comparative research on journalism profiles is hindered by the assumption that countries have homogeneous characteristics. As Stephen D. Reese (2001: 178) puts it, the internal regional differences in countries may implicitly intervene in cross-national comparisons. In addition, it would be interesting to start comparative research on other than 'nationality variables'. In other words, it might be interesting to focus on differences in the hierarchical position and career paths of journalists, medium specific elements, age, educational level, etc. And it will be most important to reduce bias and to construct international standardized survey instruments. The German researcher Thomas Hanitzsch (2007) is hoping for a 'World Journalism Survey' – a collective survey of journalists all over the world as a counter-programme of the 'World Values Survey' (conducted by Ronald Inglehart) – that is collecting data for more than 80 countries. Briefly, the main line of comparative journalism surveys conducted during the 1980s and 1990s can be summarized as follows: the typical journalist is male and highly educated; female journalists and journalists from an ethnic minority rooted background remain under-represented in the media; there is very limited consensus among journalists of different countries about professional values (as observed, only statements that focus on the importance of transmitting news as quickly as possible can aggregate consensual acceptance amongst journalists); large differences in attitudes on statements related to ethical aspects of journalism are rooted in cultural differences and journalistic development traditions between different countries (Weaver and Wilhoit 1986, 1996; Weaver et al. 2007). Interestingly enough, an identical result was obtained in a research study which aimed to investigate how innovations associated with the Internet were perceived by journalists in eleven European countries (Fortunati et al. 2009). The survey of responses, which came from 239 journalists working for 40 of the most-read print and online news outlets, shows that even in a setting of internationally converging professional practices and norms, online journalism culture is very strongly influenced by the national background, namely the economic and cultural conditions.

In conclusion, there is more stability than change in journalistic professionalization practices: although affected by external influences (diffusion of new technologies), journalism is strongly influenced by situational factors, such as traditions and values of national journalism culture. At the same time, there are some very important shifts to notice: the gender gap is getting less steep although gender differences still play an important role in the higher ranked professional journalist functions. Another very obvious observation is that journalists in many countries around Europe work in basically similar professional environments: they use similar equipment and new media technologies, and share certain ideas (e.g. informational function of journalism) in their occupational ideology.

The Impact of New Technologies on Newsroom Organization and Job Descriptions of Journalists

In the last twenty years, major shifts have taken place in European newsrooms. Digitization and convergence, especially, have changed the journalistic profession thoroughly. This has had an impact on newsroom organization but also on the job description of journalists. The package of journalistic professional tasks and skills has been transformed, and the traditional relationships between media owners and media professionals have also shifted (Franklin et al. 2006). Walters et al. (2006) conclude that those shifts result in the fact that more and more journalists are employed in a-typical professional circumstances. Although this can result into positive outcomes (extra availability of sources, more ample news coverage, larger reach), a majority of scholars refer to more negative aspects on workload (Franklin et al. 2008; Singer 2004; Dupagne and Garrison 2006; Meier 2007). In 2006, the International Labour Organization (ILO) warned for the increase of a-typical working conditions in media firms. In relation to this topic, they refer to the growing amount of freelancers, the shortening of labour contracts, the downward pressure on financial remuneration, the working hours that are difficult to combine with a regular family life and the limited chances for upward function mobility. A specialized research project among Flemish journalists (Teugels et al. 2009) and among Russian journalists (Verbitskaya 2005) demonstrates that the risk for burn-out pathology is more present among journalists than in workers from other professions. According to this research, journalists working with a freelance contract are especially vulnerable.

Research results on changing job descriptions for journalists focus on the growing demand for multi-skilled journalists. The trend for convergence implies that journalists have to work for more than one type of medium. The average journalist does not work exclusively anymore for a print medium; he/she also provides content for the online environment and – increasingly so – for an audio-visual format (photo and filmed material). This multi-skilled profile demands a lot of flexibility from journalists (Dupagne and Garrison 2006). Also, the technical job demands come to the forefront. For instance, journalists in an online newsroom spend a great deal of their attention to technical aspects related to the medium. In this respect, their job description goes beyond the traditional definition of news gathering. On the other hand, journalists working in an online environment have fewer opportunities to go outside of the newsroom to gather stories, and this implies that they have a larger focus on desk journalism.

The interactive logic of Internet media has also made a dramatic impact on journalists' professional identities. Instead of just being gatekeepers, online professional journalists must also become sense-makers; instead of being agenda-setters they must become interpreters of whatever is both credible and valuable (Singer 2006). In other words, professional journalists working online are now being asked to acquire new professional competences and, in addition to being good reporters and communicators, they must also become critics, interpreters and evaluators, as well as watchdogs of political and economic power (Balčytienė and Harro-Loit 2009).

As reported in different research studies, the urgency to adapt to cross-medium skills was first experienced by journalists working for local media. Local media were the first to ask for a combination of print journalism, online journalism and broadcast journalism, and they were often the first to integrate user-generated content. This puts a lot of innovative stress-related elements in the job description of local journalists. It is interesting to notice that survey results reveal that journalists working for that type of media have a younger average profile; many of them have started their careers in local and regional media (Deuze 2007).

In spite of certain drawbacks associated with new requests on professional performance, the Internet has indeed become a great asset to the work of journalists. It provides immediate access to an enormous amount of information which helps the news-gathering procedures and journalistic working routines. Especially in situations where deadlines are the major characteristic of the job, this is a positive shift. However, this new situation makes journalists experience an ever bigger workload due to the fact that newsroom management assumes that the news production process could be speeded up. The expanding possibilities with the Internet, mobile phones and other devices also eroded the dividing wall between the journalists' personal and working environment (Perrons 2003; Rintala and Suolanen 2005).

All these changes have dramatic effects on how journalists work and what online reporting strategies they apply in their everyday practices. As demonstrated, many of these strategies are focused on using other kinds of publicly available information (such as PR news, promotional writing, translations from other online information sources, etc.) rather than developing original journalism online (Lund 2002). In this context, a particular concern with the online production of news is the originality of production – to put it more accurately: the amount of real journalistic input provided by communications professionals.

The multiplicity of online media actors does not necessarily result to a great deal of news diversity: it appears that most mainstream online journalism simply offers new ways of consuming journalism of the same content, which is topically grouped with toolbars that allow quick linking.

One more line of analysis of academic research on professionalization shifts, focuses on the relationship between digitization and the career paths of media professionals. Different research studies report a growing number of employees in the audio-visual and multimedia industries, while at the same time many other professional journalists' job opportunities are affected negatively. Many traditional journalistic jobs in the media industries have changed into new jobs that are specifically tailored for young ICT-wise newcomers, most of whom prefer working in freelance jobs (Dupagne and Garrison 2006; Perrons 2003; Saltzis and Dickinson 2008).

Job opportunities within the journalistic field are now more and more linked to technical skills, and media firms have the luxury to pick and choose as there are more volunteers for a job in the newsrooms than there are jobs available (Hollifield et al. 2001; Alysen 2005). The recent financial crisis of 2008–09 and its shift into one of the major economical crises of the last decades has indeed worsened the emerging situation. Many media firms have reduced their newsroom staff referring to the breakdown of advertising revenues. Recent research, pre-crisis however, already shows that traditional criteria for the selection of journalistic staff (such as diploma, knowledge of foreign languages, writing and interviewing skills) are becoming less prominent in the final decision process. Next to the desirability for technical skills, the flexibility to adapt to rapidly changing working conditions, as well as memberships to different social and professional digital networks are becoming more prominent elements in the recruitment evaluation procedures for new newsroom staff members (Austin and Cokley 2006; Becker et al. 1993). These shifts in job selection variables are more evident in audio-visual media jobs than jobs in print-related media (Hollifield et al. 2001).

Constraints and Opportunities for Content Production

Journalists who work in multi-tasking job environments also have to establish more public-oriented attitudes. Hence, one of the new phenomena in journalism is the growing impact of user-generated content procedures.

As already mentioned, in the environment of pressing deadlines and shorter newsbeat procedures, journalists have adapted new routines that help them to manage the ever growing news flow. Some of these new routines are reflected in the sourcing practices. On the one hand, we observe that journalists prefer to give priority to authoritative sources (Ericson et al. 1989; Fishman 1980; Gans 1979). The type of information these sources provide is analyzed as more reliable, and therefore limits the amount of time that has to be spent checking and double-checking (Dimitrova and Strömbäck 2009; Hampton 2008). On the other hand, although this routine has proven to be useful, a negative trend is also observed. A growing number of political, institutional and economical actors provide ready-made press information and press releases that are processed in the media content often with limited – or even without any – journalistic mediation (Brennen 2009; O'Neill and O'Connor 2007). According to Balčytienė and Harro-Loit (2009), in this context, two content production strategies can be observed as emerging online: journalistic production as interpretation and translation. The mode of interpreting requires journalists to analyze, re-think and re-visit issues obtained from source information. Online journalists working as interpreters are changing journalistic discourse: they are checking and double-checking the information, finding missing angles in the story, conducting additional interviews, etc. The translating mode of online information production, in contrast, deals with the process of adaptation of journalistic text from one medium to fit the requirements of the other (online) medium. Translating does not require changing the discourse but the structure of the text through the addition of hypertext links, finding and indicating sub-topics in the text, adding multimedia elements and other kinds of online functionality.

In addition to relying on PR and other ready-made sources of news (such as news agency material), another time-saving procedure of reporting is the use of media content from other media groups what results in content mainstreaming and, to some extent, also in information redundancy (Deuze 2008; Erdal 2009). This copy and pasting type of journalism is more prevalent amongst online journalists (Cassidy 2008; Phillips et al. 2009). This is a result not only of their heavy workload and continuous deadlines, but also of the desk journalism that is a major defining characteristic in their job description (Boczkowski 2009; Machill and Beiler 2009).

As a paradox to these top-down and competing media sourcing practices, journalism is confronted with bottom-up initiatives. Due to the new digitization processes, the classical sections of 'Letters to the Editor' have now competition from online user-generated content. The traditional sources that dominate the public sphere have now broadened with the voices of the citizens themselves (Bivens 2008; Singer 2006; Dimitrova and Strömbäck 2009; Messner and DiStaso 2008). Journalists who gather local news have especially integrated those civic actors into their news production routines. This sub-group of journalists is also facing an excessive workload in newsrooms that are shrinking in terms of staff, and their job description is about all-round production while they cannot that easily adapt to a copy-paste journalism which has originated in content from competing media (Davies 2008).

For journalists, the preferred news sources are other media (Boczkowski 2009), news agencies (Machill and Beiler 2009) and press releases (Lewis et al. 2008). This preference in sourcing is induced by the growing importance of desk journalism instead of the traditional journalistic news gathering which is more time consuming (Raviola and Hartman 2009). The new information technologies offer a lot of immediate access to valuable information through search engines (Machill et al. 2008; Jha 2008; Phillips et al. 2009). Some scholars raise their voice to criticize the qualitative effect of these routines (Pavlik 2000; Machill and Beiler 2009). One should not be blind to the cost- and time-efficiency possibilities that are generated, but prudence is called for. It is not unthinkable that media owners will urge journalists to use this type of ready-made sources as a general rule. It is especially the journalists facing the hardest workloads who are driven into this pattern of hyper efficiency that directly leads towards poorer journalism diversity and quality (Bird 1999; Erdal 2009; Fengler and Russ-Mohl 2008). Online newsrooms journalists adapt particularly easily to this type of secondary sourcing, again due to the continuous deadlines and pressures they face. This is even more so because of the fact that online news floors are by definition more open for testing and experimenting with new technological formats and new information generating channels (Chung 2007).

The second major line that digitization has opened is the communication line between newsrooms and the public. Weblogs are well established and have proven to be a promising bridge between journalists and their public. Journalists use weblogs to restore, and keep, contact with their public (Bivens 2008; Domingo and Heinonen 2008; Robinson 2006). With the emerging popularity and applicability of new interactive technologies, a wide array of alternative online communication platforms have emerged offering all kinds of insights into global political matters and certain problem areas such as environmental issues, health safety, fraud and corruption, assuring security, fighting terrorism, etc. Some of these online applications of social character offer specialized information, while others are accessed by general audiences. An important and distinctive feature of these platforms is their global and transnational orientation, which is especially useful for journalists in accessing background material on important issues. Some research studies also confirm that reporting on European politics, for example, increases in the European media with the advent of a younger generation of professional journalists, who rely on a clearer and more active understanding of the European dimension involved in their daily trade (AIM Research Consortium 2007). Younger journalists are also the ones who use the Internet as a primary source for background information, useful sources and critical views – these journalists have new media skills and understand the European dimension; they also have a critical approach to issues communicated by officials, thus they rely on new opportunities for analytical and investigative reporting offered by new media.

Alternatively, weblogs also offer the public a possibility to enter the journalistic news process; the user-generated content can become a positive stimulus and challenge traditional journalism (Messner and DiStaso 2008; Regan 2003; Usher 2008). Both points of view remain rather theoretical. Only few journalists expand their activities with a weblog, and if they do so it is often under pressure from their employers. And at the same time, the content of the majority of blogs on the public side are non-journalistic. But even if the few exceptional informational public blogs are taken into consideration, one has to admit that traditional media are not eager to tap into their provided content. Only in extraordinary situations (e.g. tsunami catastrophe, London metro bombings) is the provided information from the public used for traditional media content (Domingo and Heinonen 2008).

Shifts in Journalism Quality

The trends of technological innovation and digitization described in this chapter are in line with the long-standing evolution of journalism labelled as 'tabloidization'. Since media institutions are more and more keen on maximizing their audiences, they end up adapting to mainstream taste and interest shifts. In his book *Flat Earth News* (2008), Nick Davies very vividly describes how this process of cheap production and tabloidization was merged with the negative aspects of technological diffusion and innovation as described above. According to Davies, journalism becomes hostage to the large content directing campaigns, and the cost-reducing news gathering routines as we described earlier are preventing that media content in playing its role as a key factor to the Fourth Estate: 'Generally journalists, like any other professionals, prefer to do their job well. I say it because this profession has become damaged to the point where most of the times, most of its members are no longer able to do their job. They work in structures which positively prevent them discovering the truth [...] The ethic of honesty has been overwhelmed by the mass production of ignorance' (Davies 2008: 28).

Davies accuses the media for not taking seriously the baselines of quality journalism anymore. Even the fact-checking part of the reporting process is often neglected. He gives some blood-curdling examples that provoked media hypes, as well as policy hypes (e.g. the millennium bug), and concludes eloquently: 'Journalism without checking is like a human body without an immune system. If the primary purpose of journalism is to tell the truth, then it follows that the primary function of journalists must be to check and to reject whatever is not true. But something has changed, and that essential immune system has started to collapse. In a strange, alarming and generally unnoticed development, journalists are pumping out stories without checking them – stories which then circle the planet' (Davies 2008: 51).

Generally, many of the journalistic practices described above are technologically driven, however far more important changes in journalistic production are driven by the financial cutbacks in the newsrooms. Davies describes modern newsrooms as news factories and he defines journalism as 'churnalism', which according to Davies, is a manifestation of journalists failing to perform the simple basic functions of their profession, i.e. journalists are quite unable to tell their readers the truth about what is happening on their path. Such journalists are no longer out gathering news, but their professional roles have instead been reduced to passive processors of whatever material comes their way, churning out stories, whether real event or PR artifice, important or trivial, true or false (Davies 2008). Indeed, different research studies disclose that journalistic outcome in many conventional media is in most cases just cutting and pasting practices. For example, researchers from Cardiff University measured the input of ready-made content by third parties in so-called quality newspapers and reported astonishing results: the highest scores were for The Times, a newspaper with a long pedigree, which adapted 69 per cent of its content from wire input, while The Guardian scored the lowest rates, although almost half of its content was wire-based (Lewis et al. 2008).

Discussion

Generally, two visions can be drawn from this discussion on how changes in production technologies will affect the profession of journalism. One of them sees structural changes, such as changes in institutional and organizational conditions of how journalists work and what discourses they construct in the new media enriched environments. This view also sees online journalism development and professionalization as processes of active learning and re-learning, with a need to rapidly adapt to changing external demands (rapidly changing technological and economic conditions, as well as audience requests) and working conditions. The other vision strongly relies on contextual factors and relates to the particularities of communication histories and traditions of national context and national communication culture, and their impact on working routines and messages communicated. All in all, these two visions disclose two conflicting paradigms of globalization and localism. As discussed above, journalistic production is strongly affected by the rapid diffusion of technological innovations. At the same time, European journalism also remains highly culturally sensitive, specific and framed through situational factors such as national traditions, values and norms.

References

AIM Research Consortium (ed.) (2007), *Understanding the Logic of EU Reporting from Brussels: Analysis of Interviews with EU Correspondents and Spokespersons*, in Adequate Information Management in Europe (AIM), Working Papers, 2007/3, Bochum and Freiburg: Projekt Verlag.

Alysen, B. (2005), *The Disappearing Cadetship: Trends in Entry Level Journalism Employment 1995–2005*, Sydney: University of Western Sydney.

Austin, J. and Cokley, J. (2006), *The Key Hiring Criteria Used by Journalism Employers: Australian Studies in Journalism*, Queensland: The School of Journalism and Communication.

Balčytienė, A. and Harro-Loit, H. (2009), 'Between Reality and Illusion: Re-Examining the Diversity of Media and Online Professional Journalism in the Baltic States', *Journal of Baltic Studies*, 40: 4, pp. 517–30.

Becker, L. B., Kosicki, G. M., Engleman, T. and Viswanath, K. (1993), 'Finding Work and Getting Paid: Predictors of Success in the Mass Communications Job Market', *Journalism & Mass Communication Quarterly*, 70: 4, pp. 919–33.

Becker, L. B., Lauf, E. and Lowrey, W. (1999), 'Differential Employment Rates in the Journalism and Mass Communication Labor Force Based on Gender, Race and Ethnicity: Exploring the Impact of Affirmative Action', *Journalism & Mass Communication Quarterly*, 76: 4, pp. 631–45.

Bird, S. E., 'Tabloidization: What Is it, and Does it Really Matter?', in Zelizer, B. (ed.) (1999), *The Changing Faces of Journalism: Tabloidization, Technology & Truthiness*, New York: Routledge, pp. 40–50.

Bivens, R. K. (2008), 'The Internet, Mobile Phones and Blogging: How Media Are Transforming Traditional Journalism', *Journalism Practice*, 2: 1, pp. 113–29.

Boczkowski, P. (2004), 'The Processes of Adopting Multimedia and Interactivity in Three Online Newsrooms', *Journal of Communication*, 54: 2, pp. 197–213.

—— 'Materiality and Mimicry in the Journalism Field', in Zelizer, B. (ed.) (2009), *The Changing Faces of Journalism: Tabloidization, Technology & Truthiness*, New York: Routledge, pp. 56–67.

Breed, W. (1955), 'Social Control in the Newsroom: A Functional Analysis', *Social Forces*, 33: 4, pp. 326–35.

Brennen, B. (2009), 'The Future of Journalism', *Journalism*, 10: 3, pp. 300–2.

Cassidy, W. P. (2008), 'Outside Influences: Extramedia Forces and the Newsworthiness Conceptions of Online Newspaper Journalists', *First Monday*, 13: 1. Available at: http: //firstmonday.org/htbin/ cgiwrap/bin/ojs/index.php/fm/article/view/2051/1922. Accessed 22 February 2010.

Chung, D. S. (2007), 'Profits and Perils: Online News Producers' Perceptions of Interactivity and Uses of Interactive Features', *Convergence: The International Journal of Research into New Media Technologies*, 13: 1, pp. 43–61.

Coleman, S. (2005), 'New Mediation and Direct Representation: Reconceptualizing Representation in the Digital Age', *New Media & Society*, 7: 2, pp. 177–98.

Cook, B. and Banks, S. (1993), 'Predictors of Job Burnout in Reporters and Copy Editors', *Journalism Quarterly*, 70: 1, pp. 108–17.

Dahlgren, P., 'The Troubling Evolution of Journalism', in Zelizer, B. (ed.) (1999), *The Changing Faces of Journalism: Tabloidization, Technology & Truthiness*, New York: Routledge, pp. 146–61.

Davies, N. (2008), *Flat Earth News: An Award-Winning Reporter Exposes Falsehood, Distortion and Propaganda in the Global Media*, London: Vintage Books.

Deuze, M. (2007), *Media Work*, Cambridge: Polity Press.

—— 'Understanding Journalism as Newswork: How it Changes, and how it Remains the Same', *Westminster Papers in Communication and Culture*, 5: 2, pp. 4–23.

Dimitrova, D.V. and Strömbäck, J. (2009), 'Look who's Talking. Use of Sources in Newspaper Coverage in Sweden and the United States', *Journalism Practice*, 3: 1, pp. 75–91

Domingo, D., Quandt, T., Heinonen, A., Paulussen, S., Singer, J. and Vujnovic, M. (2008), 'Participatory Journalism Practices in the Media and Beyond: An International Comparative Study of Initiatives in Online Newspapers', *Journalism Practice*, 2: 3, pp. 326–42.

Dupagne, M. and Garrison, B. (2006), 'The Meaning and Influence of Convergence: A Qualitative Case Study of Newsroom Work at the Tampa News Center', *Journalism Studies*, 7: 2, pp. 237–55.

Dutton, W. H. (2008), 'The Fifth Estate: Democratic Social Accountability Through the Emerging Network of Networks', *Social Science Research Network*. Available at: http: //papers.ssrn.com/sol3/ papers.cfm?abstract_id=1167502. Accessed 17 February 2010.

Erdal, I. J. (2009), 'Repurposing of Content in Multi-Platform News Production: Towards a Typology of Cross-Media Journalism', *Journalism Practice*, 3: 2, pp. 178–95.

Ericson, R. V., Baranek, P. M. and Chan, J.B.L. (1989), *Negotiating Control: A Study of News Sources*, Milton Keynes: Open University Press.

Fengler, S. and Russ-Mohl, S. (2008), 'Journalists and the Information-Attention Markets: Towards an Economic Theory of Journalism', *Journalism*, 9: 6, pp. 667–90.

Fishman, M. (1980), *Manufacturing the News*, Austin: University of Texas Press.

Fortunati, L., Sarrica, M., O'Sullivan, J., Balčytienė, A., Harro-Loit, H., Macgregor, Ph., Roussou, N., Salaverria, R. and de Luca, F., 'The Influence of the Internet on European Journalism', *Journal of Computer-Mediated Communication*, 14, pp. 928–63.

Franklin, B., Lewis, J., Mosdell, N., Thomas, J. and Williams, A. (2006), 'The Quality and Independence of British Journalism: Tracking the Changes over 20 Years', *Mediawise*, 1: 64. Available at: http: //www.mediawise.org.uk/files/uploaded/Quality%20&%20Independence%20of%20British%20 Journalism.pdf. Accessed 22 February 2010.

Franklin, B., Lewis, J. and Williams, A. (2008), 'Four Rumours and an Explanation: A Political Economic Account of Journalists' Changing Newsgathering and Reporting Practices', *Journalism Practice*, 1: 2, pp. 27–45.

Galtung, J. and Ruge, M. H. (1965), 'The Structure of Foreign News: The Presentation of the Congo, Cuba and Cyprus Crises in Four Norwegian Newspapers', *Journal of Peace Research*, 2: 1, pp. 64–90.

Gans, H. J. (1979), *Deciding What's News: A Study of CBS Evening News, NBC Nightly News, Newsweek and Time*, New York: Pantheon Books.

Gurevitz, M., Coleman, S. and Blumler, J. G. (2009), 'Political Communication – Old and New Media Relationships', *The ANNALS of the American Academy of Political and Social Science*, 625, pp. 164–81.

Hampton, M. (2008) 'The "Objectivity" Ideal and its Limitations in 20th –century Britisch Journalism, *Journalism Studies*, 9: 4, pp. 477–493.

Hanitzsch, T. (2007), 'Networking Journalism Studies: Towards a World Journalism Survey', *Brazilian Journalism Research*, 3: 2, pp. 43–54.

Hollifield, C. A., Gerald, M. K. and Becker, L. B. (2001), 'Organizational vs. Professional Culture in the Newsroom: Television News Directors' and Newspaper Editors' Hiring Decisions', *Journal of Broadcasting & Electronic Media*, 45: 1, pp. 92–117.

Jenkins, H. (2006), *Convergence Culture: Where Old and New Media Collide*, New York: New York University Press.

Jha, S. (2008), 'Why They Wouldn't Cite From Sites: A Study of Journalists' Perceptions of Social Movement Web Sites and the Impact on Their Coverage of Social Protest', *Journalism*, 9: 6, pp. 711–32.

Johnstone, J.W.C., Slawski, E. J. and Bowman, W. W. (1976), *The News People: A Sociological Portrait of American Journalists and Their Work*, Urbana: University of Illinois Press.

Lewis, J., Williams, A. and Franklin, B. (2008), 'A Compromised Fourth Estate? UK News Journalism, Public Relations and News Sources', *Journalism Studies*, 9: 1, pp. 1–20.

Löffelholz, M. and Weaver, D. (2008), *Global Journalism Research: Theories, Methods, Findings, Future*, Malden: Blackwell Publishing.

Lund, A. B., 'News Ecology and Media Society: Formative Views on the Production of News', in Hurd, M., Olsson, T. and Aker, P. (eds) (2002), *Storylines Media, Power and Identity in Modern Europe*, Stockholm: Hjalmarson and Högberg, pp. 78–90.

Machill, M. and Beiler, M. (2009), 'The Importance of the Internet for Journalistic Research: A Multi-Method Study of the Research Performed by Journalists Working for Daily Newspapers, Radio, Television and Online', *Journalism Studies*, 10: 2, pp. 178–203.

Machill, M., Beiler, M. and Zenker, M. (2008). 'Search-engine Research: a European-American Overview and systematization of an interdisciplinary and international Research Field', *Media, Culture & Society*, 30: 5, pp. 591–608.

Meier, K. (2007), 'Innovations in Central European Newsrooms', *Journalism Practice*, 1: 1, pp. 4–19.

Meijer, I. C. (2006), *De toekomst van het nieuws*, Amsterdam: Otto Cramwinckel.

Messner, M. and DiStaso, M. W. (2008), 'The Source Cycle', *Journalism Studies*, 9: 3, pp. 447–63.

Mindich, D.T.Z. (2004), *Tuned Out: Why Americans Under 40 Don't Follow the News*, New York: Oxford University Press.

'O Neill, D. and 'O Connor, L. (2008), 'The Passive journalist: how Sources Dominate Local News', *Journalism Practice*, 2/3, pp. 487–500.

Paulussen, S. and Ugille, P. (2008), 'User Generated Content in the Newsroom: Professional and Organisational Constraints on Participatory Journalism', *Westminster Papers in Communication and Culture*, 5: 2, pp. 24–41.

Pavlik, J. (2000), 'The Impact of Technology on Journalism', *Journalism Studies*, 1: 2, pp. 229–37.

Perrons, D. (2003), 'The New Economy and the Work-Life Balance: Conceptual Explorations and a Case Study of New Media', *Gender, Work and Organization*, 10: 1, pp. 65–93

Phillips,A., Singer,J.B., Vlad, T. And Becker, L.B. (2009), 'Implications of Technological Change for Journalists' Tasks and Skills', *Journal of Media Business Studies*, 6: 1, pp. 61–85.

Raviola, E. And Hartman,B. (2009), 'Business Perspectives on Work in News Organizations', *Journal of Media Business Studies*, 6: 1, pp.7–36.

Reese, S. D. (2001), 'Understanding the Global Journalist: A Hierarchy-of-Influences Approach', *Journalism Studies*, 2: 2, pp. 173–87.

Regan, T. (2003), 'Weblogs Threaten and Inform Traditional Journalism', *Nieman Reports*, 57: 3, pp. 68–70.

Rintala, N. and Suolanen, S. (2005), 'The Implications of Digitalization for Job Descriptions, Competencies and the Quality of Working Life', *Nordicom Review*, 26, pp. 53–67.

Robinson, S. (2006), 'The Mission of the J-Blog: Recapturing Journalistic Authority Online', *Journalism*, 7: 1, pp. 65–83.

Rühl, M. (1969), *Die Zeitungsredaktion als Organisiertes Soziales system*, Düsseldorf: Bertelsmann Universitätsverlag

Saltzis, K. and Dickinson, R. (2008), 'Inside the Changing Newsroom: Journalists' Responses to Media Convergence', *Aslib Proceedings: New Information Perspectives*, 60: 3, pp. 216–28.

Shoemaker, P. J. and Reese, S. D. (1996), *Mediating the Message: Theories of Influences on Mass Media Content*, 2nd edn, New York: Longman.

Singer, J. B. (2004), 'Strange Bedfellows? The Diffusion of Convergence in Four News Organizations', *Journalism Studies*, 5: 1, pp. 3–18.

——— (2006), 'The Socially Responsible Existentialist: A Normative Emphasis for Journalists in a New Media Environment', *Journalism Studies*, 7: 1, pp. 2–18.

Terzis, G. (2009), *European Journalism Education*, Bristol and Chicago: Intellect.

Teugels, M., Van Hoof, E., Mory, K. and De Witte, H. (2009), 'Burn-out in de Vlaamse pers: een tijdbom onder de redacties', *De Journalist*, 122, pp. 9–12.

Tunstall, J. (1971), *Journalists at Work*, Beverly Hills: Sage.

Usher, N. B. (2008), 'Reviewing Fauxtography: A Blog-Driven Challenge to Mass Media Power without the Promises of Networked Publicity', *First Monday*, 13: 12.

Verbitskaya, Y. (2005), 'Nekontroliruemaya "mpatija: tvorchestvo na grani nevroza'" (Uncontrolled Empathy: Creativity on the Edge of Neurosis), *Mediaalmanakh*, 3, pp. 18–24.

Walters, E., Warren, C. and Dobbie, M. (2006), *The Changing Nature of Work: A Global Survey and Case Study of Atypical Work in the Media Industry*, Brussels: The International Federation of Journalists.

Weaver, D. (1998), *The Global Journalist: News People Around the World*, Cresskill: Hampton Press.

Weaver, D., Beam, R., Brownlee, B., Voakes, P. and Wilhoit, G. (2007), *The American Journalist in the 21st Century: U.S. News People at the Dawn of a New Millennium*, Mahwah: Lawrence Erlbaum Associates.

Weaver, D. and Wilhoit, G. (1986), *The American Journalist: A Portrait of U.S. News People and Their Work*, Bloomington: Indiana University Press.

—— (1996), *The American Journalist in the 1990s: U.S. News People at the End of an Era*, Mahwah: Lawrence Erlbaum Associates.

White, D. M. (1950), 'The "Gatekeeper": A Case-Study in the Selection of News', *Journalism Quarterly* 27: 4, pp. 383–90.

Chapter 13

Media and Ethnic Minorities

Leen d'Haenens and Tristan Mattelart

In today's culturally diverse societies, the media play complex, often contradictory, roles. They produce peculiar representations of the nation, creating a so-called 'imagined community' (Anderson 2006) of which they define the boundaries, including some and excluding others. However, if media can be vehicles for homogeneous dominant representations hiding the cultural diversity that comprises the nation, they are also able to offer crucial loci exposing this same cultural diversity, and 'spaces in and through which imposed identities or the interest of others can be revisited, challenged and changed' (Cottle 2000: 2).

Questioning the relationship between ethnic minorities and media in Europe thus requires considering the contradictory roles the former can play. To begin with, we will analyze the mechanisms through which the mainstream media in Europe tend to frame ethnic minorities in largely negative terms. Subsequently, we will study ethnic minorities' media uses, analyzing how, responding in part to their unfair portrayal in the main national media, they articulate their consumption between both the media of their host country and those of their country of origin, and with which social consequences. Furthermore, we will try to understand what the consumption of transnational media may entail for diversity policies. To conclude, this chapter will identify some enabling mechanisms and strengths, as well as obstacles and failures, that have been experienced in an effort to build an integrated and transformative television system in which ideally all members of society are recognized as having a right to fair portrayal practices.

Portrayal Studies

Mainstream media texts are important because they constitute the main source of our knowledge about a large number of issues; in doing so, they contribute to our 'common sense' understanding of the world. As such, media texts are believed to affect the way in which we understand the world, others and ourselves. Agenda-setting theory posits that what media write about influences the topics people talk and think about, as well as what they consider important (McCombs and Shaw 1972). This chapter proceeds on the assumption that the media at least partly construct the social fabric of people's lives, certainly in the case of topics that are unfamiliar and far removed from their daily lives, when media function as substitutes for real life experiences.

Categorizing the world and the people around us appears an inevitable and unconscious process that usually occurs on the basis of external features, such as dress and skin colour, but it can also be grounded in the attribution of less visible characteristics such as religion, culture or sexual orientation. Categorizing has the advantage of making the world less complex. It provides information on the characteristics of an individual or group, but it can also be intended as a way of maintaining a positive self-image (e.g. to draw boundaries and emphasize differences between 'us' and 'them', and to apply evaluations about others). In this categorization process, emphasis is put on differences between ourselves, the in-group, and members of an out-group perceived to be (or presented as) homogeneous (Farr and Moscovici 1984; Stangor 2000; Tajfel and Turner 1979). Stereotypes and prejudices constitute examples of beliefs and attitudes based on social categorization and evaluation processes. Most of the research in this area deals with beliefs and attitudes towards specific minority or disadvantaged groups such as women, the elderly, homosexuals, disabled people and ethnic minorities. A combination of quantitative and qualitative methods is most commonly used to assess the shaping of stereotypes and underlying prejudices in different media contents (e.g. Hartmann and Husband 1974; van Dijk 1991, 1993).

Categorizing the World

Media professionals use categorizations or 'media frames' in order to make their daily news-making practice less complex. In addition, journalists tend to adjust to the existing editorial culture of their employer and their work is affected by newsroom hierarchies and socialization, as well as by the editorial/programming policy. As to the selection of stories, deep-seated news values play a crucial role (Galtung and Ruge 1965). Journalists often seek the unusual and mostly cover the bad news. As a result, minorities (the out-groups) are associated with conflict, drama, controversy, violence and deviance (e.g. Cottle 2000). Nevertheless, these news values are not exclusive to ethnic minority reporting only; they shape other news stories as well. On top of that, when producing a story about ethnic minorities, journalists do not always have the means to consult the proper (variety of) sources and contact persons, especially not within the time limits of their deadlines. One should not forget that journalists themselves are part of a society that is pervaded by prejudices. Journalists provide information in such a way that it is in correspondence with their own world views, including widespread prejudices (Cottle 2000). They often lack specific training in terms of specific ethnic minority groups' culture, while the hiring of minority journalists leaves much to be desired, given their limited access to the media industry (Ouaj 1999).

Another important context factor influencing news production is market demand: both newspapers and broadcasters operate in a highly competitive market. These economic constraints and realities of the media business are often seen as threats; concentration of ownership is seen as an obstacle for diversity in the media market and freedom of expression (Sanders 2003). The role of the media in shaping and reinforcing audiences' already existing cognitions –including the socially shared stereotypical beliefs and prejudiced attitudes – is described by Simon Cottle (2000: 3):

The media occupy a key site and perform a crucial role in the public representation of unequal social relations and the play of cultural power. It is in and through representations, for example, that members of the media audience are variously invited to construct a sense of who 'we' are in relation to who 'we' are not, whether as 'us' and 'them', 'insider' and 'outsider', 'colonizer' and 'colonized', 'citizen' and 'foreigner', 'normal' and 'deviant', 'friend' and 'foe', 'the west' and 'the rest'.

Negative portrayal is being maintained by generalizations referring to 'the' Moroccan culture or 'the' Islam, as well as through explicit referrals to minorities' backgrounds in a predominantly negative context. Single ethnic minority members are often quoted and presented as representative spokespeople of the entire group; also Turkish/Moroccan origin is directly associated with religion (Islam), which results in a biased representation on the real meaning of being a Muslim. Portrayal is undoubtedly influential in the shaping of people's opinions about ethnic minorities, if only because most people do not have direct contact and exchange with ethnic minorities, and thus rely on hear-say and the media as their main sources for knowledge about ethnic minority groups and issues. Notwithstanding our reservations vis-à-vis the sometimes too easily assumed linear correspondence between the media and the audience agenda, research recurrently reveals that the media, in general, fail to fairly portray ethnic minorities and tend to represent them both as a problem and a threat (e.g. Ter Wal 2002; Cottle 2000; van Dijk 1991).

Monitoring Media Content in Europe

One line of research concentrates on the media content and on the fair portrayals, or lack thereof, of ethnic minorities (Ter Wal 2004; Ter Wal, d'Haenens and Koeman 2005; Bonfadelli, Bucher and Piga 2007), assuming that there is a connection between the ways in which the media deal with ethnic minorities and the degree of their integration into the host society. Although many media monitoring studies have assessed the position of ethnic minorities in the news, there are few whose scope goes beyond the national borders. Moreover, the existing single-country studies are incomparable as they use different selection criteria (cf. Ter Wal 2002). The study by Ter Wal et al. (2005) was the first in which a wide variety of press sources from all the 'old' fifteen European Union (EU) member states. These press sources were analyzed in terms of their (re)presentation of the multicultural society and their portrayal of ethno-cultural minorities, immigration and asylum issues, by using uniform standardized categories and criteria at the European level for the coding and analysis of news contents. Unlike former studies on minorities and the media, the analysis by Ter Wal et al. (2005) included all domestic news and thus not just the news coverage of ethnic issues only. This inclusive approach was new in that it allowed this coverage to be compared with 'other' news. In 2003, national teams in the fifteen 'old' EU member states content-analyzed one day's (13 November) domestic coverage in national and regional daily press, for a total of ten different newspapers per country. The following question was central: to what extent and in what way are ethnic minorities (re)presented in the news? The patterns emerging from the content analysis (frequency of topics, actors and actor roles) provided insight into the visibility given to ethnic minorities in the media; the preferred roles, the labels and news contexts in which they tend to appear the most or conversely, from which they are absent. The overall selection produced a vast amount of news stories (2802) originated from quality, popular and free dailies.

This content analysis revealed a disparity in the coverage of minority and migrant issues, compared to the treatment of general issues. On the basis of a number of indicators – minority actors were less present as main actors in ethnic stories, they were quoted less than majority actors, and they were more often presented in negative news contexts and roles – news about migrants and ethnic minorities was found to be often more negative than general news. In terms of representation, minority actors were slightly more often the objects of negative portrayal and of questioned credibility when quoted. In other words, this material confirmed the often-found communication of a stereotypical image of minorities as relegated to specific secluded spheres of society linked to crime and deviance at the negative end and celebrities at the positive end. In addition, ethnic minorities or migrants became a focus when identity issues such as fundamentalism and religion were discussed. Everyday ethnic relations were often covered without consulting the views and perspectives of the minority protagonists. Even in stories about their own position, minorities were quoted less than their majority counterparts. Furthermore, the negative portrayal was not by itself determined by ethnicity, but by the frequent association of minorities with particularly negative news contexts, such as religious fundamentalism and illegal immigration, and in particular the over-representation of minorities in crime news. This finding is a confirmation of the importance of news-selection mechanisms and of news and public agendas on the portrayal of minorities in the media.

In short, ethno-cultural diversity in mainstream programming in Europe faces many challenges. In recent years, however, European journalists and media makers have begun to address some of the above-mentioned gaps, and producers have established television series that try to remedy this lack of ethno-cultural diversity. Even though the number of intercultural programming stays quite limited, overall there is far more going on in North-western Europe than in southern Europe in this respect. As budgetary constraints impose their limits on broadcasters and producers, and as more and more takeovers occur in the European commercial media landscape, we will likely see even smaller investments in innovative intercultural series in the future. The initiatives taken by the public broadcasters will prove all the more important.

This brings us to the fundamental issue of the ways of representing diversity in the media in Europe. Among programme makers, two diverging opinions emerge on the depiction of diversity: some believe that equality is achieved when differences become irrelevant, thereby achieving a state of colour-blindness in casting procedures and storytelling, while others believe diversity is achieved when qualities are accounted for as different yet equal. In practice, this issue is of particular relevance because it affects the evaluation of the successful representation and portrayal of diversity. For the first group, an assimilationist model aimed at the normalization of ethnic differences would be the goal; for the second, it is important to illuminate ethnic and cultural differences in an effort to further the acceptance and understanding of diversity.

Ethnic Minorities' Media Uses

Studies of ethnic minorities' media uses have been for a long time under-researched. However, in the 1990s, these studies came to figure prominently in the agenda of the research on media and migration in Europe. The emphasis on diasporas and their hybrid cultures (Cottle 2000; Mattelart 2007), which coincided with research on active audiences, contributed to the development of an important literature devoted to media consumption practices among ethnic minority families. New questions began to be raised: how do migrants organize their media consumption between the media of their host country and those of their country of origin? How do these uses impinge on their cultural experiences? The bulk of this literature focuses on television reception. Indeed, the small screen, often used as an aural background medium, continues to be the most important medium for migrant groups in Europe, as a literature review by Bonfadelli et al. (2007) shows.

Research on Media Reception by Ethnic Minorities in Europe

One of the pioneering studies in this field is the ethnography of media consumption conducted by Marie Gillespie among Punjabi families living in Southall, south of London. Doing her fieldwork between 1988 and 1991, Marie Gillespie analyzes how the video cassette recorder is used by the parents or the grandparents as a medium to show mainly Hindi films to their offspring, and, as such, as a medium to reassert the necessity of conforming to Punjabi cultural traditions. But young Punjabis also use the small screen to watch western soaps that convey very different cultural values that are dangerous in the eyes of the parents. The interest of Gillespie's work lies in her analyses of young Punjabis' cultural negotiations in front of their television sets. She shows more particularly how they scrutinize western teenagers' ways of life deployed on the screen, using these images as a 'cultural resource' to transform aspects of their own families' traditions (Gillespie 1995).

Marie Gillespie did her fieldwork just before the emergence of direct to home satellite television. The rise of satellite dishes in the 1990s constitutes an important cultural fact for migrant populations and ethnic minorities in Europe. Before direct broadcasting by satellite, they had to watch the channels of their host country. With the advent of satellite television, they are now able to watch the programmes of the countries, or the regions, from which they left.

This rise of satellite dishes in migrant homes has raised concerns in different European countries. Indeed, in France and in Germany, these satellite dishes have often been criticized for contributing to a 'media isolation' of migrants (Güntürk 1999), or to the rise of 'media ghettos' (Hafez 2002) among migrant populations, thus impeding their integration in their host countries (see also Hargreaves and Mahdjoub 1997). Reception studies carried out in this field have nonetheless come to relativize these fears. Among the first works studying satellite television viewing in ethnic homes, there is the qualitative survey carried out in the mid-1990s by Hargreaves and Mahdjoub within families of mainly Maghrebi origin in the South of France. Following Gillespie's study, they show how first generation respondents devote a lot of time watching the televisions of their country of origin, not without nostalgia, and how they use the satellite dish to convey their culture of origin to their children. However, Hargreaves and Mahdjoub also make the point that first generation respondents keep on watching French television, including news broadcasts. Interestingly, second generation respondents are, for their part, described in this study as consuming above all French private television or, as far as satellite television is concerned, American-style channels like MTV, TNT or CNN, rather than Maghreb channels (Hargreaves and Mahdjoub 1997).

Several other studies have pointed in the same direction, analyzing the generation gaps in television viewing among families with migrant origins (Georgiou 2006). Indeed, various studies stress the similarity of television preferences of minority and majority youth: in these studies, typical youth cultural patterns in media use appear as being more significant than cultural differences (e.g. Bonfadelli and Bucher 2006; Granato 2001; Milikowski 2000). When looking at ethnic minority youngsters primarily, television socio-demographic factors seem to have more influence on media use patterns than ethno-cultural origin or orientation (d'Haenens et al. 2002). If second generation ethnic minorities use media from their home country, they mention affective motives, or see them as a particular form of education regarding language and general knowledge of their country of origin (e.g. Milikowski 2000).

Another variable of importance that has to be taken into account is the socio-economic variable. The higher the socio-economic milieu and educational level of ethnic minorities, the longer the period of living in the host country and the better the language skills, the higher is the use of the host country's majority media (e.g. Weiss and Trebbe 2001). The 'direct integration thesis', suggesting that a higher use of majority media by ethnic minorities has a positive influence on their level of integration is confirmed in many studies, but cannot be generalized. According to Peeters and d'Haenens (2005), a positive correlation exists between integration and general media use in so far as well integrated ethnic minorities use majority media more often than less integrated minorities. This is not the case with television use, however, as ethnic minorities with a lower level of integration have more access to satellite television and spend on average considerably more time watching homeland channels. In Switzerland, for example, the integration function for mainstream television use in the host country language is fulfilled for young people from Italian families, but not for the Turkish youngsters. For ethnic groups, however, there is a negative correlation between use of television in the native language and integration into Swiss culture (Bonfadelli and Bucher 2006; Bucher and Bonfadelli 2007a, 2007b).

Kevin Robins and Asu Aksoy, for their part, propose a move away from the national frame of thinking underpinning questions around the integrative role of the media, and plead in favour of a more transnational frame of thinking, which would study more closely the way ethnic minorities are, thanks to their day-to-day viewing practices, participating simultaneously in various cultures. These authors have in particular gone a bit further in the destruction of the thesis according to which transnational television channels would integrate their diasporic viewers in an isolated media space exclusively dominated by the culture of their country of origin. Studying the way Turkish television is received in the homes of Turkish-speaking minorities in London, they show how these channels provide to their viewers an ordinary link with Turkey, helping them to live in synchrony with Turkish realities. They argue that this daily televized contact with Turkey, full of violent and tragic news, prevents them from developing an idealized image of the country they left, or from developing uncritical nostalgic feelings towards it (Aksoy and Robins 2003; Milikowski 2000).

The ordinary character of Turkish minorities' viewing practices is at the heart of Aksoy and Robins' argument. Turkish minorities have to be seen, they assert, as seeking ordinary television pleasures, such as familiarity, confirmation, like other British viewers. But, if they are seeking ordinary pleasures, Turkish minorities live nonetheless a very specific cultural experience: through their television viewing, they are daily moving between at least two cultures, the Turkish one and British one. Thanks to this specific cultural experience, Turkish minority viewers have acquired a very specific competence: they have learned to move across two or more distinct cultural spaces. As such, they have developed a highly 'mobile culture', or better, to quote the title of one of Aksoy and Robins' papers, a 'banal transnationalism'. Turkish viewers are indeed described as constantly comparing Turkish and British channels, freeing themselves from a 'monocultural (national) vision'. Through their television viewing, they may thus 'become more reflexively aware of the arbitrariness and provisionality of cultural orders' (Aksoy and Robins 2003: 101–102).

A qualitative reception research undertaken by d'Haenens et al. (2000) among ethnic minority youngsters and adults residing in the Netherlands confirms these results. It shows that these groups are critical media users because they can compare Dutch media with those in their country of origin, thus acquiring a wider view of the news. Moreover, their hunger for news and information about their own group, as well as for their home country, is only partly satisfied by the media in the Netherlands. This finding applies to all age groups: ethnic minorities have a strong need for information about their country of origin and turn to alternative means, especially foreign media, to find the news they are interested in.

News Reception and Ethnic Publics in Europe

In the aftermath of September 11, and the subsequent war on Islamist terrorism, new concerns have been raised about the 'parallel societies' and 'ghettos' that Arab television channels would feed in Europe (Hafez 2007). Even in the United Kingdom, with its long-established multiculturalist tradition, the loyalty of ethnic minorities began to be questioned, and Arab transnational channels started to be seen as a challenge to national integration (Aksoy 2006). In this situation, the issue of news consumption by ethnic minorities has become quite sensitive. Watching non-western transnational news stations has been more and more regarded, deplores Asu Aksoy, as 'jeopardizing the migrants' tenuous link to the "host" country' (Aksoy 2006: 925).

It is in this context that one of the rare research projects devoted to television news reception among families with migrant origins has been carried out in the United Kingdom, under the direction of Marie Gillespie. This collective work, gathering twenty researchers who interviewed over 300 people, mainly in the United Kingdom, studies how minority viewers – above all Muslim viewers – with Middle Eastern, Afghan, Somalian or Turkish origins, have responded to the television coverage of September 11 and of the military intervention in Afghanistan that followed. Presenting itself as a collective audience ethnography, it apprehends the way viewers with migrant origins negotiate the news, be they local, national or transnational (Gillespie 2006).

One of the main results emerging from the different contributions is the critical view expressed by minority publics against their representation in the media of their host country (Miladi 2006). What is called into question is not only how these minorities are represented as such in British media, but also how the realities of the Arab or Muslim world – to which they are in one way or another associated – are depicted in the same media, with all the negative consequences these representations may have for Muslims living in the United Kingdom (Harb and Bessaiso 2006; Matar 2006; Ahmad 2006). Interestingly, ethnic minority viewers equally criticize television news programmes of the state channels of their countries of origin, accusing them of lacking editorial independence.

These criticisms give an insight into the reasons why Al Jazeera established itself as a source of reference in many homes of the Arab or Muslim diaspora. Part of its success is due to its ability to bring news that break the logics of censorship organizing much of the circulation of information in the Arab world, as well as to its capacity to offer non-western perspectives on the conflicts of the Muslim world (Ahmad 2006; Matar 2006). First generation respondents are the more prone to show their interest in Al Jazeera's news. However, September 11, 2001, seems to have aroused also the curiosity of younger viewers for the Qatari channel. Unable to understand the comments, these had – until then – not paid a lot of attention to its programmes. Nevertheless, after the September 11 attacks, they have started to watch Al Jazeera's news with their parents, the latter playing a central role in the translation and explanation of programmes to their children (Harb and Bessaiso 2006).

If Arab channels are seen as providers of information, they are also described as an important medium for diasporic viewers through allowing them to maintain a link with their countries of origin. State national television is criticized by these viewers for its narrow perspectives, but it is still watched by them so that they can create ties with the 'home culture' and convey it to their children (Miladi 2006). Moreover, pan-Arab channels are seen as linking their viewers in the United Kingdom to an Arab 'transnational community' (Ahmad

2006). These channels are alternately described as connecting their diasporic publics to the world of 'the ummah' (Gillespie 2006: 908), to an 'emerging transnational Arab public sphere' (Miladi 2006: 953), or to a 'pan-Arabic and Muslim transnational public sphere' (Harb and Bessaiso 2006: 1073).

Still, this research shows that Arab diasporic publics continue to be viewers of western channels, be they satellite or terrestrial channels. These publics carry on watching domestic channels for their sport, entertainment or news programmes, but with a critical eye, as an informed audience, enriched by the perspectives gleaned on Arab channels (Harb and Bessaiso 2006; Miladi 2006).

In the continuity of previous works, diasporic viewers are here described as being eminently active, as constantly comparing various sources of information, as being 'highly critical new consumers' (Gillespie 2006: 913). In her contribution to this collective research, Asu Aksoy, studying the reception of television news by Turkish viewers 'doubly estranged, fully identifying neither with the West nor with Islam', goes as far as to say that these have been much more active in the decoding of September 11 than 'monocultural' publics. Oscillating between Turkish channels and British ones, Turkish viewers, she explains, have developed – thanks to their cultural ambivalence – a scepticism towards these channels, and have done a lot of thinking by themselves to give meaning to the events (Aksoy 2006: 935–943).

However, not all the viewers benefit in the same way from this situation of cultural ambivalence. Indeed, Asu Aksoy opposes the 'flexible thinking' that sustains some viewers, fed by a plurality of information sources, to a 'dogmatic thinking' sustained by other viewers embedded in a cultural environment shaped up 'by experiences of persecution and dogmas about persecution'. In this instance, 'the potentially creative possibilities that might emerge from the position of cultural ambivalence are closed down' (Aksoy 2006: 939–41).

The Impact of European Media in Emigration Countries

Focusing above all on minorities' reception practices in their host countries, the research on media consumption within migrant homes has largely neglected another field of study: the role media play in fuelling the desire to emigrate in European countries. Only a handful of studies tackle this question. Among them, there is the ethnographic work carried out by Tarik Sabry among young Amazighs living in the Moroccan Atlas mountains. He shows how their 'desire to emigrate' is nourished, not only by the difficult socio-economic context in which they live, but also by the images of the western world broadcast by Moroccan television and the ostentatious signs of success displayed by migrants coming back to their village for the holidays. These images then shape a positive 'mental geography of the West', associated with the ideas of happiness, leisure and wealth, with all the dangerous illusions it conveys (Sabry 2004: 41–43).

In the same vein, Nicola Mai shows how the signals of the luxuriant Italian television, by crossing the Adriatic Sea, offered Albania a window on the western way of life for years. So much so that in 1991, when they were able to leave their country, young Albanians 'driven by economic necessity to be sure, but lured by images of success provided by the imaginary world of television', tried at all costs to reach 'the country that fuelled their hopes and desires' (Mai 2001: 95, 104). Nevertheless, when confronted with the harsh realities of emigration, they were soon to discover the mystifying power of images.

If television can feed individuals' desire to emigrate, it may also have a more deterrent effect by depicting, in a not so positive way, the realities of immigration countries. With the satellite dish, the issue of minorities' media representation in Europe has been increasingly transnationalized. Studying the uses of satellite television in Algeria in the 1990s, Lotfi Madani shows for example how the main French television channels spread in the intimacy of Algerian homes to show images of immigrants appearing with stereotypical features, under the sign of an irreconcilable difference and as 'a polymorphic and continuous menace' (Madani 2002: 198).

Redefining Policies of Media Inclusion

The 1990s have witnessed the development of hundreds of channels – be they public, state-run, commercial – aimed at diasporic populations living in Europe. Coming from all over the world, their mapping nonetheless reveals 'immense inequalities'. Indeed, the contrast is high between the important Turkish satellite output offered to its diasporic public and the 'almost non-existent' sub-Saharan African transnational broadcasting (Georgiou 2005: 44–45). However unequal their geography, these channels have profoundly transformed the European television landscape.

If their reception in migrant homes has begun to be well documented, the political stakes they raise have been largely understudied. Yet, some of these channels have been at the heart of heated political debates in different European countries. Since its creation in the second half of the 1990s, the Turkish state has tried to fight the Kurdish transnational television: it has deployed intense diplomatic activity against it, forcing it to move its headquarters several times (Hassanpour 2003; Akpinar 2007). Afraid of its possible influence on viewers with migrant origins, the French regulatory body, the Conseil supérieur de l'audiovisuel (CSA), cancelled in 2005 the broadcasting authorization it had granted to Al-Manar, the Hezbollah satellite television station, accusing it of anti-Semitism (Ferjani 2007).

Moreover, these channels raise important issues for the policies of inclusion of ethnic minority populations in the European media landscape. For years, policies have been fostered trying to improve the representation of ethnic minorities in the main national media of the different countries of Europe. Some European countries in North-western Europe have played a leadership role in the development of multiculturalism and its use in broadcasting as an integrative tool for cultural and racial constituency groups. Public service broadcasters, more than their commercial counterparts, and media watchdog organizations have set as their goals the increased portrayal of ethnic diversity in programming and employment.

However, these diversity policies have their limits, as illustrated in the various monitors of diversity that exist across Europe (e.g. Macé 2008). In addition, ethnic minorities' consumption of diasporic channels challenges these policies. They find 'in transnational broadcasting the kinds of services that they have been missing in national broadcasting schedules' (Robins 2006: 154).

From our own snapshot view of media experiences with ethnic minorities in Europe, it becomes clear that more intercultural contents in mainstream media would allow to provoke a process in which audiences could reach out to others, to reconcile value differences, to work on conflict resolution and generally motivate everyone to go beyond their own interests. In effect, a dialogically-based multicultural television service – and public broadcasters should broadly take up this function – could help people build social capital beyond their own ethnic community boundaries. Multicultural media output has a role in building social cohesion in globalized societies that are becoming more fragmented by the day, as it is often the only way of intercultural dialogue and engagement people happen to be exposed to. Hence, media authorities in European countries need to develop a new policy frame which fosters a cross-cultural dialogue aimed at bridging and understanding, and which will stimulate media makers to become truly intercultural in their output.

References

Ahmad, F. (2006), 'British Muslim Perceptions and Opinions on News Coverage of September 11', *Journal of Ethnic and Migration Studies*, 32: 6, pp. 961–82.

Akpinar, Z., 'L'État turc face aux télévisions transfrontières kurdes', in Mattelart, T. (ed.) (2007), *Médias, migrations et cultures transnationales*, Paris-Brussels: Ina-De Boeck, pp. 89–103.

Aksoy, A. (2006), 'Transnational Virtues and Cool Loyalties: Responses of Turkish-Speaking Migrants in London to September 11', *Journal of Ethnic and Migration Studies*, 32: 6, pp. 923–46.

Aksoy, A. and Robins, K., 'Banal Transnationalism: The Difference that Television Makes', in Karim, K. H. (ed.) (2003), *The Media of Diaspora*, London: Routledge, pp. 89–104.

Anderson, B. (2006), *Imagined Communities: Reflections on the Origin and Spread of Nationalism*, London: Verso.

Barker, C. (1997), 'Television and the Reflexive Project of the Self: Soaps, Teenage Talk and Hybrid Identities', *British Journal of Sociology*, 48: 4, pp. 611–28.

Bonfadelli, H. and Bucher, P., 'Jugendliche mit und ohne Migrationshintergrund: Gemeinsamkeiten und Unterschiede im Umgang mit Medien' (Young People with and without Migration Background: Similarities and Differences in Media Use), in Lothar, M., Hoffmann, D. and Winter, R. (eds) (2007a), *Mediennutzung, Identität und Identifikationen*, Weinheim: Juventa, pp. 223–45.

—— 'Mediennutzung von Jugendlichen mit Migrationshintergrund in der Schweiz' (Media Use by Adolescents with Migrant Background in Switzerland), in Bonfadelli, H. and Moser, H. (eds) (2007b), *Medien und Migration: Europa als multikultureller Raum*, Wiesbaden: VS Verlag, pp. 119–45.

—— 'Mediennutzung von Jugendlichen mit Migrationshintergrund: Inklusion oder Exklusion' (Media Use of Young People with Migrant Background: Inclusion or Exclusion?), in Imhof, K., Blum, R., Jarren, O. and Bonfadelli, H. (eds), *Demokratie in der Mediengesellschaft*, Wiesbaden: VS Verlag, pp. 319–40.

Bonfadelli, H., Bucher, P. and Piga, A. (2007), 'Use of Old and New Media by Ethnic Minority Youth in Europe with a Special Emphasis on Switzerland', *Communications*, 32: 2, pp. 141–70.

Cottle, S. (2000), *Ethnic Minorities and the Media: Changing Cultural Boundaries*, Buckingham: The Open University Press.

d'Haenens, L., Beentjes, H. and Bink, S. (2000), 'The Media Experience of Ethnic Minorities in the Netherlands: A Qualitative Study', *Communications: The European Journal of Communication Research*, 25: 3, pp. 325–41.

d'Haenens, L., Van Summeren, C., Kokhuis, M. and Beentjes, J. (2002), 'Ownership and Use of "Old" and "New" Media Among Ethnic Minority Youth in the Netherlands. The Role of the Ethno-Cultural Position', *Communications: The European Journal of Communication Research*, 27: 3, pp. 365–393.

Farr, R. M. and Moscovici, S. (1984), *Social Representations*, Cambridge: Cambridge University Press.

Ferjani, R., 'Les télévisions arabophones en France: une transnationalité postcoloniale', in Mattelart, T. (ed.) (2007), *Médias, migrations et cultures transnationales*, Paris-Brussels: Ina-De Boeck, pp. 102–20.

Galtung, J. and Ruge, M. H. (1965), 'The Structure of Foreign News', *Journal of Peace Research*, 2, pp. 64–91.

Geissler, R. (2006), 'Multikulturalismus in Kanada – Modell für Deutschland' (Multiculturalism in Canada – A Model for Germany?), *Politik und Zeitgeschichte*, B26, pp. 19–25.

Georgiou, M. (2006), *Diaspora, Identity, and the Media. Diasporic Transnationalism and Mediated Spatialities*, Cresskill: Hampton Press.

—— 'Mapping Diasporic Media Cultures: A Transnational Cultural Approach to Exclusion', in Silverstone, R. (ed.) (2005), *Media, Technology, and Everyday Life in Europe: From Information to Communication*, London: Ashgate Publishing, pp. 33–52.

Gillespie, M. (1995), *Television, Ethnicity, and Cultural Change*, London: Routledge.

—— (2006), 'Transnational Television Audiences after September 11', *Journal of Ethnic and Migration Studies*, 32: 6, pp. 903–21.

Granato, M. (2001), *Freizeitgestaltung und Mediennutzung bei Kindern türkischer Herkunft*, Eine Untersuchung des Presse- und Informationsamtes der Bundesregierung (BPA) zur Mediennutzung und Integration der türkischen Bevölkerung in Deutschland und zur Mediennutzung und Integration türkischer Kinder (A Study of Media Use and Integration of the Turkish Population in Germany by the Federal Press and Information Office), Bonn: BPA.

Güntürk, R., 'Mediennutzung der Migranten – mediale Isolation' (Media Use by Migrants – Media Isolation?), in Butterwegge, Ch., Hentges, G. and Sarigöz, F. (eds) (1999), *Medien und multikulturelle Gesellschaft*, Opladen: Westdeutscher Verlag, pp. 136–43.

Hafez, K. (2007), *The Myth of Media Globalization*, Cambridge: Polity Press.

—— *Türkische Mediennutzung in Deutschland: Hemmnis oder Chance der gesellschaftlichen Integration?* Eine qualitative Studie im Auftrag des Presse- und Informationsamtes der Bundesregierung (Turkish Media Use in Germany: Barrier or Chance to Social Integration), Hamburg and Berlin: Deutsches Orient-Institut.

Harb, Z. and Bessaiso, E. (2006), 'British Arab Muslim Audiences and Television after September 11', *Journal of Ethnic and Migration Studies*, 32: 6, pp. 1063–76.

Hargreaves, A. and Mahdjoub, M. (1997), 'Satellite Television Viewing among Ethnic Minorities in France', *European Journal of Communication*, 12: 4, pp. 459–77.

Hartmann, P. and Husband, C. (1974), *Racism and the Mass Media*, London: Davis Poynter.

Hassanpour, A., 'Diaspora, Homeland and Communication Technologies', in Karim, K. H. (ed.) (2003), *The Media of Diaspora*, London: Routledge, pp. 76–88.

Koeman, J., Peeters, A. and d'Haenens, L. (2007), 'Diversity Monitor 2005: Diversity as a Quality Aspect of Television in the Netherlands', *Communications*, 32, pp. 97–121.

Leurdijk, A. (2006), 'In Search of Common Ground: Strategies of Multicultural Television Producers in Europe', *Cultural Studies*, 9: 1, pp. 25–46.

Macé, E. (2008), *Perception de la diversité dans les programmes de télévision. Rapport au Conseil supérieur de l'audiovisuel*, Paris: CSA (Conseil supérieur de l'audiovisuel).

Madani, L., 'L'antenne parabolique en Algérie, entre dominations et résistances', in Mattelart, T. (ed.) (2002), *La mondialisation des médias contre la censure: Tiers Monde et audiovisuel sans frontières*, Paris-Brussels: Ina-De Boeck, pp. 177–210.

Madianou, M. (2005), 'Contested Communicative Spaces: Rethinking Identities, Boundaries and the Role of the Media among Turkish Speakers in Greece', *Journal of Ethnic and Migration Studies*, 31: 3, pp. 521–41.

Mai, N., '"Italy is Beautiful": The Role of Italian Television in Albanian Migration to Italy', in King, R. and Wood, N. (eds) (2001), *Media and Migration: Constructions of Mobility and Difference*, London: Routledge, pp. 95–109.

Matar, D. (2006), 'Diverse Diasporas, One Meta-Narrative: Palestinians in the UK Talking about 11 September 2001', *Journal of Ethnic and Migration Studies*, 32: 6, pp. 1027–40.

Mattelart, T. (2007), *Médias, migrations et cultures transnationales*, Paris-Brussels: Ina-De Boeck.

McCombs, M. E. and Shaw, D. L. (1972), 'The Agenda-Setting Function of Mass Media', *Public Opinion Quarterly*, 36, pp. 176–87.

Miladi, N. (2006), 'Satellite TV News and the Arab Diaspora in Britain: Comparing Al-Jazeera, the BBC and CNN', *Journal of Ethnic and Migration Studies*, 32: 6, pp. 947–60.

Milikowski, M. (2000), 'Exploring a Model of De-Ethnicization: The Case of Turkish Television in the Netherlands', *European Journal of Communication*, 15: 4, pp. 443–68.

Nilan, P. and Feixa, C. (eds) (2006), *Global Youth? Hybrid Identities, Plural Worlds*, London and New York: Routledge.

Ogan, C. (2001), *Communication and Identity in the Diaspora: Turkish Migrants in Amsterdam and Their Use of Media*, Lanham: Lexington Books.

Ouaj, J. (1999), *More Colour in the Media: Employment and Access of 'Ethnic Minorities' to the Television Industry in Germany, the UK, France, the Netherlands and Finland*, Düsseldorf: The European Institute for the Media.

Peeters, A. and d'Haenens, L. (2005), 'Bridging or Bonding? Relationships between Integration and Media Use among Ethnic Minorities in the Netherlands', *Communications: The European Journal for Communication Research*, 30: 2, pp. 201–31.

Robins, K., 'Transnational Media, Cultural Diversity and New Public Cultures', in Robins, K. (ed.) (2006), *The Challenge of Transcultural Diversities: Transversal Study on the Theme of Cultural Policy and Cultural Diversity*, Strasbourg: Council of Europe Publishing, pp. 143–56.

Sabry, T. (2004), 'Young Amazighs, the Land of Eromen and Pamela Anderson as the Embodiment of Modernity', *Westminster Papers in Communication and Culture*, 1: 1, pp. 41–48.

Sanders, K. (2003), *Ethics and Journalism*, London: Sage.

Sreberny, A. (1999), *Include Me In. Rethinking Ethnicity on Television: Audience and Producer Perspectives*. Available at: http://www.ofcom.org.uk/static/archive/bsc/pdfs/research/Include.pdf. Accessed 31 May 2010.

Stangor, C. (ed.) (2000), *Stereotypes & Prejudice: Essential Readings*, Philadelphia, PA: Psychology Press.

Tajfel, H. and Turner, J. C., 'An Integrative Theory of Intergroup Conflict', in Austin, W. G. and Worchel, S. (eds) (1979), *The Social Psychology of Intergroup Relations*, Monterey, CA: Brooks-Cole, pp. 33–47.

Ter Wal, J. (2004), *European Day of Media Monitoring: Quantitative Analysis of Daily Press and TV Contents in the 15 EU Member States*, Pilot study in the framework of the Online/More Colour in the Media project 'European Day of Media Monitoring', Utrecht: ERCOMER, University of Utrecht.

—— (2002), *Racism and Cultural Diversity in the Mass Media: An Overview of Research and Examples of Good Practice in the EU Member States, 1995–2000*, Vienna: EUMC (European Monitoring Centre on Racism and Xenophobia).

Ter Wal, J., d'Haenens, L. and Koeman, J. (2005), '(Re)presentation of Ethnicity in EU and Dutch Domestic News: A Quantitative Analysis', *Media, Culture & Society*, 27: 6, pp. 937–50.

van Dijk, T. A. (1991), *Racism and the Press*, London: Routledge.

—— (1993), *Elite Discourse and Racism*, London: Sage.

Weber-Menges, S., 'Ethnomedien in Deutschland' (Ethnomedia in Germany), in Geißler, R. and Pöttker, H. (eds) (2006), *Integration durch Massenmedien (Mass Media-Integration)*, Bielefeld: Transcript Verlag, pp. 121–45.

Weiss, H. J. and Trebbe, J. (2001), *Mediennutzung und Integration der türkischen Bevölkerung in Deutschland*, Ergebnisse einer Umfrage des Presse- und Informationsamtes der Bundesregierung (Results of a Survey by the Federal Press and Information Office), Potsdam: GöfaK Medienforschung GmbH.

Chapter 14

Europe as World News Leader

Jeremy Tunstall

This chapter argues that for more than 150 years, world news leadership has been exercised by Europe and/or the United States. US world news leadership peaked around 1947; but Europe has been the world news leader since at least 1990.

What is world 'news leadership'? It's certainly not *The Elite Press* as defined by John C. Merrill (1968: 3–54). Merrill's *Elite Press* included Pravda (USSR) and the South African daily, Die Burger, which at the time supported the Nationalist Party government and its apartheid policies. Since there is no accepted definition of news leadership, here is my suggested definition. News leadership requires:

- Independence, most obviously from government and business. To be convincing, independence needs to be put in evidence through criticism of, and investigation into, big government and big business.
- News leadership needs to be deployed on a not-for-profit or not-primarily-for-profit basis. In the past, the obvious example was the newspaper which pursued prestige rather than profit. Today, the most obvious not-for-profit example is the public broadcaster (so long as it can also demonstrate a significant degree of independence from government and political parties).
- Media can only exercise news leadership by establishing a reputation for credibility, both nationally and internationally. Credibility especially refers to 'facts' in the sense of C. P. Scott's 1926 statement in the Manchester Guardian: 'Comment is free but facts are sacred.'

British, French and American News Leadership, 1830–1945

For over 100 years, world news leadership was shared between Britain, France and the United States. Within this threesome, American news gradually became of greater world importance and was clearly in the lead by 1945. Throughout this long period, the 'free flow of news' was inhibited by empire, war, governments generally, advertising and monopolistic media behaviour.

Since the 1850s, a small number of British, French and American news agencies have been the main suppliers of international news to most of the world's media. Still today most of the world's media (print, radio, TV and Internet) rely for their world news on news agencies based in New York, London and Paris. Most of the world's TV viewers receive most of their video foreign news from Reuters and the Associated Press (AP); each of these two agencies says that its TV images reach one billion people per day and two billion people per week. Both agencies' TV services locate their central world 'hub' in London, but (since the sale of Reuters to Thomson of Canada) neither is now British owned.

During the years 1830–70, Britain was the world news leader. In this period The Times of London was the world's most quoted and influential newspaper (History of The Times 1935, 1939: vols 1–2). The Times had a monopolistic advantage, because newspaper taxation enabled this one up-market daily to dominate in circulation. By 1855, The Times had established a unique foreign news operation with a strong focus on the growing British Empire and imperial wars, and use of the electric telegraph. But only four years later (1859), The Times began subscribing to Julius Reuter's news service. From the 1850s onwards, Reuters has been a world news leader (Read, 1992). But it had many difficulties along the way – especially during the two world wars. Despite being seen by many as the semi-official agency of the British Empire, Reuters was widely regarded as being the least partisan world news service.

France was the other main early leader in selling world news to the world. Agence Havas began in 1835. In 1856, Havas and Reuter began exchanging news with Wolff – establishing a French-British-German grouping. This group dominated the flow of international news in the world until 1914.

Agence Havas of France exemplified the tendency of news leadership to become news monopoly. During 1860–1900, Havas had the monopoly for domestic as well as foreign news. Havas became the dominant supplier of both news and advertising to the growing French press; Havas also had close news and advertising relationships with both the French business community and the French government (Boyd-Barrett 1980: 122–26).

During the years 1860–1914, the Associated Press and all US newspapers were dependent on the Europeans for world news. Havas monopolized Latin America; Reuters monopolized the British Empire and Asia; Africa was shared between Havas and Reuters; Wolff controlled news from eastern Europe and Russia. The Associated Press was only allowed to 'own' US news.

But by 1900 the United States was already the leader in popular newspapers. The New York and Chicago popular papers during 1890–1914 had close ties with popular newspapers in London, Paris and Berlin. The leading German popular newspaper owners in this period copied many American press characteristics, not least the heavy reliance on 'human interest', advertising and low (or nil) price (Tunstall 1977: 145–46).

During the 1890s, the US daily press became the world circulation leader. But the American prestige up-market daily emerged more slowly. In 1898, the New York Times had a daily sale of 25,000 and was near death. However, by 1901 – with a price cut from three cents to one cent – it was selling 100,000 copies daily (Emery and Emery 1996: 239).

By 1935, the United States had established itself as a world news leader. The United States now had no less than three big national-and-international news agencies: Associated Press (AP), United Press (UP) and International News Service (INS). In addition to this trio of news agencies, the United States was in the 1930s establishing a lead in three new types of news outlets: namely radio news, news magazines (such as Time) and picture news magazines (such as Life). Meanwhile, European news leadership was rapidly evaporating not only in Germany, Italy and Spain, but also in France. The years 1935–39 also marked a bad period for the London press and Reuters, while the BBC still had no news of its own.

It was during 1939–45 that the United States at last achieved unambiguous world news leadership. About twenty separate US news organizations sent significant teams of correspondents to Europe, North Africa and Asia to cover World War II. These twenty organizations included three news agencies, three radio networks, ten daily newspapers and several magazines. About 800 American correspondents were abroad at any one time, but 2600 individuals spent some time doing foreign war reporting (Desmond 1984: 231–465). Forty nine American and eighteen British journalists were killed while covering the war.

American media were the news leaders of 1939–45, but the British media were also prominent. By 1943, the BBC was broadcasting in all the main European languages and in a total of 45 languages (Briggs 1970). The main American wartime radio effort was in the Pacific.

1945–85: The Cold War as the Golden Age of American News

For the four decades of the Cold War, American news media led the news around the world, with the exception of the Communist countries. American news led in western, but not eastern, Europe.

The high point of American news pre-eminence was during 1945–48. The media of most of the other big nations were in ruins. American films and magazines around 1946 were still entering the Soviet Union and China. The United States accounted for more than half of the entire world consumption of newsprint in 1948 (Tunstall 1977).

Two American news agencies (AP and UP), with some help from the British Reuters, dominated the flow of world news. The old Havas agency had collaborated with the Nazis during 1940–44 and the new Agence France-Presse (AFP) only gradually grew into international importance. A high point for the American news agencies was their Vietnam reporting in the 1960s, and especially in the earlier phases of major American involvement (1962–65). AP was blessed in its Saigon bureau with three exceptionally talented journalists; only one, Mal Browne, was American, while Peter Arnett was a New Zealander and Horst Faas, the photographer, was German (Reporters of the Associated Press 2007).

But much other American foreign reporting during 1945–85 lacked any serious attempt at objectivity. Most American foreign reporting (and silence) was heavily biased to support official American foreign and military policy. Here for example is Richard Fryklund, the award-winning Pentagon reporter of the then highly respected Washington Evening Star:

> I know of no other beat in which reporters assume that their phones are tapped […] We were lied to about the U-2 flights over Russia. I did not really mind that. I think that an espionage operation as important as that one ought to be lied about. It ought to endure as long as possible. (Hiebert 1966: 167–71)

The fact that US U-2 spy aircraft were routinely flying across the Soviet Union was revealed not by American journalists, but by the Soviet leader Nikita Khrushchev, when breaking off talks with the United States in 1960.

The New York Times loyally supported the Central Intelligence Agency (CIA) in numerous sponsored military coups; for example, it assisted the CIA in the military overthrow of the elected government of Guatemala in 1954 (Grandin 2004: 67). The New York Times also supported American policy in Iran from the CIA-generated coup of 1953 and across the ensuing decades. A content analysis study of 1600 New York Times stories about Iran, during 1951–78, showed that the newspaper always closely supported official American policy and broadly supported the coup-installed Shah (Dorman and Farhang: 1987). These authors used the term 'deference' to describe the New York Times attitude to official US policy.

James Reston of the New York Times was widely regarded as the leading American political journalist in the 1960s and 1970s. But a detailed analysis of his career and output shows that he allowed himself to become a media mouthpiece for the makers of American foreign policy, including John Kennedy and Henry Kissinger (Stacks 2003).

Throughout the Cold War period, the American media applauded the status of the United States as a military superpower. But, in terms of infantry boots-on-the-ground, the American military have had a fairly weak record ever since 1945. The title of 'Bombing Superpower' might have been thought more appropriate by the citizens of Korea, Vietnam and Cambodia (and subsequently by the citizens of Iraq).

Behind their apparent strength on the world scene, the US media also looked to be extraordinarily strong at home. It was during these four Cold War decades that the Washington Post and the Los Angeles Times joined the New York Times as papers that carried a lot of foreign news and had big teams of foreign correspondents. These three dailies developed two large syndication services, whose news appeared in publications around the world. In these Cold War years, three big TV networks developed big national and international news operations; the CBS, NBC and ABC evening news shows were by 1980 attracting a combined audience of over 60 million people each evening.

But by 1980, anti-monopoly laws and rules were already having unanticipated consequences for both press and TV news. Because the big newspapers were forbidden to own nearby suburban dailies, the bigger dailies decided not only to kill their central city competitors, but also to compete in the outer suburbs and exurban areas against much smaller suburban dailies. The prestige of the big dailies was built upon local monopoly. The Washington Post achieved its local morning monopoly in 1954, the Los Angeles Times in 1962 and the New York Times in 1967. As these big newspapers moved aggressively into their suburban areas, they developed separate editions for specific areas. By 1980, the Los Angeles Times had editions for counties (such as San Diego county) over 100 miles from the central location. With massive weekend editions and separate local daily editions, these three big newspapers were each routinely printing over 1000 (large) pages per week and each was employing about 1000 journalists. These were local monopoly dailies seeking to be county, city, state, national and international newspapers within a package financed by advertising, especially local classified advertising.

By 1980, the American TV networks were also subject to important anti-monopoly regulation. They made their own prestige news (in New York) but were required to buy the bulk of their national programming from separate producers (in Hollywood). These three big networks also had somewhat lopsided business plans. Their profits were largely generated by their groups of 'owned and operated' local TV stations in the largest cities.

It was after 1981 (under President Reagan) that 'deregulation' became the Washington fashion (Tunstall 1986). But communications deregulation was initially mainly aimed at the giant AT&T telephone monopoly. The media were broadly seen in Washington as doing a fairly good job both at home and abroad. These attitudes were supported by the emerging success of USA Today and the appearance of CNN in 1980.

As the Cold War was coming to an end in the 1980s, the American media still had a world lead in news. But paradoxically the American people were less informed about the world than were the people of almost any other nation. Both American newspapers and television adopted a 'home news abroad' approach to all foreign news. Foreign news focused on American political, military and business involvement in specific countries. During the Cold War, this led to a very close connection between American foreign news and American foreign policy. American reporters located in Germany or Israel or Venezuela or India were expected to report on American involvement and policy in that specific country. This meant that American foreign correspondents needed to be close to major American businesses (such as oil companies) as well as to the American embassy and, very often, to the local CIA people. American foreign news was usually closely allied not only with American embassies abroad (Pedelty 1995), but also with the State Department and with the CIA, and other spy agencies in Washington.

Nineteen eighty was a pivotal year in another respect. In 1980 UNESCO produced 'Many Voices, One World', the report of a commission chaired by Seán MacBride, Ireland's former foreign minister. This report called for 'a more just and more efficient world information and communication order' (MacBride 1980, sub-title). Three countries subsequently resigned from UNESCO in protest. These countries were the United States, the United Kingdom and Singapore (notorious for its restrictive media policies). While the Reagan and Thatcher administrations (supported by the big news agencies) rejected the (mild) UNESCO critique, all of Europe (except the United Kingdom) was in favour. Europe, it seemed, was in step with the world, while the US and UK governments and news media were not.

1985–2000: Europe Takes the World News Lead

By 1990, western Europe had become the world news leader (Tunstall 1992). By 1990, there was no major world region in which the United States was the main supplier of world news. The UP (and the UPI) news agency had traditionally been strong in Latin America; but by 1990

UPI had ceased to be a significant news agency – and in Latin America AP was outgunned by the Spanish EFE, the French AFP and the British Reuters. The US news media were paying the price for Washington's relentless support for Latin American military regimes.

Europe is geographically closer to the rest of the world than the United States is. It's an example of what a popular UK real estate TV show calls 'Location, Location, Location'. Foreign reporters based in London or Paris or Rome are literally 'closer to the story' (than Washington-based reporters) when the story is in Europe, Africa or the Middle East. These three regions are, in fact, regarded as a single time-zone market by the big news agencies and by other large foreign news players such as the BBC.

The biggest world news story in the years after 1985 was the collapse of Communism in the Soviet Union and eastern Europe. The Europeans had several advantages in covering this story – not only geographical proximity, but also past and present cultural proximity. The German media in general – and the DPA news agency in particular – were uniquely placed to cover this story, not least because of the East/West split in Germany itself, but also because of the historical location of German population clusters across eastern Europe. News coverage, not only of the break-up of the Soviet Union but also of the break-up of Yugoslavia, was led by the Europeans. For the media of Austria, Italy and Greece, Yugoslavia was a neighbour.

By 1990, historical animosity towards Germany had largely disappeared as had animosity towards the former European empires. By 1990, it was a great news and cultural advantage to have been an imperialist. European media had language (and other) ties with Latin America, Africa, the Middle East, South Asia and South East Asia.

Europe has no foreign policy or foreign news headquarters comparable to the twin cities of Washington and New York. Brussels is only one of about ten major European locations for foreign news operations and for correspondents from foreign media (Kuhn and Neveu 2002). In these foreign news locations, there is a mix of foreign news experts from the host country with foreign correspondents from other European countries, as well as correspondents from outside Europe. Brussels has the largest number of foreign correspondents. One 1985 study showed London to have 69 US foreign correspondents, 42 Germans, 113 from other European countries, 31 Japanese, 34 from Australia and New Zealand, 19 from the Middle East and 53 from the 'Third World' including South Africa (Morrison and Tumber 1985).

European correspondents who report on other European countries, help to ensure that Europe's big total supply of foreign news is actively passed around the continent each day. One relevant study is about Italian correspondents based in Paris; not surprisingly they closely monitor the French media and the available press conferences (Mazzoleni and Splendore 2007).

In the 1990s, each European capital city had the following components engaged in foreign policy and foreign news:

- A national External Affairs Ministry
- Embassies and diplomats of foreign countries

- A national news agency which typically also employed some foreign correspondents
- A public service broadcaster and several commercial broadcasters
- Domestic newspapers, employing some foreign correspondents
- Universities and institutes with relevant language skills, specializing for example in former colonies and their politics
- Immigrant media and media-in-exile

In each of the larger centres (such as Berlin, London, Madrid and Paris), several thousand people are thus involved. Across Europe's numerous smaller capitals, there will be many further thousands of such diplomatic, foreign policy and foreign news people at work.

In one of these smaller capitals – e.g. in one of the Scandinavian countries – there is a wealth of foreign news expertise which would not be found in a loosely equivalent American location such as Idaho or Minnesota.

Since 2000: The US News Decline Continued

Since 2000, there has been a collapse of the traditional US news media in general and of the foreign news component in particular. The not-primarily-for-profit element in both American press and broadcasting has largely disappeared. Increasingly since 2000, the US traditional media have been aiming solely at profit, but have still been making losses. The Internet's impact has looked so damaging partly because the US news media were already suffering from other illnesses.

During this period, Joseph S. Nye (of Harvard University and formerly of the Clinton Department of Defense) has been arguing that the United States can achieve 'success in world politics' by using its 'Soft Power' (Nye 2004). Like so much else written and spoken about the US media, 'Soft Power' refers back nostalgically to the American Golden Age of the Cold War.

The American media – unlike the media of most European countries – were remarkably uncritical of President George W. Bush's advance into the quagmires of Iraq and Afghanistan. But the US media were also extremely slow to recognize huge business and financial scandals. These included two very high profile large companies – WorldCom and Enron – both of which made financial claims which should have sounded false and improbable to any business journalist. Then came the massive Wall Street crash of 2008, which was accurately predicted by Paul Krugman over a lengthy period in the columns of the New York Times (as well as in a sequence of books) (Krugman 2003). But Krugman was only an academic economist from Princeton, so the New York Times (and the Washington and New York banking authorities) ignored what he and other economists were saying.

One reason for the US media's lack of interest in the impending financial scandal and disaster was that virtually all of American television had become part of the show business industry. This does not merely refer to the kind of news which appeared on the screen.

During the 1980s and early 1990s, the increasingly deregulated broadcast media had been 'bulking up for digital' (Tunstall and Machin 1999: 53–67). Previous regulatory constraints on vertical integration were removed; all of the main broadcast television and cable and satellite networks came to be owned by the big Hollywood entertainment companies. The ABC network was the most dramatic early example. In 1984, the 'Broadcast Networks Trembled' when ABC was acquired by the much smaller, but much more profitable Capital Cities (Tunstall 1986: 142–61). Then in 1995 the 'Mouse House Swallowed the Alphabet Net', when Disney acquired the ABC-Capital Cities combine (Tunstall and Machin 1999: 53–76). Subsequently both NBC and CBS (the traditional broadcast news leaders) also became part of vertically integrated entertainment companies.

Under the deregulatory rules, the new show business owners of the network news no longer needed to impress the Washington regulators with some not-primarily-for-profit news. There were now more TV networks and much smaller audiences for TV news. The inevitable business logic was to cut back on staff in general, and on foreign news bureaus and staff in particular. CNN remained the most serious dispenser of foreign TV news. But CNN's not-primarily-for-profit approach eventually succumbed to competition from Fox News and its shock-jock style borrowed from the far-right radio talk stations. Fox News, of course, was owned by the News Corporation, whose main business activity was Hollywood film and TV entertainment (Kitty 2005).

Serious news, and in particular foreign news, suffered even more severely in the big newspapers. Back in 1985, the leading US newspapers were seen by the business world as a 'high margin business', although they were never quite as profitable as the larger TV station groups. The Los Angeles Times, which in 1980 was still expanding its revenue and profits, subsequently went through a series of financial crises and ownership changes; it was acquired by the (traditionally profitable) Chicago Tribune press and TV group. In December 2008, the Tribune Company itself filed for 'Chapter Eleven' bankruptcy protection. By this time there had already been huge cuts in journalist numbers, and especially in both papers' foreign news operations.

The Washington Post, after its few years of Watergate glory in 1973–74, also moved to the political right and found it increasingly difficult to extract enough revenue from the Maryland and Virginia suburbs. Bob Woodward used his prestige to gain remarkable access into the two George W. Bush administrations, but most of this material appeared in a sequence of books.

Meanwhile the New York Times was also in trouble. The 'grey lady' of American journalism had three big problems. Firstly, its business plan was defective. Secondly, its journalism was marred by scandal. Thirdly, it failed to be independent of the George Bush government, especially in 2001–04.

For over a century, the New York Times had been controlled by the Ochs-Sulzberger dynasty (Tifft and Jones 1999). But the majority of shares were owned by others. This resulted in a confused business plan (Bianco 2005). The New York Times in the 1980s and 1990s tried to combine prestige and profit, and to appeal to local, national and international audiences.

It made bad decisions about office buildings and printing plants, and it mistakenly acquired the sinking Boston Globe in 1993. By seeking to compete on the US national scene, the New York Times found itself at a disadvantage against USA Today and the Wall Street Journal.

Further mistakes were made with the International Herald Tribune (IHT); the New York Times bullied the Washington Post management into selling their 50 per cent share. But, while the IHT's main sale is in Europe, it sells daily into 180 countries; this partly explains why the IHT carries (especially by US standards) so little advertising.

The scandalous behaviour of certain individual journalists has included the notorious case of Jayson Blair, a reporter who simply invented (or plagiarized) a long succession of stories (Columbia Journalism Review 2003: 3–22). The important point of these scandals was what they indicated about the New York Times' lack of internal editorial competence. The list of journalists who once worked for the New York Times is much more distinguished than the list of journalists who currently work for the paper. Seymour Hersh, for example, as a lone investigative reporter generated a series of Afghanistan and Iraq expose stories (Hersh 2004) which put to shame the huge current team of journalists working for the New York Times.

The New York Times made a series of big editorial mistakes in relation to George W. Bush during 2000–04. The paper assigned a reporter called Frank Bruni to follow George Bush on his 2000 presidential campaign. Bruni gave Bush a remarkably easy time and failed to follow up several dubious elements in Bush's recent past (Bruni 2002). Subsequently this same Frank Bruni became the ferociously critical restaurant critic of the great newspaper.

For the six months following September 11, 2001, the New York Times gave massive day-by-day coverage to 'Portraits of Grief' and other post-September 11 themes. This coverage was awarded a Pulitzer Prize, one of seven awarded to the New York Times in early 2002. But the focus meant that the newspaper took its eye off the ball in Iraq. A New York Times correspondent in Asia, interviewed by this author at this time, told me that he couldn't get anything into the paper because of its obsession with the September 11 hometown story.

During the winter of 2002–03, the New York Times was very mildly sceptical about the need for an invasion of Iraq. However, when the 2003 invasion occurred, the paper supported the invasion with patriotic enthusiasm (Purdum 2003). Subsequently, of course, the paper reflected the more sceptical national mood and became much more critical of the Bush Iraq adventure. But it was too late.

By 2005–06, many voices inside the United States were bewailing the inadequacies of the press and TV news in general, and of foreign news in particular. The numerous books of this kind included such titles as When The Press Fails (Bennett et al. 2007) and Losing the News (Jones 2009). These books bewail the tendency of both foreigners and US citizens not to believe what the American media and the American government are saying. These particular criticisms were made before the American news media's inadequate performance in relation to Wall Street and the international financial crash of 2008–09.

Both Jones and Bennett (like other US commentators) would seem to many Europeans to be missing a key point. Within the American media, a mind-set still prevails which harks back to the golden age of the Cold War. Then, as now, many decent American journalists (with a few exceptions) supported the activities of the military, the State Department, the CIA, the US Special Forces, the bombing and the targeted assassinations. Most Europeans, and many others around the world, beg to differ.

Since 2000: Europe Still Ahead but Also in Relative News Decline

During the 2000–10 decade, Europe seems to have remained ahead of the United States in terms of international news. Paradoxically this happened despite America's spectacular Internet success. United States companies now provide low-audience channels across Europe via satellite and cable (Chalaby 2009). The International Herald Tribune and the Wall Street Journal are still available each day in all European capital cities. The (Murdoch) News Corporation has moved out from its regional base in London to make significant advances in other European countries, notably Italy.

These American incursions largely support the Hollywood presence in Europe, which dates back about 90 years. Easily the most important American news presence in Europe is that of the Associated Press. AP stories are prominently available on every single TV screen in Europe, and in newspaper text and pictures. Newer news phenomena, such as political blogging and user-generated content have close connections with the AP. It is noticeable that AP is the only American news organization which employs large numbers of news personnel from across Europe and across the world.

Like AP, most of Europe's news agencies are not-primarily-for-profit. Europe's other big not-for-profit news providers have been the public service broadcasters and linked services, especially Euronews.

However, the European Union has failed to actively link public service broadcasting and the Internet at either the European or national levels. A key case is Germany where the public service broadcasters have been separated from Internet provision.

During the 2000–10 decade, the London-based BBC expanded its foreign coverage 'on radio, on TV, on-line'. The BBC has significant worldwide operations in both TV and radio; what is less well known is that the BBC's online operation makes use of much material from domestic Radio Four, which is well funded and generates large quantities of news features, comment and public affairs material. Some people claim that the BBC is now operating the world's leading electronic newspaper. Audience research in many countries, and over several decades, has shown that around the world the BBC is regarded as more objective, or less partisan, than all other rival services. But it is far from certain that incumbent British governments will allow the BBC to remain so big and so well financed.

Until 2008, London might have claimed to be the hub of the world news system. But in 2008 Reuters was acquired by Thomson of Canada. Reuters, which had led the world data business (especially during 1975–95) was swallowed by a rival data company. Neither the British government nor the European Union made any attempt to stop this takeover.

Currently the Reuters editorial hub (for all types of news, including television) remains in London. But at some point in the future the hub could be moved to Toronto, or to New York, or to somewhere in Asia.

It seems probable that Europe and the United States will continue to lead the worldwide provision of news. But it was already evident in 2005 that neither European nor American media had much impact in the world's eleven largest countries where 60 per cent of the world's population live. This was especially true of China and India (Tunstall 2008: 125–231). As these two countries' economies become more important, news generated by Indian and Chinese journalists will inevitably become more important on the world scene.

Europe was the world news leader during 1990–2010; if the European Union – and the governments of the larger European countries – so wished, Europe could remain the world news leader. But if European not-primarily-for-profit journalism is allowed to become less salient, Europe could eventually find itself in fourth place behind not only the United States, but also behind India and China.

To summarize: there have been three separate historical periods for world news leadership. Firstly Europe (mainly France and Britain) was the leader of world news, through an international news cartel operated by the leading European news agencies. This lasted for about 100 years – from 1830 to 1930. Secondly, the United States media were the leaders of world news for about 50 years, from 1930 to 1980. Thirdly, from about 1990 onwards, the European news media reasserted their old leadership of world news. But in the future both Europe and the United States may have to share world news leadership with the great powers of Asia.

References

Anon, History of The Times (1935, 1939), 'The Thunderer' in the Making, 1785–1841 (Vol 1) and The Tradition Established, 1841–1884 (Vol 2), London: The Times.

Anon (2003), 'The Times After the Storm', Columbia Journalism Review, July/August pp. 3–22.

Bennett, W. L., Lawrence, R. and Livingstone, S. (2007), When the Press Fails: Political Power and the News Media from Iraq to Katrina, Chicago: University of Chicago Press.

Bianco, A. (2005), 'The Future of the New York Times', in Business Week, January 24 2005: 52–55.

Boyd-Barrett, O. (1980), The International News Agencies, London: Constable and Beverly Hills: Sage.

Briggs, A. (1970), The War of Words: The History of Broadcasting in the United Kingdom, Volume 3, Oxford: Oxford University Press.

Bruni, F. (2002), Ambling into History: The Unlikely Odyssey of George W. Bush, New York: HarperCollins.

Chalaby, J. K. (2009), Transnational Television in Europe, London: I.B. Tauris.

Cranberg, G., Bezanson, R. and Soloski, J. (2001), Taking Stock: Journalism and the Publicly Traded Newspaper Company, Ames: Iowa University Press.

Desmond, R. W. (1984), Tides of War: World News Reporting, 1931–45, Iowa City: University of Iowa Press.

Dorman, W. A. and Farhang, M. (1987), *The US Press and Iran: Foreign Policy and the Journalism of Deference*, Berkeley: University of California Press.

Emery, M. and Emery, E. (1996), *The Press in America*, 8th edn, Boston: Allyn and Bacon.

Fenby, J. (1986), *The International News Services*, New York: Schocken Books.

Grandin, G. (2004), *The Last Colonial Massacre: Latin America in the Cold War*, Chicago: University of Chicago Press.

Hersh, S. M. (2004), *Chain of Command: The Road from 9/11 to Abu Ghraib*, London: Allen Lane, Penguin.

Hiebert, R. E. (ed.) (1966), *The Press in Washington*, New York: Dodd, Mead and Company.

Jones, A. S. (2009), *Losing the News: The Future of the News that Feeds Democracy*, New York: Oxford University Press.

Kitty, A. (2005), *OutFoxed: Rupert Murdoch's War on Journalism*, New York: Disinformation.

Krugman, P. (2003), *The Great Unraveling: Losing Our Way in the New Century*, New York: W.W. Norton.

Kuhn, R. and Neveu, E. (eds) (2002), *Political Journalism: New Challenges, New Practices*, London: Routledge.

MacBride, S. (ed.) (1980), *Many Voices, One World*, Paris and London: UNESCO.

Mazzoleni, G. and Splendore, S., 'Italian Foreign Correspondents: Fashioning Representation of France', in Palmer, M. and Aubert, A. (eds) (2007), *L'Actualité Internationale Vue Depuis La France*, Paris: Université Sorbonne Nouvelle.

Merrill, J. C. (1968), *The Elite Press: Great Newspapers of the World*, New York: Pitman Publishing.

Morrison, D. E. and Tumber, H. (1985), 'The Foreign Correspondent: Date-Line London', *Media, Culture and Society*, 7, pp. 445–70.

Nye, J. S. (2004), *Soft Power: The Means to Success in World Politics*, New York: Public Affairs.

Pedelty, M. (1995), *War Stories: The Culture of Foreign Correspondents*, New York: Routledge.

Purdum, T. S. and the staff of the New York Times (2003), *'At a Time of Our Choosing': America's War in Iraq*, New York: Times Books.

Read, D. (1992), *The Power of News: The History of Reuters, 1849–1989*, Oxford: Oxford University Press.

Reporters of the Associated Press (2007), *Breaking News: How the Associated Press Has Covered War, Peace and Everything Else*, New York: Princeton Architectural Press.

Stacks, J. F. (2003), *Scotty: James B. Reston and the Rise and Fall of American Journalism*, Boston: Little, Brown.

Tifft, S. E. and Jones, A. S. (1999), *The Trust: The Private and Powerful Family behind The New York Times*, Boston: Little, Brown.

Tunstall, J. (1986), *Communications Deregulation: The Unleashing of America's Communications Industry*, Oxford: Basil Blackwell.

____ (1992), 'Europe as World News Leader', *Journal of Communication*, 42, pp. 84–99.

____ (1977), *The Media Are American: Anglo-American Media in the World*, London: Constable and New York: Columbia University Press.

____ (2008), *The Media Were American: US Mass Media in Decline*, New York: Oxford University Press.

Tunstall, J. and Machin, D. (1999), *The Anglo-American Media Connection*, Oxford: Oxford University Press.

Biographical Notes

The Euromedia Research Group is a network of European researchers that began life in 1982. Since then it has continued on its own initiative, changing in membership over time, but with the same working methods and purposes. It aims to collect and exchange information, and to develop and apply frameworks that help to describe and analyze developments in media structure and policy in Europe. The core activity of the group has been to produce a sequence of books, following from regular meetings in each other's countries.

Website: www.euromediagroup.org

Group Members and Contributors to this Book

Auksė Balčytienė, Department of Public Communications, Faculty of Political Science and Diplomacy, Vytautas Magnus University, Lithuania.

Laura Bergés Saura, Department of Media, Communication and Culture, Universitat Autònoma de Barcelona, Spain.

Leen d'Haenens, Centre for Media Culture and Communication Technology, Katholieke Universiteit Leuven (KU Leuven), Belgium and Department of Communication, Radboud Universiteit Nijmegen, Netherlands.

Gunn Sara Enli, Department of Media and Communication, University of Oslo, Norway.

Olof Hultén, School of Communication and Design, Kalmar University College, Sweden.

Hans J. Kleinsteuber, Institute for Political Science, University of Hamburg, Germany.

Anker Brink Lund, Copenhagen Business School, Denmark.

Tristan Mattelart, Department of Culture and Communication, University of Paris VIII, France.

Denis McQuail, Amsterdam School of Communication Research, University of Amsterdam, Netherlands.

Werner A. Meier, Institute of Mass Communication and Media Research, University of Zurich, Switzerland.

Hannu Nieminen, Department of Social Research, Media and Communication Studies, University of Helsinki, Finland.

Stylianos Papathanassopoulos, Faculty of Communication and Media Studies, National and Kapodistrian University of Athens, Greece.

Karin Raeymaeckers, Center for Journalism Studies, Department of Communication Sciences, Faculty of Political and Social Sciences, Ghent University, Belgium.

Helena Sousa, Communication and Society Research Centre, University of Minho, Portugal.

Jeanette Steemers, School of Media, Arts and Design, University of Westminster, United Kingdom.

Barbara Thomass, Institute for Media Studies, University of Bochum, Germany.

Josef Trappel, Department of Communication Research, University of Salzburg, Austria.

Jeremy Tunstall, Department of Sociology, City University, United Kingdom.

Elena Vartanova, Faculty of Journalism, Moscow State University, Russia.

Index